Academic Advising

for Student Success and Retention™

Participant Book/ Resource Guide

Michael Hovland, Ph.D.

Edward "Chip" Anderson, Ph.D.

William G. McGuire, Ph.D.

David Crockett

Juliet Kaufman, Ph.D.

David Woodward

Noel-Levitz™

a USA Group company

Academic Advising for Student Success and Retention™ developed by:

Michael Hovland, Vice President, Advancement of Educational Practice, USA Group Noel-Levitz

Edward "Chip" Anderson, Program Coordinator, Graduate School of Education and Information Studies, UCLA

William G. McGuire, Associate Director for Student Support Services and Retention, Pittsburg State University

David Crockett, Senior Vice President, USA Group Noel-Levitz

Juliet Kaufmann, Director, Undergraduate Academic Advising Center, The University of Iowa

Video Production

David Woodward, President, Conwood Enterprises, Inc.

Layout and Design

Pam Jennings, Director of Marketing Communications, USA Group Noel-Levitz

Ron Bissell, Designer, USA Group Noel-Levitz

Tyrrell Albaugh, Project Coordinator, USA Group Noel-Levitz

ISBN 1-887842-12-8 (Participant Book/Resource Guide)
ISBN 1-887842-10-1 (Complete program)

USA Group Noel-Levitz
2101 ACT Circle
Iowa City, Iowa 52245-9581
USA

Table of Contents

Acknowledgments v

Foreword vii

UNIT ONE: Introduction and Foundation 1

    SECTION 1: Advising for Student Growth and Development 3

    SECTION 2: Advising for Student and Institutional Success 7

    SECTION 3: Advising to Promote Student Learning 15

    SECTION 4: Making a Difference Through Advising 17

    SECTION 5: Building for the Future Through Good Course Selection 21

    SECTION 6: Helping Students Get Connected 27

    SECTION 7: Planning for Careers and Life After College 33

    SECTION 8: A Strengths-Based Approach to Advising 39

UNIT TWO: Communication and Relational Skills 43

    SECTION 1: Conducting an Effective Advising Interview 45

    SECTION 2: Showing Students You Care 55

    SECTION 3: Listening With Understanding 59

    SECTION 4: Questioning Skills That Uncover Student Needs 61

    SECTION 5: Taking the First Step: Reaching Out to Students 67

    SECTION 6: Challenging Students to Clarify Attitudes and Actions 77

    SECTION 7: Helping Students Evaluate Alternatives and Make Decisions ... 81

    SECTION 8: Accessing and Activating Campus Resources 85

UNIT THREE: Advising Special Populations 89

    SECTION 1: Making the Connection With Adult Students 91

    SECTION 2: Building Schedules That Fit Adult Student Priorities 97

    SECTION 3: Motivating Underprepared Students by Building on Strengths ... 101

    SECTION 4: Moving Toward Informed Decisions With Undecided Students ... 105

    SECTION 5: Helping Honors Students Bring Focus to Multiple Talents ... 115

    SECTION 6: Understanding and Meeting the Needs of Students of Color ... 119

    SECTION 7: Building Bridges With Students of Color Through Effective Communication ... 123

    SECTION 8: Building Success Plans With Students of Color 127

UNIT FOUR: Key Issues in Advising 129

    SECTION 1: Building on Your Strengths as an Advisor 131

    SECTION 2: Ethical Implications and Practices of Advising 139

    SECTION 3: Avoiding Bias in Advising 147

    SECTION 4: Meeting Challenging Legal Issues in Advising 151

Appendix 159

    Advising for Excellence (Edward "Chip" Anderson) 161

    The Relationship Between Teaching and Advising (Carol Ryan) 169

    Developmental Advising (Steven C. Ender) 171

    Student Development Theory Into Practice: Implications for Advisors
        (Virginia Gordon) 177

    Advisor Resources (Thomas J. Kerr) 183

    Referral Skills (Faye Vowell) 191

    Communication Skills (Margaret C. "Peggy" King) 195

    Advising Undecided/Exploratory Students (Virginia Gordon) 201

    Advising Graduate Students (Cheryl J. Polson) 207

    Advising Transfer Students (Thomas J. Kerr and Margaret C. "Peggy" King) 215

    Advising Students of Color (Thomas Brown and Mario Rivas) 223

    Advising Adult Learners (Cheryl J. Polson) 235

    Developing an Advising Portfolio (Faye Vowell) 241

    Ethics and Values in Academic Advising (Marc Lowenstein) 247

    Legal Issues in Academic Advising (Susan J. Daniell) 251

Group Session Evaluation Form 257

Acknowledgments

The staff at USA Group Noel-Levitz want to publicly express our appreciation to the following advising specialists who served on the national Advisory Panel that helped to design and develop the program.

Unit Coordinators

Virginia Gordon, Assistant Dean Emerita, The Ohio State University

Thomas Grites, Special Assistant to the Vice President for Academic Affairs, Richard Stockton College of New Jersey

Advisory Panel Members

Thomas Brown, Dean of Advising Services, Saint Mary's College of California

David Crockett, Senior Vice President, USA Group Noel-Levitz

Susan J. Daniell, Associate Registrar and Director of Admissions, Gainesville College

Steven C. Ender, Professor, Learning Center, Indiana University of Pennsylvania

David Goldenberg, Executive Dean, The Sage Colleges

Thomas J. Kerr, Associate Provost, Rowan College of New Jersey

Margaret C. "Peggy" King, Assistant Dean for Student Development, Schenectady County Community College

Marc Lowenstein, Assistant Vice President for Academic Affairs, Richard Stockton College of New Jersey

Sidney McPhee, Vice Provost for Academic Affairs, University of Memphis

Cheryl J. Polson, Associate Professor, College of Education, Kansas State University

Buddy Ramos, Regional Manager, USA Group TRG

Mario Rivas, Director of the Advising Center and Director of the Learning Assistance Center, San Francisco State University

Carol Ryan, Dean, First College and Coordinator of University Advising, Metropolitan State University

Faye Vowell, Dean, School of Library and Information Management, Emporia State University

Nancy Walburn, Director, General Studies, The University of Alabama at Birmingham

In addition, with respect and appreciation we acknowledge the advisors, teachers and other educators who through their on-camera roles enrich the program with their experience and expertise.

Edward "Chip" Anderson, Program Coordinator, Graduate School of Education and Information Studies, UCLA

David Ball, Academic Advisor, Kirkwood Community College

Thomas Brown, Dean of Advising Services, Saint Mary's College of California

Patricia Mason-Browne, Academic Advisor, The University of Iowa

George Carter, Jr., Director, Undergraduate Academic Services, Clemson University

David Crockett, Senior Vice President, USA Group Noel-Levitz

John Gardner, Professor and Director, National Resource Center for the Study of the Freshman Year Experience, University of South Carolina

David Goldenberg, Executive Dean, The Sage Colleges

Virginia Gordon, Assistant Dean Emerita, The Ohio State University

Thomas Grites, Special Assistant to the Vice President for Academic Affairs, Richard Stockton College of New Jersey

Jeanne L. Higbee, Associate Professor of Counseling, The University of Georgia

Juliet Kaufmann, Director, Undergraduate Academic Advising Center, The University of Iowa

Thomas Kerr, Associate Provost, Rowan College of New Jersey

Margaret C. "Peggy" King, Assistant Dean for Student Development, Schenectady County Community College

Jack Levin, Professor of Sociology and Criminology, Northeastern University

Bette Mayes, Academic Advisor, The University of Iowa

Sidney McPhee, Vice Provost for Academic Affairs, University of Memphis

Cheryl Polson, Associate Professor, College of Education, Kansas State University

Mario Rivas, Director of the Advising Center and Director of the Learning Assistance Center, San Francisco State University

Carol Ryan, Dean, First College and Coordinator of University Advising, Metropolitan State University

Laurie Schreiner, Associate Professor of Psychology, Eastern College

Faye Vowell, Dean, School of Library and Information Management, Emporia State University

Foreword

Academic Advising for Student Success and Retention: An Advising Perspective

Edward "Chip" Anderson, Ph.D.
Program Coordinator, Graduate School of Education and Information Studies, UCLA

William G. McGuire, Ph.D.
Associate Director for Student Support Services and Retention, Pittsburg State University

Participant Note. The following advising perspective, written by two of the program's authors, discusses the strengths-based approach to advising and the role this approach can have in promoting student retention and student success.

The focus of Academic Advising for Student Success and Retention is on students, and on advising students in ways that promote the development of talent within students. At the same time, we hope that the program will also add to the development of faculty members and the professional and paraprofessional advisors who participate.

The ultimate aim is for college students to gain maximum benefits from the college experience and to come alive to the possibilities of lifelong learning, growth and development. And we are convinced that for this to become a reality, students must experience advising of the highest order—advising based on standards of excellence—advising that is driven by a commitment to excellence and that defines excellence in terms of the development of the talents of its students.

For the faculty member, the hallmarks of excellence and desired change might occur along such dimensions as teaching, advising, mentoring and scholarly ability and productivity. In a similar manner, all those who have responsibilities for the educational mission of the institution would be expected to experience growth and development as a result of being in the educational institution. Therefore, excellence in a framework of the development of human talents would include an emphasis on the intellectual and personal development of all advisors, counselors, learning specialists and student service professionals.

Can you imagine anything more exciting than working in an educational institution that is truly devoted and committed to the development of human talent? Can you imagine a better institution of higher education than one that is truly devoted and committed to the intellectual and personal development of its students, its faculty and its professional staff? Can you imagine how alive, how vibrant and how exciting it would be to work at an institution that truly defined itself, truly strove for excellence in terms of fully developing its students, its faculty and its staff?

- Would such an institution have difficulty recruiting students, faculty and staff?

- Would such an institution have drop-out and attrition problems?

- Who wouldn't want to be at an institution that was *alive* with growing and developing people?

- Who wouldn't want to attend an institution that was helping you discover your talents and abilities, and then encouraging you to develop those talents fully?

- Who wouldn't want to persist and become fully involved at an institution where you were becoming more alive intellectually and personally as you developed your talents?

- Who wouldn't want to achieve at an institution that was actively helping you discover new talents and abilities and helping you grow toward your fullest capacity?

What do you suppose might happen over the course of the lives of students who experienced an institution that really helped them fully develop intellectually and personally? Don't you imagine that such alumni would become fully functioning, high achieving, healthy professionals? Would such an institution have much difficulty generating donations, gifts and endowments from its alumni? Alumni would likely be very generous because they would know that their alma mater was devoted to talent development and because they would have experienced the benefits of such an institution.

A Strengths-Based, Talent-Development Approach to Advising

A strengths-based, talent-development approach to academic advising:

- Explicitly attempts to promote excellence—specifically the academic achievement, persistence and maximum development of students.

- Uses student strengths and talents as the basis for educational planning and excelling.

- Recognizes that student motivation is the single most important factor determining achievement, persistence and intellectual as well as personal development; thus student motivation must be central to advising.

- Recognizes that excellence only occurs when individuals capitalize on their strengths and talents, and invest the time and energy needed to excel.

- Sets forth an organized and proactive approach to advising based on the strengths-based, talent-development theme.

- Provides specific strategies and interview methods designed to promote student achievement, persistence and maximum development (i.e., excellence) that advisors can use in their advising sessions.

- Provides specific activities and exercises that advisors can use to reinforce advising sessions and help students prepare for subsequent sessions.

Some Premises of the Program

Excellence is a central value in all of higher education:

- Colleges and universities want to be known and recognized for their excellence.

- Excellence is a core value of every faculty member—every person in the academic community.

- Maintaining excellence defines the credibility, status and prestige of colleges and universities.

- Advising for Student Success and Retention emphasizes the educational mission of a college or university as it defines excellence in terms of student learning, growth and development.

Rationale for the Strengths-Based, Talent-Development Approach

Excellence—as both (a) the process of excelling to higher levels of achievement and (b) performing at the highest levels—is most likely to occur when individuals:

- Capitalize on their strengths.

- Fully utilize their talents and abilities.

- Invest the time and energy necessary to achieve.

Excellence, while based on strengths and talents, is dependent upon the motivation to invest the time and energy needed to achieve. Individuals are more likely to be motivated, remain motivated and thus invest the time and energy necessary to achieve if they are utilizing and working to develop their strengths, talents and abilities. Conversely, individuals who are forced to use, work on and strive to overcome their weaknesses, deficiencies and lack of talent will likely become discouraged, demoralized and suffer a lack of motivation that will reduce the probability of achieving, persisting and investing the time and energy needed for excellence.

Intents and Themes of the Strengths-Based, Talent-Development Approach

- To increase student awareness of strengths, talents and abilities.

- To encourage students to develop their strengths, talents and abilities to the maximum extent.

- To focus on building and developing strengths, talents and abilities first in order to build and sustain motivation, and build confidence/efficacy to achieve.

- To help students believe they can reach levels of excellence as a direct extension of developing their strengths and talents.

- To help students address areas where they need to be successful by applying their strengths, talents and abilities.

- To facilitate student adjustments and adaptations by applying their strengths and talents where changes need to be made.

- To facilitate career planning that extends from, fully utilizes and allows further development of strengths, talents and abilities.

What Are Strengths?

Strengths are the attributes that enable a person to do specific things well. These include:

- **Skills**. Specific thinking and behavior patterns that increase effectiveness and efficiency and improve problem solving.

- **Abilities**. Attributes that were developed from experience and enable a person to efficiently learn and complete certain tasks.

- **Gifts**. Seemingly natural inclinations and capabilities to do certain things very well.

- **Beliefs**. Thought patterns that enable a person to be effective and successful.

- **Habits**. Those recurring behaviors and thought patterns that ensure growth, development and achievement.

- **Knowledge**. The accumulated information, insights and understandings that **come** from previous learning experiences and that form the basis for future learning.

- **Curiosity**. The seemingly natural instinct to ask questions and desire answers to certain questions—the innate motivation to learn, know and understand.

In essence, a person's strengths are the unique combination of attributes that enable a person to do certain things at levels of excellence! The strengths-based talent-development approach advocates that attention and effort be directed toward strengths and to the full development of those strengths. Full development of strengths is the most effective and efficient means of promoting achievement.

The Uniquely Important Role of Advising in Promoting Excellence

Advising provides a unique opportunity:

- To help students form accurate perceptions of the college experience, correct misperceptions leading to adjustment problems and form accurate perceptions about excellence.

- To help personalize the college experience and help students become personally connected in the college environment.

- To help students personally experience two of the hallmark processes that lead to excellence: inquiry and reflection. As advisors use their questioning/inquiry skills and as advisors and students reflect on the answers that emerge, students can learn skills essential for excellence.

- To help students experience and learn from an "advanced learner/scholar" about the personal aspects of what excites him or her to learn and pursue excellence. Advisors and students can also discuss how that pursuit of excellence has emerged and has changed during a professional career. In this process, students can learn the importance of taking their interests seriously and trusting the validity of their experiences.

Advising is thought of in terms of sets of activities and a process that could occur in a variety of programs and services. It is unlikely that an academic advisor could do all of what is proposed in the program, Academic Advising for Student Success and Retention, and some components may not be appropriate at some colleges and universities.

When we use the term "advising," we are talking about a mode of interacting and intervening in the lives of students. Some of these "advising" interventions could occur in orientation programs, pre-registration or registration conferences, summer instructional programs, traditional academic advising interviews, college success/orientation courses and/or career/life planning workshops.

Advisors and the Strengths-Based, Talent-Development Approach

The same approaches that lead to success for students produce similar outcomes for advisors, namely that fully utilizing and capitalizing on strengths and talents will lead to excellence and maximize effectiveness.

While institutions differ in terms of who performs advising services—staff, faculty, graduate students and/or undergraduate students—one thing is clear: they are all advanced learners in one way or another. It is this fact, this strength and this talent we want to encourage advisors to use. As advanced learners, advisors at every level have developed a talent for asking informed questions and learning in response to their inquiries. Asking informed, relevant and timely questions is the most important skill and ability any advisor can develop.

This program attempts to organize advising and structure advising interactions into groups of questions that address various aspects of the three major issues advisors typically confront:

- Course selection

- Adjusting to demands/requirements of college

- Choosing a career

The second most important skill advisors need to use this approach is to listen carefully and reflect back (or mirror) what they hear from students. This simple process is profound in helping students become clearer, more focused and less confused. Listening and reflecting is essential in all advising sessions that involve planning, decision making and/or problem solving.

The third most important skill advisors need in this approach is the ability to help students identify appropriate and relevant opportunities, options, resources and services. We anticipate that utilizing this skill will involve advisors sharing their knowledge and experience and/or making timely referrals.

There are four overarching qualities that make advisors particularly effective:

- Caring and expressing compassion toward students

- Encouraging students by reminding them of their strengths and success patterns

- Sharing with students experiences or reactions that are similar to those experienced by students

- Expressing confidence in students and affirming a personal belief in what they can do

The Advisor's Role in the Strengths-Based, Talent-Development Approach

There are significant differences between the roles of a traditional advisor and the roles of an advisor who adopts the strengths-based, talent-development approach. The biggest role difference emanates from a strengths-based advisor's attempts to discover and develop a student's strengths/talents as opposed to identifying and remediating the student's deficiencies and/or weaknesses.

The specific roles of a strengths-based, talent-development advisor are as follows:

- **Assessing strengths.** This role is demanding in that it requires an understanding of (1) which strengths are needed for achievement in specific courses and (2) which strengths are needed to persist and gain maximum benefits from the college experience. In addition, the strengths-based advisor must have interviewing skills and an ability to administer and interpret inventories designed to identify strengths, talents and abilities. In reality, most assessments will be informal interviews rather than standardized tests. The key to the strengths assessment process is an advisor who actively seeks to know and understand students as persons and who agrees with the idea that achievement will result most effectively from identifying and building upon a student's strengths.

- **Mirroring strengths and increasing awareness of strengths.** This is the most important role of a strengths-based advisor. It demands outstanding interpersonal skills, because strengths must be reflected in a way that raises the student's awareness of his or her strengths, talents and abilities. Students must come to see, accept and appreciate their strengths in order to increase their motivation, confidence and efficacy, and thereby increase their achievement.

- **Orchestrating opportunities to build strengths.** The strengths-based advisor is determined to build a pattern of achievement within students by first having them build and develop their strengths. But this requires getting students into appropriate courses, services, clubs, organizations and recreational activities. Like an orchestra conductor, the strengths-based advisor tries to pull together services and opportunities so that students can use, build and expand their strengths to their maximum capacity.

- **Affirming and celebrating progress.** In some ways, the strengths-based advisor is like a detective and investigator, but the focus is on the positive. Instead of trying to "catch" someone doing something wrong, this approach tries to "catch" students doing things right and making it possible for them to excel, gain confidence and develop their strengths. As strengths are discovered, as progress (rather than perfection) is accomplished, as students experience themselves "soaring with their strengths," the strengths-based advisor affirms and celebrates the achievement.

As Donald Clifton and Paula Nelson state in their book, *Soar With Your Strengths* (1992, New York: Delacorte Press), strengths and talents develop best within the context of a supportive relationship. If an advisor makes use of the four attributes listed above, there is little doubt that students will experience a supportive relationship.

Introduction and Foundation

EDWARD "CHIP" ANDERSON

LAURIE SCHREINER

JULIET KAUFMANN

*"Academic advising is a planning process
that helps students to approach their education
in an organized and meaningful way."*

EDWARD "CHIP" ANDERSON, UCLA

*"A good advisor is someone who's pro-student—
who's a student advocate, who is able to cut
through some of the red tape of the bureaucracy
if necessary and who looks at the system through
a student's eyes."*

LAURIE SCHREINER, EASTERN COLLEGE

*"Academic advising is a process of teaching
students how to become responsible consumers of
their own educations."*

JULIET KAUFMANN, THE UNIVERSITY OF IOWA

Advising for Student Growth and Development

Key Learning Points

1. Academic advising is a planning process that helps students to approach their education in an organized and meaningful way. Advising brings together all of the major dynamics in a student's life.

2. Advising is a process of giving students guidance, support and encouragement.

3. Academic advising is a process of teaching students how to become responsible consumers of their own educations. It's also a process that involves teaching students how to make viable academic decisions.

4. There is quite a difference between ideal advising and how students view advising.

5. Advising is about helping students become self-sufficient.

6. Informed academic advising can help students progress and grow and your campus thrive.

7. Advising is a process that involves the entire campus, from freshman orientation to career counseling to graduation.

8. Advising is a process of helping students diminish the confusion that comes with a new environment, clarify their goals and get the most out of their education.

9. Academic advising is the central process by which you can personalize the whole college experience and help make it relevant to the student.

10. Informed academic advising is guided by the notions of progress and growth. Advising is a process that helps students discover their strengths and build on them to achieve their goals.

11. The ultimate goal of academic advising is students getting the very most out of their college experience. Advising promotes excellence.

12. Effective advisors care about students and want to make a difference in their lives.

13. Good advising is interactive. Both the student and the advisor contribute.

Discussion Questions

Question 1. What are some characteristics of an effective academic advisor?

Question 2. What do you think students expect from their advisor and the advising process? Is this different at different times?

Question 3. The video segment presents a contrast between student perceptions of advising and faculty comments about what advising ideally could be. How would students and faculty on your campus describe advising?

- How would students describe the strengths of advising?

- How would students describe the weaknesses of advising?

- How would faculty describe the strengths of advising?

- How would faculty describe the weaknesses of advising?

Question 4. Why is there a gap between the perception many students have of advising and the ideal of what advising can be? How might you go about closing that gap?

Question 5. What is your view of ideal academic advising?

Question 6. What has been your most rewarding experience as an academic advisor? Why?

Question 7. An advisor in the video segment suggests that advising is the central opportunity to personalize a student's college experience.

- How does this happen?

- What is the value of this?

Question 8. An advisor in the video segment suggests that advising is the central opportunity to help make a student's entire college experience more relevant.

- How does this happen?

- What is the value of this?

Question 9. The video suggests that informed advising promotes student progress and growth. What does progress and growth mean for students?

Question 10. An advisor in the video segment suggests that advisors know they have done their job when they are no longer necessary to students. In what ways are advisors more necessary in the beginning? What do students learn that makes advisors less necessary?

Question 11. What do students need to survive on your campus? What do they need to thrive?

Question 12. In the video segment, an advisor talks about excelling. What does it mean at your institution for students to excel?

Question 13. In the video segment, an advisor talks about students who come to college expecting to "receive" knowledge. In what ways do students come to college expecting to "receive" advising?

Question 14. Discovery is one of the main purposes of higher education. What role does advising play in achieving this purpose?

Question 15. In addition to faculty and professional advisors in formal advising situations, where else does advising happen on the campus?

Activities

Self-Assessment: Goals of Advising

Directions. The advisors in the video segment mention several goals of ideal academic advising, some of which are listed below. In the first column, number the items in rank order according to your view of their importance. In the second column, number the items in rank order according to your personal advising strengths.

Importance	Advising is ...	Strengths
_____	A planning process that promotes the maximum *academic* development of students.	_____
_____	A planning process that promotes the maximum *personal* development of students.	_____
_____	A planning process that promotes the maximum *social* development of students.	_____
_____	A planning process that promotes the maximum *career* development of students.	_____
_____	A process that helps students discover and access the support services on campus.	_____
_____	A process of helping students diminish the confusion that comes with a new environment and clarify their goals.	_____
_____	A process that increases student motivation to succeed and excel.	_____
_____	A process to help students learn to make independent decisions.	_____
_____	A process that gets students to think.	_____
_____	A process that provides guidance, support and encouragement.	_____
_____	A process that teaches students to be responsible consumers of their own educations.	_____

END OF SECTION 1

Advising for Student and Institutional Success

Key Learning Points

1. Advising is a key to student retention. The best way to keep students enrolled is to keep them stimulated, challenged and progressing toward a meaningful goal. The best way to do that—especially among new students—is through informed academic advising.

2. Good advising is vital to the long-term success of the institution.

3. Students who stay in college and who graduate are much more likely to be students who developed a relationship with one significant person in the employ of the college. Advisors are in an excellent position to be that significant person.

4. The advisor is the link between the student and the institution.

5. Advising can make a difference. Advisors can take a student who might otherwise leave the university or the college and reshape that student to some extent so that the student stays and excels and feels good about him or herself.

6. First- and second-year students can be overwhelmed by the college experience. The reality is that many new students have trouble coping with so many new experiences.

7. Academic preparation does not always equip students to persist and succeed academically. Attitude and motivation are powerful predictors of student success in college.

8. Most students don't come to school knowing how to make academic decisions.

9. Advisors teach students how to gather information, how to make decisions and how to test the results.

Discussion Questions

Question 1. In the video segment, a student says that she was misadvised. What are ways for students and advisors to assure this doesn't happen?

Question 2. The video segment suggests that students will be more likely to stay enrolled when they are stimulated, challenged and making progress toward a meaningful goal.

- How can advisors stimulate students?

- How can advisors challenge students?

- How can advisors help students identify and make progress toward meaningful goals?

Question 3. In what other ways can advisors help students stay enrolled?

Question 4. What would your reaction be if you heard someone say to a student, "I'm not going to let you fail."

Question 5. Why is it important that students stay enrolled and be successful?

Question 6. How do colleges and universities succeed and excel when students succeed and excel?

Question 7. If you were to craft a prevention plan to keep students from failing or leaving the institution, what would it include?

Question 8. If you were to craft a success plan to help students gather information to make good decisions and to test out the results, what would it include?

Question 9. What are the outcomes associated with the delivery of high quality academic advising? Consider each of the following:

- Student academic outcomes

- Student personal outcomes

- Student social outcomes

- Student career outcomes

- Faculty outcomes

- Advisor outcomes

- Institutional outcomes

Question 10. The video segment refers to advising for excellence. What does excellence mean to you and how could you use advising to bring that out?

Activities

Campus Goals and Academic Advising

Every college or university has academic, personal and career goals for its students. Academic goals might include students becoming broadly educated, developing the capacity for lifelong learning, or developing solid communication skills. Personal goals might be students developing aesthetic appreciation, becoming more open to new ideas, or valuing diversity. Career goals might include helping students develop a solid work ethic, flexibility to adapt to the needs of changing workplace, or the ability to transfer and apply knowledge.

Goals will and should vary widely from institution to institution. The goals of a research university will be different from those of a community college or a liberal arts college. Some goals will speak directly to the special mission of some institutions. For instance, a church-related college might have as one of its goals that students strengthen their faith or that they develop a strong service orientation by performing community service. A trade or technical program might be concerned primarily with giving students the personal, social and technical skills required for entry-level jobs.

In other words, the goals you have for students should arise directly from your institution's mission and should serve as a vehicle to set your institution apart from others. What do you want your graduates to know? What do you want your graduates to be able to do? What do you want your graduates to value? These questions are central to your institution and central to advising because advising will likely be the chief vehicle for realizing the goals of the mission statement.

One reason some people don't take mission statements seriously is that often there is such a wide gap between lofty institutional goals and daily realities. Take general education requirements, for example. Many institutions have a central goal of students becoming more liberally or broadly educated, developing critical thinking skills and acquiring knowledge and appreciation of literature and fine arts. The vehicle most institutions use to institutionalize those goals is general education or distribution requirements.

The reality is that many students do not take these courses seriously. They want to get through as quickly and with as little pain as possible. Why? Because they don't see the value of general education. They don't understand the institutional goals and they don't see how these courses fit into their lives and their interests. They want to get on to what they call "the good stuff," the content majors in which they are interested.

Few would argue that simply fulfilling a series of course requirements will automatically make students more liberally educated. If student goals and interests are to be aligned with institutional and faculty goals, it is up to faculty and advisors to help students make the connections between coursework and student goals, to put the students' coursework in a context that the students will value. When students say they aren't interested in taking certain courses, advisors and faculty need to be able to answer the nuts and bolts practical questions: How is music appreciation going to help me? Why should I be interested in the history of Western civilization? How does introduction to poetry fit in with accounting or engineering? Students seek relevance.

Advising is the ideal vehicle for bringing institutional mission alive and for aligning student and institutional expectations. Some students will drop out because they don't value what the institution values. Values and goals need to be carefully presented to students as early as the recruitment cycle. After students enroll, faculty and advisors need to probe students to discover their interests and values. Then they need to motivate students to get excited to see the value in what they will be required to do.

Directions. On the grid below, take the mission statement of your institution and write down in the first column some of the academic, personal, career or other goals the institution has for students. If your institution's mission statement does not contain specific goals, come up with some goals as a group that address the following questions: What do you want your graduates to know? What do you want your graduates to be able to do? What do you want your graduates to value? Then, in the second column, list the advising challenges for each goal. Finally, in the third column, list strategies and techniques advisors can use to help students meet these goals.

Academic, Personal and Career Goals for Students	Advising Challenges	Advising Strategies and Techniques to Help Achieve Goals
1.		
2.		
3.		
4.		
5.		
6.		

Alternative Activity on Campus Goals and Student Development

Directions. While not institution-specific, the lists below contain common institutional goals for student academic, personal and career development. Identify the goals in each of the three lists that fit your institution and discuss how advising could help students achieve each of the goals.

Academic	Personal	Career
Skills for lifelong learning	Sense of self-identity	Ability to market self
Understanding the value of learning	Leadership, responsibility	Clear career direction
Solid research skills	Flexibility, self-confidence	Sense of employment potential
Appreciation for other disciplines	Assertiveness, poise	Skills to determine capabilities
Effective oral and written communication	Sense of self-worth	Knowledge of what success requires
Effective study skills	Sense of values, honesty	Awareness of gender and ethnic issues in workplace
Ability to integrate course work	Tolerance of differences	Ability to develop inroads into marketplace, network
Ability to transfer and apply knowledge	Caring attitude	Job-hunting skills
Critical thinking skills	Willingness to question	Ability to get along with co-workers
Ability to acquire new knowledge	Human relations skills	Work values and ethics; honesty
Understanding of processes and outcomes	Ability to identify personal goals	Entry-level job competence
Enjoy the learning process	Ability to think globally	Skill in using and learning equipment
Ability to learn independently	Ability to act professionally	Preparation for future trends
Active curiosity	Attention to detail and follow-through	Flexibility and adaptability
Ability to discover talents	Decision-making skills	Mastery of theoretical background of field
Intellectual tolerance	Ability to accept change	Understanding that skills are transferable
Aesthetic appreciation	Social responsibility	Experience with technology
	Independence	
	Clear personal values	
	Understanding strengths	
	Health and well-being	

Analyzing Gaps Among Institutional, Faculty and Student Goals

While institutional mission statements often lay out lofty educational goals for students, common student goals may be very different, including such things as:

- Make more money

- Have a better life

- Get a job

- Get out of the house

- Satisfy parental desires

- Stay on parent health insurance

- Collect VA benefits or qualify for public assistance

- Develop avocational skills

The most effective advisors understand student goals and use them as a point of departure. They help students make connections between their goals and the goals of the institution. This is crucial to promoting student retention.

Directions. Working in small groups or as a large group, identify key institutional, faculty and student goals at your institution and write them down on the grid below. What are some differences between student, faculty/staff and institutional goals, and what are the implications for advisors?

Institutional Goals	Faculty/Staff Goals	Student Goals
1. _____	_____	_____
_____	_____	_____
2. _____	_____	_____
_____	_____	_____
3. _____	_____	_____
_____	_____	_____
4. _____	_____	_____
_____	_____	_____
5. _____	_____	_____
_____	_____	_____
6. _____	_____	_____
_____	_____	_____

Characteristics of Successful and Unsuccessful Students

Directions. Using the lists below as a starting point, identify the characteristics of unsuccessful/attrition-prone students at your institution and the characteristics of successful students.

Selected Characteristics of Attrition-Prone Students, Unsuccessful Students	**Selected Characteristics of Successful Students**
Poor self-management skills	Self-discipline
Lack of family expectations/support	Strong family support
Misperceptions or incorrect expectations of institution or program	Clear sense of academic expectations and what it takes to meet them
Poor study habits	Good study habits
Apathetic, uninvolved, disconnected	Involved in school activities, enthusiastic
Poor academic skills	Good academic skills
Lack of curiosity and intellectual interests	Curiosity, intellectual orientation
Closed to new ideas and new experience	Open-minded
Easily persuaded, subject to peer pressure	Independent thinker
Poor time management	Effective time management
Low self-esteem	High self-esteem
Lack of confidence in abilities	Self-confidence
Lack of career and educational goals	Focus, aims, goals
Lack of receptivity to help	Receptive to academic support and advising
Frustration with scheduling problems and administrative errors	Ability to understand and function with institutional bureaucracy and demands
Lack of commitment	Strong work ethic
Stressed, insecure, troubled	Emotionally healthy and mature
Underprepared	Good academic preparation
Part-time attendance, stop-out behavior	Special reason for choosing the institution
Socially isolated	Strong peer support
Lack of fit with institutional mission and goals	Full-time attendance, steady progress toward degree
Home/family difficulties	Highly motivated
Personal problems	Commitment to getting degree
Financial problems	Integration into college environment
Health problems	Willingness to seek help
Excessive socializing	
Chemical dependency	

Directions. After you have identified the characteristics, choose 10 that you as a group feel are the most significant for your institution and list them in the first column. Then brainstorm and discuss advising strategies and techniques that could be used to help students be more successful. List some of these strategies and techniques in the second column.

Characteristics of Attrition-Prone Students, Unsuccessful Students	Advising Strategies and Techniques to Help Students Be More Successful
1. _____	1. _____
2. _____	2. _____
3 _____	3 _____
4. _____	4. _____
5. _____	5. _____
6. _____	6. _____
7. _____	7. _____
8. _____	8. _____
9. _____	9. _____
10. _____	10. _____

Institution-Specific Issues

Directions. Discuss important factors in student retention that have been identified at your institution. For instance, you may want to look at:

• Varying retention rates among different student populations

• Retention rates, course pass rates, course drop rates, graduation rates, etc.

• Special retention issues or retention goals

Question 1. What are the key retention issues and retention goals at your institution? What role can advisors play in addressing these retention issues and goals?

END OF SECTION 2

SECTION 3

Advising to Promote Student Learning

Participant Note. For more information about the relationship between advising and teaching, see the resource article by Carol Ryan, "The Relationship Between Teaching and Advising," on page 169 in the appendix of the Participant Book.

Key Learning Points

1. The success of students and the success of institutions are inseparable.

2. Most faculty already practice the basics of informed advising in the classroom.

3. Teaching and advising require the same skills. Advisors and teachers have to really care about students, and want to make a difference in their lives. They get personal satisfaction out of having an impact, changing students in a positive way so that they can fulfill the goals they seek.

4. Teaching and advising are similar activities. Teachers help students learn to collect information, to weigh alternatives, to understand the pros and cons of different choices. Advisors teach students how to make decisions and how to engage in the various steps of decision making.

5. The best teachers and advisors make students think.

6. Advising is an extension of the teaching role.

7. When faculty have students in classes who want to be there and who are appropriately prepared to be there, it creates a whole different atmosphere in the classroom.

Discussion Questions

Question 1. The video suggests that the success of students and institutions are inseparable. Do you agree with this? How are the success of students and institutions inseparable?

Question 2. How is good advising vital to the long-term success of the institution?

Question 3. The video suggests that the best advisors and the best teachers make students think. Do you agree with this? How do the best advisors make students think?

Question 4. The video suggests that well-advised students make better students. Do you agree with this? In what ways are students better? What benefits are there for faculty in the classroom when students are appropriately advised?

Question 5. The video suggests that students need to be placed into classes for which they are well-informed, appropriately prepared and for which they have appropriate motivation and skills. What do advisors need to know about students to make this happen? What do advisors need to know about courses to make this happen?

Question 6. What are some other benefits to faculty of well-advised students?

Activities

Characteristics of Outstanding Teachers and Advisors

What are characteristics of outstanding teachers? How are these characteristics consonant with the characteristics of outstanding advisors?

Directions. In the two columns below, list the characteristics of outstanding teachers and advisors and discuss the ways in which the lists are similar.

Characteristics of Outstanding Teachers

1. _____
2. _____
3 _____
4. _____
5. _____
6. _____
7. _____
8. _____

Characteristics of Outstanding Advisors

1. _____
2. _____
3 _____
4. _____
5. _____
6. _____
7. _____
8. _____

END OF SECTION 3

Making a Difference Through Advising

Key Learning Points

1. An advisor is like an academic tour guide—helping a student wind that student's way through the college experience. In order to be an effective tour guide, advisors need to know where the student is starting from and where the student wants to go.

2. Effective advisors are caring, compassionate, concerned and excited about meeting students and helping to direct students.

3. A good advisor is someone who is pro-student, who is a student advocate, who is able to cut through some of the red tape of the bureaucracy when necessary and who looks at the system through a student's eyes as well.

4. Being an advocate for students, empathizing with students, caring for students—all are vehicles that can carry the advising effort down the road toward helping a student discover and build strengths and in the process apply them to achieve goals.

Discussion Questions

Question 1. Several advisors in the first video segments suggest that you have to want to make a difference in the lives of students. Do you agree with that? How do you make a difference through teaching? How do you make a difference through advising?

Question 2. How do you communicate to students that you care about them and their concerns?

Question 3. What are some means by which advisors can keep in contact with their advisees during the year?

Question 4. Can anyone share samples of letters or notes you send student advisees? These might include welcome/invitation letters inviting new students or new advisees to come to see you early in the term; letters concerning poor academic performance (from faculty referrals or mid-term grade reports); letters about specific academic issues, planning deadlines, etc.

Question 5. Sometimes advisors will need to call students. However, students are not always easy to reach by phone. Can anyone share ideas or techniques concerning the following:

- What is the best time of day to reach students?

- How do you reach students whose phones have been disconnected?

- When you leave a message for a student, what steps can you take to assure that the student will receive and act on the message?

Question 6. Most advisors will need to address questions of availability. Can anyone share ideas concerning the following:

- Do you share your home phone number with students and invite students to call you there?

- To what extent are you available outside posted office hours?

Question 7. What are some other ways to communicate effectively with students?

Question 8. Can anyone share examples of communicating with students by computer through e-mail or with intranet home pages?

Question 9. What are examples of bureaucracy or red tape you've had to confront on behalf of students?

Activities

Develop an Advising Contact Plan

Advisors will be more effective in identifying and meeting student needs if they meet with students regularly throughout the academic year.

> **Directions.** Working in small groups or as a large group, outline the components of an effective month-by-month advising contact plan for new students at your institution. Consider the following when developing the plan:

- If you were planning to meet with your advisees three to five times a term, what are the key times when your meetings might make the most difference to student success and retention? Consider key institutional events such as pre-registration and mid-term grades. Consider institutional deadlines such as drop/add and financial aid.

- At what points would face-to-face meetings be desirable or necessary? What follow-up meetings are desirable or necessary?

- At what points would phone, written or electronic communication be adequate?

Meeting Recruiting Promises

Question 1. What does your institution's recruitment literature say about academic advising?

Question 2. What does your institution's recruitment literature say about the personal attention and help students can expect from faculty and advisors?

Question 3. How does academic advising at your institution actually compare to the claims about advising presented in the recruitment literature?

Question 4. What could advisors do to help the institution match the reality of advising to the picture presented in the recruitment literature?

Tools

Ten Ways to Show Students You Care About Them and Their Concerns

1. Post office hours that meet students' needs—and keep advising appointments.

2. During advising meetings, show students you're listening carefully by taking notes, asking frequent questions and using appropriate body language.

3. Review your notes before the next student appointment.

4. Anticipate student needs and be prepared to meet them. Remember that students often don't know what they don't know.

5. Follow up on recommendations and referrals.

6. Remember advisee names and use them.

7. _____

8. _____

9. _____

10. _____

END OF SECTION 4

SECTION 5

Building for the Future Through Good Course Selection

Participant Note. For more information about advising for effective course selection, see the resource article by Edward "Chip" Anderson, "Advising for Excellence," on page 161 in the appendix of the Participant Book. The chart on page 168 provides a helpful summary of the five C's of student concerns and the role of advising in addressing each of them.

Five C's
- Course Selection
- Connection
- Confusion
- Confidence
- Career Selection

Key Learning Points

1. To help students develop strengths, advisors need to understand the five C's of student concerns: course selection, connection, confusion, confidence, and career selection.

2. Students create a college education by the decisions they make, by what they become involved in. Selecting classes is an important part of the college student involvement process.

3. Course selection is a primary concern of all students. Getting the right courses in the right order concerns most students, whether they are incoming freshmen, transfer students or fifth-year seniors. Informed course selection considers more than course sequencing.

4. Informed course selection involves three factors that need to come together to inform every single course decision: the motivation of the student, the preparation of the student, and the way the course fits into the student's life and requirements.

5. Advisors need to understand student curiosities and help students select classes that reflect those curiosities.

Discussion Questions

Question 1. What specific role and responsibility do advisors have with course selection and with the concerns students have about course selection?

Question 2. The video suggests that informed course selection meets the student from the standpoint of motivation, preparation and fit. What is the value of this?

Question 3. Who can share techniques or strategies you have found effective in dealing with the following issues:

- How can you best "sell" institutional course requirements to students?

- How can you be more creative in promoting the value of required courses?
- How do you motivate students to take required courses in which they have little interest?

Question 4. What transferable skills are taught in general education courses?

Question 5. What are some questions to ask students to assess motivation?

Question 6. What are some questions to ask students to assess preparation?

Question 7. What are some questions to ask students to assess fit?

Question 8. What are common course scheduling mistakes made at your institution by *students*? How could they be minimized or eliminated?

Question 9. What are common course scheduling mistakes made at your institution by *advisors*? How could they be minimized or eliminated?

Question 10. What aspects of a student's lifestyle will impact his or her ability to succeed in specific courses?

Question 11. How can students use general education courses to explore majors?

Question 12. It has been suggested that faculty aren't good at course selection for students who aren't like themselves. Do you agree?

Question 13. Courses vary in the patterns and kinds of work students are expected to do. For example, some courses are "reading courses" that may have widely dispersed writing assignments. Courses in areas such as math, accounting and foreign languages may demand significant amounts of time in daily assignments. Other courses may require students to spend several hours a week in labs. Can anyone share ideas on how you help students put together schedules that take into account these different patterns and kinds of work?

Activities

Role Plays

Situation. A new student at a community college is having difficulty distinguishing between college transfer and vocational-technical courses with similar titles.

Situation. A new student comes to see her advisor and says, "Tell me what I should take."

Situation. A second-year student comes in for pre-registration advising and says that she is changing majors from accounting to music.

Situation. A continuing student says, "Last term was a little rough. Do you have any easy courses?"

Situation. A new student comes to see his advisor and says, "Please sign my proposed schedule. I know it's blank, but I'll fill it in later."

Situation. A new student comes to see her advisor and says, "Why do I have to take all these required courses? I already know what I want to be."

Situation. A new student comes to see her advisor and says, "I don't want any courses that require a lot of reading. I don't like to read."

Situation. A new student comes to see her advisor and says, "I know I didn't do well in math in high school, but I know I can do calculus here."

Situation. A student comes to see his advisor and says, "I need a full schedule, but I can't take any courses before 10 a.m. or after 3:30 p.m. What have you got for me?"

Situation. A new student plans to attend a community college for two years and then transfer to a four-year institution to complete a degree. The student has not yet chosen a major or a transfer institution.

Institutional Recommendations

What policy recommendations might you make about improving course scheduling on your campus? In particular, consider some of the following:

- Course information and resources available to students and advisors

- Advisor training on using assessment and academic information about students in course placement

- The use and effectiveness of institutional course placement tests

- The impact of course availability on course selection

- The effectiveness of course prerequisites in promoting student success

- The extent to which students and advisors are provided with accurate and progressively updated information on which program and institutional requirements students have satisfied

- The usefulness of transcripts in aiding advisors and students in identifying what requirements have been satisfied

- Existing problems such as excessive course-drops that could be addressed by advisors or through policies

Accuracy of Course Scheduling Information

With respect to course scheduling, perhaps the most important issue to students is accuracy. Students expect to get from advisors accurate answers to many questions, including the following:

- Are the course and/or section numbers accurate?

- Do any of these courses conflict?

- Do I have the necessary prerequisites, co-requisites, placement scores or other preparation to take the course?

- What specific distribution, program or elective requirements will each course satisfy? How do the courses fit with past requirements I have satisfied? How many do I have left?

- Am I taking any courses for "institutional credit only" that would not likely transfer to another institution?

- If I am interested in more than one program, am I taking courses that will satisfy multiple requirements?

- Am I taking courses in the proper sequence?

- Do I need to take any courses this term that aren't offered in other terms?

- Have any course requirements changed since I began my program (especially important for students who have stopped out)?

- If I take this course on a pass/fail basis, will it still count to meet the requirements?

- Will this course count if I change majors?

Directions. Working in small groups or as a large group, discuss the issues of accuracy listed above. In particular, focus on the following:

1. Do advisors have the necessary information and resources to answer these common student questions and concerns? If not, what do they need?

2. Do advisors have the training to accurately and definitively answer these questions?

3. If advisors are unsure of the answers to these questions, what are the best resources on campus to help students and advisors?

Tools

Questions to Ask Students Concerning Course Selection

Use the space below to build a list of helpful questions to ask students to get at motivation, preparation and fit with respect to course scheduling.

1. What courses would you take if you had no requirements?

2. If you have a career in mind, what are the kinds of things you'd need to know to be successful in it?

3. Apart from career goals, where do you see yourself in 10 years? In 20 years? What's it going to take to get there?

4. _____

5. _____

6. _____

7. _____

8. _____

9. _____

10. _____

Advising Issues and Implications

Question 1. What is a good balance for students between general education and other institutional requirements and courses in areas of the major or minor?

Question 2. If motivation, preparation and fit are key factors in helping students build a course schedule in which they can succeed and thrive, what is the effect on students if they are encouraged to take a "standard" or "set" program?

Preparation for First Course Selection Advising Session: Student Worksheet

Participant Note. The following worksheet provides a sample list of student questions that advisors might find useful when working with students on course selection. Students could complete this worksheet in advance, or advisors could ask students to answer these questions during the advising meeting.

I. Areas of Interest and Preparation

A. What are the three courses (high school or college) you have most enjoyed?

B. In which academic areas do you feel you are most thoroughly prepared?

C. What do you consider the two most interesting books you have ever read?

D. What academic/school project has given you the greatest pride?

E. As a result of your college experience, what aspect of the world around you would you most like to better understand?

II. Complete the Following Sentences:

A. In my opinion, my greatest personal assets are _____

B. I feel best when _____

C. I feel most positive about my ability to _____

D. The part of my educational plan I feel best about is _____

E. The part of my educational plan I feel most concerned about is _____

_____

F. As a student, I am most proud of _____

G. Upon graduation from college, I will feel most satisfied if _____

H. Ten years after college, I will feel fulfilled and successful if_____

_____

III. Time Commitments

A. If you plan to work this term, how many hours per week do you plan to work?

B. What *school* activities will you be involved in this term? How many hours per week?

C. What *non-school* activities do you plan to be involved in this term? How many hours per week?

D. What family and/or child care commitments will you have this term?

E. Any other scheduled commitments of your time?

END OF SECTION 5

Helping Students Get Connected

Participant Note. For more information about the role advising plays in helping students get connected, see the resource article by Edward "Chip" Anderson, "Advising for Excellence," on page 161 in the appendix of the Participant Book. The chart on page 168 provides a helpful summary of the five C's of student concerns and the role of advising in addressing each of them.

> **Five C's**
> • Course Selection
> • Connection
> • Confusion
> • Confidence
> • Career Selection

Key Learning Points

1. Connecting a student to the campus, giving the student a sense of belonging both academically and socially, is key to the success of both the student and the institution.

2. The chance for students to persist is greatly enhanced when they are integrated in the social and academic environment of an institution.

3. The number one student problem is confusion. Successful advisors help guide the student toward clarity.

4. Good advisors ask questions and hold a mirror up to students.

5. Many students lack confidence.

6. First and foremost advisors should make sure that students get a good start, learn and understand their strengths and grow with the confidence of successful experience.

Discussion Questions

Question 1. Do advisors have a role and responsibility in addressing students' concerns about becoming "connected" to the college environment? If so, what is the nature of that role and responsibility? If not, who does have that responsibility?

Question 2. Do advisors have a role and responsibility in addressing students' concerns about their confusion? If so, what is the nature of that role and responsibility? If not, who does have that responsibility?

Question 3. Do advisors have a role and responsibility in addressing students' concerns about their confidence? If so, what is the nature of that role and responsibility? If not, who does have that responsibility?

Question 4. When they begin college, many students are anxious, overwhelmed and confused by their new life.

- What are some simple things advisors can do to help students feel less anxious?

- What are some simple things advisors can do to help students feel less overwhelmed?

- What are some simple things advisors can do to help students feel less confused?

Question 5. Sometimes students find it difficult to talk about personal feelings of anxiety, insecurity and lack of confidence. With these students it is often helpful for advisors to ask probing questions in a more abstract way. For instance:

- I had a student the other day who told me such-and-such; what do you think about that?

- What kinds of problems do you see other new students trying to deal with?

Can anyone share examples of other questions you use to get at personal issues in an indirect way?

Question 6. What are some questions you find it helpful to ask to get at issues of connection to the institution, students and faculty?

Question 7. What are some questions you find it helpful to ask to get at issues of confusion?

Question 8. What are some questions you find it helpful to ask to get at issues of confidence?

Activities

Role Plays

Situation. A new student finds there's not enough money to afford everything. He comes in to drop courses so he can work part time.

Situation. A new student at a community college is living at the only residence hall. The student feels very isolated and lonely at the largely commuting campus.

Situation. A new student finds that her roommate's behavior in their room is keeping her from studying after the library closes.

Situation. An entering student tells you she plans to commute home every weekend to work at the family business.

Situation. An entering student tells you he plans to study "about five hours a week."

New Student Experiences and Advising Implications

Directions. List the key experiences new students may be going through for the first time on your campus. What are some of the potential problems associated with each? What are some of the ways that advisors and/or the institution as a whole can respond to each?

New Experience	Potential Problems	Advisor and/or Institutional Response
1. First checkbook, first credit card/s, first phone account, first time needing to manage money	• Overspending • May need to drop out of school to pay bills, etc. • May need to work more and take less course-work	• Advisor can help identify misuse of money problems • Institutions can address money management through workshops, orientation courses, etc.
2. First time living away from home	• Loneliness, depression, isolation • Inability to wisely handle new freedoms	• On-campus jobs can be a retention strategy • Advisor can help identify problems and get students connected with people and organizations on campus
3. First time sharing a room	• Conflict, unhappiness, negative effects on academic work	• Advisor referrals to counseling, residence life and other offices • Advisor can discuss problem or refer to residence life
4. _____	_____	_____
5. _____	_____	_____
6. _____	_____	_____

Organizing Student Involvement and Personal Development

Many institutions have implemented student development or co-curricular transcripts. Whether maintained in a formal way by the institution or maintained by students and advisors, these transcripts provide a record of such things as:

- Involvement in activities, organizations or programs

- Non-credit academic experiences, workshops, internships, etc.

- Competencies attained

- Participation in community service or community organizations

- Leadership development

- Campus or volunteer work

- Honors, awards and recognition

Besides providing students with a personal development record to share with employers, these transcripts provide advisors an excellent *planning* document to help new students plan their personal development and involvement.

Directions. Working in small groups or as a large group, discuss how your institution could develop a student development transcript or could develop a student development planning worksheet advisors could use when working with new students.

Organizing Student Development to Promote Institutional Values

Whether stated explicitly or implied, every college or university has student development goals tied to institutional mission and values. These goals typically fall in several areas, such as academic, career, interpersonal, aesthetic, wellness, social responsibility, spiritual, and so forth. Here are examples of typical goals:

1. Work ethic, vocational and interpersonal skills necessary for entry-level employment

2. Effective study skills and habits

3. Appreciation of the creative and performing arts

4. Ability to critically examine ideas and information

5. Ability to understand and value people from diverse backgrounds

6. Ability to work with others

7. Written and oral communication skills

Directions. Working in small groups or as a large group, identify and list key institutional goals for students in academic, personal, career, social, spiritual or any other areas appropriate to the institution. (Note: If you completed the activity in Unit Two, Section 2, Campus Goals and Academic Advising, you will already have identified many or most of these goals.)

Identify opportunities at your institution for students to reach each of these goals, including the following:

- Course-based opportunities

- Academic and personal programs and services, workshops, etc.

- Organizations and activities

- Volunteer or work opportunities

This information can serve as a key resource for advisors. It can also serve as a student development planning worksheet advisors could use when working with students.

Tools

Show Students They Aren't Alone

Many students feel that they are the only ones experiencing a particular problem. It is often a great relief to them to discover that their problems may be shared by many other students. Advisors can do a real service to students by letting students know through questions and comments that the problems they may be experiencing are common and natural.

Help Students Get Connected

As you have learned earlier in the program, advising presents an ideal opportunity to bring institutional values alive for students. For instance, your institution may have learned through research or anecdotal experience that students who are involved in campus activities are retained at a higher rate and have higher grade point averages than students who are not involved in campus activities. Further-more, your institution believes that involvement in activities is important to student development. In other words, involving students in activities is an "institutional value" that can be furthered through advising.

Here are some ways to actively try to get students connected to activities:

1. Rather than asking a student, "Are you planning to be involved with any activities this term?" reword the question to assume that the student will be involved in something: "What activities are you planning to be involved with this term?"

2. Ask students questions about the activities they were involved with in the past. Then go over with students a list of all school organizations and activities to discover any that seem like a good fit with student time and interests.

3. Encourage students to attend any activity fairs sponsored by your institution.

4. Give students an "assignment" to attend a meeting of at least two campus organizations and to report back on what they discovered.

5. If a student is fairly set on a major area and/or career, help them identify campus organizations, activities or volunteer opportunities that might be related or helpful.

Questions to Ask Students

Use the space below to build a list of helpful questions to ask students concerning connection, confusion and confidence.

1. How are your parents doing without you?

2. Have you met a faculty member you'd like to get to know better?

3. What has been your most surprising experience here so far?

4. What do you like best and least about being here?

5. How is the school different from what you thought it would be?

6. What are you spending more time on than you thought you would?

7. What are some of the feelings you've experienced about being away from home?

8. What are some of the feelings you've experienced about being in college?

9. If you were starting a journal about new things you are learning about yourself, what are some of the things you would list?

10. What advice would you give a brand-new student, based on what you've learned so far?

11. _____

12. _____

13. _____

14. _____

15. _____

END OF SECTION 6

Planning for Careers and Life After College

Participant Note. For more information about advising for effective career planning, see the resource article by Edward "Chip" Anderson, "Advising for Excellence," on page 161 in the appendix of the Participant Book. The chart on page 168 provides a helpful summary of the five C's of student concerns and the role of advising in addressing each of them.

Five C's
- Course Selection
- Connection
- Confusion
- Confidence
- Career Selection

Key Learning Points

1. Most students are very concerned with their life after school.

2. Many advisors feel uncomfortable talking about careers. They think that they aren't career counselors. However, there's a certain level of expertise that every academic advisor needs to have in the area of careers, simply because this is an area that students are so concerned with.

3. Educational, career and life planning are the fundamental purposes of academic advising.

4. Many students come to college and choose a major not based on what they personally like, but on what they have heard is practical or what their parents told them to do. That's a great place for an advisor to make an impact, to make a difference, to discuss majors and careers.

5. Helping students develop a life purpose is a central focus for many advisors who practice developmental advising concepts.

6. Developing a life purpose requires that students clarify what is really important to them in their personal lives and how their personal lives will relate to their vocational lives.

7. Part of career advising is helping students build a portfolio of skills they can use in one or more careers.

8. Successful advisors help steer students in directions that will help them succeed and develop the ability to make informed decisions—a skill that will last a lifetime.

Discussion Questions

Question 1. How concerned about careers are students at your institution? How do they demonstrate this?

Question 2. Do advisors have a role and responsibility in addressing students' concerns about career decisions? If so, what is the nature of that role and responsibility? If not, who does have that responsibility?

Question 3. What are some helpful questions you ask students to discover their level of knowledge about particular careers?

Question 4. What are some helpful questions you ask students to discover their motivation and personal interest in particular careers?

Question 5. What are examples of advising "assignments" you give students with respect to educational and career planning?

Question 6. Do you find many students who make mistakes by equating educational and career planning? How do you get students to see the important differences?

Question 7. The video suggests that helping students develop a life purpose is central to advising. What does it mean to develop a life purpose and how can advisors help students with this task?

Question 8. In your advising, do you feel comfortable talking with students about careers? If you feel uncomfortable, what training or information would help you feel more comfortable?

Question 9. In your advising, how can you help students develop a portfolio of skills that will help them in their careers?

Question 10. What majors at your institution lead directly to careers?

Question 11. For those who teach in departments, what are examples of careers in which your graduates have been successful?

Question 12. Given the strong career interest of many students, how do advisors help students broaden their horizons beyond narrow career interests?

Activities

Role Plays

Situation. An undecided student wants to major in something like public relations that the school may not have as a program but for which the school has more than enough appropriate courses.

Situation. A new student says, "I don't know what I want to do, so how can I choose what courses to take?"

Situation. A student chooses a very challenging major, such as biology or computer science, for which he appears to have neither the preparation nor the academic skills to succeed.

Situation. A new student has "excessive careerism"—she only wants to take courses that directly relate to a particular career (such as accounting) and does not see the value of taking anything else.

Situation. A new student says, "I want to do something where I can help people."

Organizing Student Development to Promote Career Planning

One of the central goals of academic advising is to help students make informed academic and career decisions.

Directions. Working in small groups or as a large group, develop a career planning worksheet that advisors can use with students to plan experiences that complement a student's career goals, including the following components:

- Credit and non-credit courses

- Academic and personal programs and services, workshops, etc.

- Organizations and activities

- Volunteer or work opportunities

This information can serve as a key resource for advisors and students.

Using Career Development Resources on Your Campus

Directions. Working in small groups or as a large group, identify the career development resources at your institution. Here are some questions to consider:

1. What career development resources are available to and recommended for new students?

2. What vocational and/or aptitude tests are offered to students?

3. What career development software is available to students?

4. How do students find out about and arrange internships and research opportunities?

5. What workshops or seminars are offered to students on topics such as writing effective resumes and job application letters?

6. How do career development professionals like to handle student referrals?

Use this information as a resource when discussing career development with students.

Helping Students See Distinctions Between Academic Programs and Careers

Directions. Working in small groups or as a large group, identify and list the academic programs at your institution that are designed to lead to specific careers or that are required for entry into specific careers. Use this information as a resource when discussing with students the distinctions between academic programs and careers.

Identifying Career Opportunities for Graduates of Your Institution

Directions. Working in small groups or as a large group, identify and list by academic program what graduates typically do after they leave your institution. This can include employment as well as further education. Use this information as a resource when discussing career opportunities with students. This information is also very useful to have for recruiting new students.

Institution-Specific Issues

Directions. Working in small groups or as a large group, discuss enrollment patterns at your institution and the implications for advising. Focus particular attention on the following:

• The numbers of new students enrolling in each program

• The numbers of students graduating in each program

- What actually happens to graduates (kinds of jobs, graduate and professional school, further training, etc.)

- Frequency of major changes

- What happens to undecided or undeclared students

- Retention rates by academic program

Also discuss institutional rules and policies concerning academic progress toward degree completion. For instance, must undecided students choose a program after they have completed a certain number of hours?

Tools

Transferable Skills: Help Students Make the Connection

A majority of college students hold part-time jobs either on- or off-campus. Although most students don't work in areas that are directly related to their career interests, part-time jobs can often provide a wealth of experience. Ask students questions about their work, such as "What are you doing in your job that will be helpful to you in a career?"

Help Students Build a Résumé

It's common for students to finish a program and then realize that they may not have planned well for their chosen career. Advisors can help by focusing student attention on developing transferable skills. When students have fairly clear academic and vocational goals, give them one or two sample résumés and ask them to think through what academic background, work experience and competencies they would need to be competitive for a job in their intended career. Then work with them to "build a résumé"—to plan courses, activities and experiences that make them ready for employment.

Questions to Ask Students About Careers and Life After College

Use the space below to build a list of helpful questions to ask students concerning connection, confusion and confidence.

1. What academic areas are you currently considering? What do you like about these areas?

2. What occupations are you considering? What about these occupations attracts you?

3. How do your strengths and skills fit the tasks necessary to succeed in these areas?

4. Will these occupations provide the rewards and satisfactions you want for your life? Why?

5. What are the differences among the occupations you are considering? The similarities?

6. Who has influenced your ideas about these alternatives?

7. In what kind of work environment do you picture yourself five years after you have finished school?

8. _____

9. _____

10. _____

11. _____

12. _____

END OF SECTION 7

SECTION 8

A Strengths-Based Approach to Advising

Participant Note. For more information about the strengths-based approach to advising, see the resource article by Edward "Chip" Anderson and William G. McGuire, "Academic Advising for Student Success and Retention: An Advising Perspective," on page vii in the Participant Book.

Key Learning Points

Five C's
- Course Selection
- Connection
- Confusion
- Confidence
- Career Selection

1. If you address the five C's of student concerns, students will be in a better position to excel and succeed. The best way to guide students toward this end is to help them capitalize on their strengths.

2. Advisors help students discover and explore strengths. A student can be led to discover existing strengths, use them to succeed and invest the time and energy needed to bolster other areas.

3. Information is critical to the advisor in assessing and building on strengths.

4. The notion of progress, not perfection, is central to helping students develop their strengths.

5. Objective assessment information presents only a partial snapshot of a student. Advisors also need to tap into student attitudes and motivation.

6. Advising needs to be an ongoing relationship.

7. Advising is a progressive process that moves students from dependence to independence. This involves increasingly shifting responsibility to the student.

8. Part of the advising process is helping students develop realistic expectations of the college experience.

Discussion Questions

Question 1. As an advisor, how can you lead students to discover existing strengths, utilize them to succeed and invest the time and energy needed to bolster other areas?

Question 2. What questions do you ask to tap into student strengths?

Question 3. How do you build on strengths when students have multiple weaknesses?

Question 4. Of the information you currently receive about students, what helps you best assess their strengths and weaknesses?

Question 5. What questions do you ask students to discover if the assessment information you have about them presents an accurate picture of the student?

Question 6. What are some positive expectations you want students to have about college and how can the advising process be used to develop them?

Question 7. What questions do you ask to tap into student motivation?

Question 8. How is building on strengths different from focusing on limitations and weaknesses?

Question 9. What expectations should advisors have of their advisees?

Question 10. We talk about the responsibilities of students. What are the responsibilities of advisors?

Question 11. How do you help students take responsibility for their own learning and education?

Question 12. What are some misconceptions and misperceptions that new students have about postsecondary education and/or advising? How can advisors help students identify and change these misconceptions and misperceptions?

Activities

Role Plays

Situation. In the first meeting with a new student, an advisor focuses entirely on all the deficits in the student's record.

Situation. In the first meeting with a new student, an advisor focuses almost exclusively on identifying and tapping into student strengths and motivations.

Situation. A student direct from high school has a very uneven record: good grade point average but below average test scores and average scores on institutional placement tests.

Situation. A student direct from high school has a great many personal but few academic strengths. The advisor needs to help the student build on these personal strengths to achieve more academic success.

Using Student Information to Build on Strengths

Directions. As a group, go over all the kinds of information advisors typically receive for new students, such as ACT or SAT scores, College Student Inventory™ results, high school transcripts, high school GPAs and scores on institutional placement tests. Discuss how advisors use the information to identify student strengths. What questions do advisors find helpful to ask using this information as a starting point?

You may want to include the following questions in your discussion:

Question 1. At your institution, what information about *new* students is available to advisors? Is the information sufficient to conduct effective advising?

Question 2. At your institution, what information about *continuing* students is available to advisors? Is the information sufficient to conduct effective advising?

Tools

Questions to Ask to Tap Into Student Strengths

Use the space below to build a list of helpful questions to tap into student strengths.

1. What are you especially good at?

2. What do you do well enough that you could teach someone else?

3. As you compare yourself with other students here, what would you say are your academic and personal strengths?

4. _____

5. _____

6. _____

Questions to Ask to Tap Into Student Motivation

Use the space below to build a list of helpful questions to tap into student motivation. **Note:** Questions about strengths and motivation are counterintuitive for many students who have been conditioned to make decisions about what they "ought to do" or "ought to like."

1. What do you like to do?

2. When you're not in school or working, how do you like to spend your time?

3. What kinds of things make you feel most fulfilled?

4. _____

5. _____

6. _____

END OF SECTION 8

UNIT TWO
Communication and Relational Skills

THOMAS BROWN

PATRICIA MASON-BROWNE

THOMAS GRITES

*"What is really important in that first inter-
action with the student is that you demonstrate
you have something to offer, that you have some
skills, that you are interested in that student: you
are committed to that student's success."*

THOMAS BROWN, ST. MARY'S COLLEGE OF CALIFORNIA

*"If we didn't ask questions about spring break, if
we didn't ask questions about living in residence
halls versus having your own apartment, if we
didn't ask what they were doing outside the class,
we wouldn't be advising the whole student."*

PATRICIA MASON-BROWNE, THE UNIVERSITY OF IOWA

*"It is still the student who is the decision-maker
and the person responsible for that decision and
the person who accepts and must accept the
results or consequences of that decision."*

THOMAS GRITES, RICHARD STOCKTON COLLEGE OF NEW JERSEY

Conducting an Effective Advising Interview

Participant Note. For more information about conducting effective advising interviews, see the resource article by Steven C. Ender, "Developmental Advising," on page 171 in the appendix of the Participant Book.

Key Learning Points

1. What is accomplished in advising is set in motion in the advising interview. Through the interview a relationship is established and a sense of caring communicated, a sense that you are interested in the student and committed to his or her success. All that develops trust.

2. The advising interview can be divided into five parts: (1) open the interview; (2) identify the problem; (3) identify possible solutions; (4) take action; (5) summarize the transaction.

3. In the opening section, ask students to state the issue or problem. Then help the student provide all the relevant facts. Where is the student? What kind of help is the student seeking? There should be agreement between the student and advisor on the issue or issues at hand and the direction of the advising.

4. When you ask students for solutions, focus on concrete details, such as: What is to be done? When? By whom? How? Also help the student identify any other resources that are needed to solve the problem. Finally discuss the implications of these decisions.

5. You get to know students by asking questions about family, hometown, etc.

6. You never get a second chance to make a first impression.

7. It's vital to respond to students' immediate needs.

8. Tapping into students' intellectual interests and curiosities is the toughest part of advising.

Discussion Questions

Question 1. The video mentions that the advising interview develops trust. What are some things that trust means both to an advisor and to a student?

Question 2. The content experts mention several keys to the first advising interview: showing students you care about them as individuals, having students perceive you as thorough, being an advisor who provides a lot of options and information, communicating interest in the students and commitment to their success, and encouraging students to make their own decisions.

How do you show students you care about them as individuals?

Question 3. How do you show students your willingness to work together?

Question 4. How do you show students you are thorough and well-informed?

Question 5. How do you show students your willingness to let them make their own decisions?

Question 6. If it's important for you to get to know students, is it equally important for students to get to know you? If yes, what is it important for students to know about you?

Question 7. How do you show students your interest in them?

Question 8. How do you show students you are committed to their success?

Question 9. One of the advisors on the video segment said that tapping into students' intellectual interests is the toughest part of advising? Why is that so?

Question 10. Why is it important that the student and the advisor agree on the issue or issues at hand and the direction of the advising?

Question 11. How can advisors help students identify, set and reach goals?

Question 12. What are helpful questions to ask students to determine openness and readiness for advising?

Question 13. How do you evaluate your student advising sessions? Can anyone share ways you solicit feedback from students?

Activities

Role Plays

Situation. A new student comes in for her initial advising session. As an advisor, you outline your expectations for advising. In return, the student indicates she doesn't need advising and doesn't want an advising relationship; she just wants to get her registration form signed.

Situation. An adult student comes in for an advising session. He is very shy, and you find out early on that he is very hard to draw out.

Situation. An entering freshman brings his parents to the first advising interview. "I have just one question," the student's mother says. "Who is going to make sure my son wakes up in time to get to class?"

Self-Assessment: Personal Goals for Student Advising Sessions

Directions. The following self-assessment will guide you in determining in an organized and objective way your expectations for advising. For each goal, rate the importance to you on a scale of 6 to 1, with 6 being high.

Each of these items will have implications for the signals you give students during your advising sessions. For instance, if you want advisees to get to know you as an individual, you can invite that by talking about your own experience as a student, your intellectual interests and curiosities, etc.

If you want to see advisees frequently, you can make that expectation clear through direct statements, advising assignments between sessions, etc. In particular, look at the goals that are very important to you. To what extent are you achieving these goals? What might you have to change in your advising approach or expectations for students to achieve the goals that are most important to you?

Goals for Student Advising Sessions	Importance to You
1. I want to get to know advisees as individuals and am interested in knowing about and discussing aspects of their personal lives.	6 5 4 3 2 1
2. I want advising sessions to focus only on academic and career areas.	6 5 4 3 2 1
3. I want advising sessions restricted to discussions of course scheduling.	6 5 4 3 2 1
4. I expect to see my advisees frequently.	6 5 4 3 2 1

5. I expect advisees to do "assignments" between advising sessions.	6 5 4 3 2 1	
6. I want advisees to get to know me as an individual.	6 5 4 3 2 1	
7. I want to establish an ongoing relationship with advisees.	6 5 4 3 2 1	
8. I want advisees to perceive me as thorough and competent.	6 5 4 3 2 1	
9. I want advisees to make their own decisions.	6 5 4 3 2 1	
10. I stress career planning with my advisees.	6 5 4 3 2 1	
11. With course scheduling, I take an approach that includes motivation, preparation, fit.	6 5 4 3 2 1	
12. I take a strengths-based approach with advisees.	6 5 4 3 2 1	

Personal Goal Statement. In the next several weeks, I will take steps to assure that I am achieving the goals that are important to me. (From the inventory items above, list the top five in order of importance, then answer questions 1-4.)

1. _____

2. _____

3. _____

4. _____

5. _____

Question 1. List several *personal* qualities you most like to see in students.

Question 2. As an advisor, what can you do to help students develop or strengthen these qualities?

Question 3. List several *academic* qualities you most like to see in students.

Question 4. As an advisor, what can you do to help students develop or strengthen these qualities?

Discussion of Sample Advising Agenda

Directions. Working in small groups or as a large group, discuss the Sample Advising Agenda printed below in the Tools section. Go over each section of the advising agenda, with particular focus on the following:

1. Given the time constraints facing advisors at your institution, which items on the agenda would be most helpful for advisors and students for the first session?

2. Which items from the agenda could be useful in a follow-up meeting to the initial advising interview?

3. What other agenda items or student questions could you add that are specific to the needs of the students you work with at your institution?

After discussing the Sample Advising Agenda, break into groups of three and take the roles of advisor, advisee and observer. Conduct an advising interview focusing on the elements of one or more of the six sections of the outline. Switch roles so that each participant has an opportunity to play the role of advisor.

Tools

Sample Advising Agenda: New Student—First Advising Session

Participant Note. This sample advising agenda presents a range of topics that advisors may want to address in a first advising session. Although there is more material included than an advisor would have time to use, the agenda provides a helpful, comprehensive list from which advisors may choose topics and approaches.

In the first unit of the program you discussed many of the ways in which academic advising is tied to student retention and student success:

*   By building relationships with students, advisors provide a personal link between students and the institution.

*   Advisors identify student expectations and goals and provide a rationale for institutional expectations and goals.

*   Advisors promote success in the classroom through informed course selection that stresses the importance of motivation, preparation and fit.

*   Advisors help students identify and build on their strengths to increase motivation and promote success.

*   Advisors help students get connected to the institution.

*   Advisors help students build confidence.

- Advisors promote student personal development.

- Advisors assist with career planning.

Now, how does all this happen? How does advising actually promote student retention and student success? It begins with the first advising interview. That's when the advisor introduces expectations and goals and begins the process of assessing motivation and student strengths.

The outline below covers the six key elements of an initial advising session:

1. Expectations of advising and of this session

2. Assessment of strengths and talents

3. Assessment of motivation

4. Assessment of preparation

5. Matching strengths and motives to opportunities

6. Fitting potential courses to demands and requirements

Within the outline, you will find a listing of goals to accomplish, items to discuss and helpful questions to ask students. Remember, the primary goals of the first advising session are to:

1. Build a positive relationship

2. Introduce the strengths-based, talent-development approach

3. Select first-term courses

1. Exploration of expectations

A. What the student expects of advising in general and wants as outcomes for this session—needs and concerns

B. What the advisor hopes to accomplish:

    1. Understanding strengths-based advising.

    2. Get acquainted in the process of initiating a relationship

    3. Identify potential courses that stem from strengths and desires/motivations.

    4. GOAL: To find classes that match the student's strengths and motivations and ensure that these classes are a realistic fit to degree requirements and the student's commitments.

C. Mesh student needs/expectations with advisor's agenda—assure student that his or her concerns will be addressed

2. Assessment of student's strengths and talents

A. Discuss high school or other prior formal learning experiences

Helpful questions to ask students:

1. What did you learn with greatest ease?

2. What did your teachers compliment you about?

3. In what areas do you feel you have the greatest academic skills?

4. What was your favorite course in high school?

5. What do your friends say they like best about you?

B. Think about learning, studying and performing

Helpful questions to ask students:

1. In what ways do you find it easiest to learn?

2. On what types of tests do you score highest?

3. What types of problems do you enjoy solving?

4. What was your favorite assignment?

5. What subjects do you most enjoy studying? Which do you like least?

6. What academic projects give you the most feelings of pride?

7. What sorts of teaching styles or classes do you find the most challenging?

8. What sort of learning do you enjoy *outside* school settings?

C. Predict achievement

Helpful questions to ask students:

1. If you were to choose three classes in which you would be most likely to achieve, what would these classes be—topics, content, classroom activities, assignments, etc.?

2. In what academic areas do you feel that you are at your best?

3. Assessment of motivation

Helpful questions to ask students:

1. What do you look forward to in college?

2. What do you want to happen during your college years? What do you hope will happen?

3. Imagine it is the end of the term and you feel great—successful and fulfilled—what will have to happen in order for you to feel this way?

4. What are the two things you most want to accomplish while you are in college?

5. What are the two things you most want to be able to do after college—as a result of college?

6. In what academic areas are you most motivated to learn?

7. What are some of the questions you have that you wish you could find answers to?

8. In what areas, academic and personal, would you like to explore and grow?

Fill in these questions with the first thing that comes to your mind:

1. I don't know why _____

2. I wish that I understood why _____

3. I would like to know how to _____

4. More than anything I want to _____

5. If I only could _____, I would feel great.

6. I feel like my life is meaningful when _____

7. No matter what, I plan to _____

8. I want my children to think of me as _____

9. I want to be more knowledgeable about _____

10. I want to be more skillful at _____

11. The types of books I really like to read are _____

12. Ideas about _____ keep running through my mind.

13. The person I aspire to be like is _____

14. The qualities of the person I want to become include _____

15. Who are the three people you most admire? Why? What are their finest traits? _____

    _____

16. Which of these traits do you already have, and which ones do you want to develop further? _____

    _____

4. Assessment of preparation

Helpful questions to ask students:

1. In what areas and subjects do you have the greatest background knowledge?

2. For which specific courses do you feel most prepared?

3. In which courses are you likely to earn your highest grades because of what you already know or have experienced?

4. What types of academic competition do you thrive on?

5. What types of academic cooperation or collaboration do you thrive on?

6. Which of your academic skills are your strongest?

7. When you have to perform to earn grades, which type of performance activities provide the best opportunities for you to achieve success?

5. Matching strengths and motives to opportunities

Helpful questions to ask students:

1. What courses would be a direct extension of your intellectual interests and curiosities?

2. What types of courses would capitalize on your strengths, talents and skills?

3. In which of the classes identified above are you most motivated to learn, grow and develop?

4. What types of extracurricular activities might stimulate your desire to grow and/or motivate you to learn?

6. Fitting potential courses to demands and requirements

A. How much time and energy does the student have, and of that, how much is he or she willing to invest in learning activities?

1. What employment or volunteer obligations?

2. What obligations to friends, spouse, children, parents?

3. Estimate of time/energy required for commuting/travel?

B. How much time and energy will selected courses require?

C. How can potential courses be used to fulfill graduation or certificate requirements, and in what areas do courses need to be found to fulfill requirements?

D. Are potential courses offered at a time that fits the student's schedule?

The bottom line of the Strengths-Based, Talent-Development Advising Approach:

- Bring to light and clarify (1) strengths, talents and skills and (2) motivations and desires to learn, grow and develop.

- Based on the foundation of the student's own strengths and motives, consider courses that directly extend from strengths and reflect motivations.

- Test potential courses (those identified through the process above) against the realities of (1) the demands of the courses compared to the student's available time and energy, and (2) the function of the courses in meeting graduation requirements.

END OF SECTION 1

Showing Students You Care

Participant Note. For more information about advising and effective communication, see the resource article by Margaret C. "Peggy" King, "Communication Skills," on page 195 in the appendix of the Participant Book.

Key Learning Points

1. Communication is critical to the advising process. The foundation of good communication is respect and caring.

2. The first and foremost thing is to take students seriously. You take students seriously as persons and seek to know and understand them from their points of view.

3. The advisor needs to ask, "Is the student getting my message?" In other words, the burden in this case is on the advisor, not the student.

4. Advisors communicate their sense of caring and concern in many different ways, some verbal, some nonverbal and some through actions.

5. As much as two-thirds of communication is done nonverbally.

6. You show students you are interested in them and what they are saying by smiling, looking at the student and maintaining good eye contact, welcoming students and making them feel comfortable, getting up to greet students and remembering them by name, sitting erect and leaning toward the student.

7. You send messages to students with your body. You also send messages with such things as how well you prepare for advising sessions.

Discussion Questions

Question 1. Think of a faculty office you have visited recently where you felt welcome and comfortable. What were the characteristics of that office that made you feel that way?

Question 2. Think of your office. How would you rearrange your office to make it more comfortable for your advisees?

Question 3. Identify three things you can do to make the student aware that you are prepared for his or her visit.

Question 4. Observe other faculty members participating in this training session. What does their body language/attending behavior convey regarding their interest in this topic?

Activities

Role Plays

Situation. Pick a partner. One person take the role of advisor and the other of advisee. Role play a short advising session in which the advisor demonstrates poor attending behavior—disinterested attitudes and body language. Discuss how that made the "advisee" feel.

Self-Assessment: Looking at Yourself Through the Eyes of Others

Question 1. What are several adjectives your family or close friends would use to describe you?

Question 2. What are several adjectives your advisees would use to describe you?

Question 3. What are several adjectives you would like advisees to use to describe you?

Question 4. What differences are there between how your advisees see you and how you would like to be seen by your advisees?

Question 5. What personal attitudes or behaviors would you need to change to bring advisee perceptions of you more in line with the perceptions you'd like them to have?

Tools

Taking the student seriously is the foundation of all effective advising, and it has implications for every aspect of advising. Think of your advising actions as responses to the following questions:

If I really took the student seriously...

1. How would I prepare for an advising interview?

2. How would I listen to the student?

3. What kinds of questions would I ask in the advising interview?

4. What would I want to know about the student?

5. How would I follow up after the advising interview?

6. How would I communicate my concern and caring during the advising interview?

7. How much time would I give the student in the advising interview?

END OF SECTION 2

Listening With Understanding

Participant Note. For more information about advising and effective communication, see the resource article by Margaret C. "Peggy" King, "Communication Skills," on page 195 in the appendix of the Participant Book.

Key Learning Points

1. Listening is critical—really hearing what the student has to say.

2. Try to listen with understanding and without judgment or criticism. What is the student really saying? What is behind her decisions?

3. Show students you're listening through behaviors such as occasionally nodding your head, making comments and asking clarifying questions.

4. Listen at the highest level—the level at which you are an active listener.

Discussion Questions

Question 1. Think for a moment about your day. How often did you listen at the highest level—the level where you are an active listener? When? With whom?

Question 2. The video suggests you can show students you're listening through behaviors such as nodding your head, making comments and asking clarifying questions. How would you describe your listening style?

Question 3. When is it helpful to repeat or paraphrase what a student has said?

Question 4. When you're talking with a student, what clues reveal that the problem a student presents isn't the real problem?

Question 5. How can you learn to listen for things the student isn't saying?

Question 6. Sometimes you have to go beyond the questions students ask to discover what they really want or need. Can anyone give any examples of this from your own work with students?

Question 7. When you're talking with students, what can you do to assure that they are really listening and giving you their full attention?

Question 8. When you are speaking to another person in a work or business situation, what are some irritating behaviors you notice that indicate people aren't listening to you?

Question 9. When you are speaking to another person in a work or business situation, what listening behaviors do you appreciate?

Activities

Role Plays

Situation. Get into pairs. For the next three minutes, one person becomes the speaker and talks about something of interest while the other person listens. Stop. Have the listener reflect back what the speaker said, noting the feeling and intent behind the words. Reverse roles and repeat the process.

Situation. Get into pairs in chairs which are placed back to back. Have a conversation for three to four minutes and note how difficult it is in the absence of facial expressions, eye contact, etc. Reverse roles and repeat the process.

Situation. Get into pairs and have a conversation for three to four minutes. Consciously make an effort to reflect and paraphrase what your partner is saying. Reverse roles and repeat the process.

Situation. Select one person to leave the room for a few minutes. Select one person from the remaining group to be a listener. Have the leader read a detailed half-page of text to the listener and the rest of the group. Invite the person who left the room back into the room. Have the person designated as listener tell the person who left the room in as much detail as possible what was read in the half-page of text.

END OF SECTION 3

Questioning Skills That Uncover Student Needs

Participant Note. For more information about advising and effective communication, see the resource article by Margaret C. "Peggy" King, "Communication Skills," on page 195 in the appendix of the Participant Book.

Key Learning Points

1. Questions are the main vehicle for establishing a relationship with advisees.

2. Questions allow you to discover what students know, what they feel, their points of view, biases, their preparation, their motivation, their strengths and weaknesses, their curiosities, expectations, to discover those things not on the computer or not in the personal record.

3. Questions open doors to the student's concerns, pave the way to discussions of critical issues and help identify real and potential trouble areas.

4. Open-ended questions are invitations for students to talk. They draw students into conversation and help students reveal valuable information about themselves.

5. Closed questions help advisors fill in the blanks about a student's history. They emphasize factual information and can often be answered briefly or with a yes or no answer. If you wish to learn something specific about a student or want to direct the conversation to a specific area, use closed questions.

6. Clarifying questions help make the conversation more clear to both you and your advisee. These questions beg for more detail, communicate to the student that you're hearing and trying to understand their concerns, and help to both uncover and clarify what is actually on the student's mind.

7. Key-word questions ask the student to continue a train of thought by providing more details.

8. One way to demonstrate that the student has been heard and encourage the student to focus on feelings is to restate or paraphrase what the student has said.

9. Advising the whole student means focusing on personal as well as academic areas.

Discussion Questions

Question 1. What open-ended questions have you found helpful to ask as conversation starters—to put students at ease and get them talking?

Question 2. Give some examples of closed questions. What are the dangers of closed questions in an advising session?

Question 3. Give some examples of clarifying questions.

Question 4. Give some examples of key-word questions to follow up conversation.

Question 5. What do students always say when you ask, "how are your classes going?" What questions could you ask to better find out the answer?

Activities

Role Plays

Directions. The role-play situations below are based on the Tools portion of Section 4, Establish Student Intentions and Expectations, on page 64 and Conversation Starters, on page 65.

Situation. Get into groups of three—one advisor, one student, one observer. The advisor will ask the student questions to establish intentions. Switch roles and repeat the process.

Situation. Get into groups of three—one advisor, one student, one observer. The advisor will ask the student questions to establish expectations. Switch roles and repeat the process.

Situation. Get into groups of three—one advisor, one student, one observer. The advisor will use some of the conversation starters listed in the Tools section to put the student at ease and begin establishing a relationship. Rotate roles and repeat the process.

Self-Assessment: Communication

Directions. The following self-assessment will give you an opportunity to review your communication skills and attitudes and to identify areas for improvement. Rate each item on a scale of 6 to 1, with 6 being high.

Interpersonal Skills	How I Would Rate Myself	How Students Would Rate Me
1. When students come into the office, I get up to greet them and call them by name.	6 5 4 3 2 1	6 5 4 3 2 1
2. I smile at advisees and show them I am interested in talking with them.	6 5 4 3 2 1	6 5 4 3 2 1
3. I look at students and maintain good eye contact while they are talking.	6 5 4 3 2 1	6 5 4 3 2 1
4. I show students I am listening by responding verbally and nonverbally.	6 5 4 3 2 1	6 5 4 3 2 1
5. I sit erect and lean toward students.	6 5 4 3 2 1	6 5 4 3 2 1
6. I listen with understanding and without judgment or criticism.	6 5 4 3 2 1	6 5 4 3 2 1
7. I ask open-ended questions to draw students into conversation.	6 5 4 3 2 1	6 5 4 3 2 1
8. I ask clarifying questions to help make the conversation more clear both to me and to students.	6 5 4 3 2 1	6 5 4 3 2 1
9. To show students I hear and understand their concerns; I repeat or paraphrase what they say.	6 5 4 3 2 1	6 5 4 3 2 1
10. I minimize interruptions (for example, by not taking phone calls) during advising sessions.	6 5 4 3 2 1	6 5 4 3 2 1
11. I show students I am listening by taking notes on what they say.	6 5 4 3 2 1	6 5 4 3 2 1

Personal Goal Statement. In the next several weeks, I will improve some of my interpersonal advising skills. (From the inventory items above, list the top five in order of importance.)

1. _____

2. _____

3. _____

4. _____

5. _____

Tools

Note to Participants. Many sections of the program include helpful questions advisors can ask students. These include:

- Unit One, Section 5: Building for the Future Through Good Course Selection (page 21)

- Unit One, Section 7: Planning for Careers and Life After College (page 33)

- Unit One, Section 8: Adopting a Strengths-Based Approach to Advising (page 39)

- Unit Two, Section 1: Conducting an Effective Advising Interview (page 45)

- Unit Two, Section 7: Helping Students Evaluate Alternatives and Make Decisions (page 81)

- Unit Three, Section 1: Making the Connection With Adult Students (page 91)

- Unit Three, Section 2: Building Schedules That Fit Adult Student Priorities (page 97)

- Unit Three, Section 3: Motivating Underprepared Students by Building on Strengths (page 101)

- Unit Three, Section 4: Moving Toward Informed Decisions With Undecided Students (page 105)

- Unit Three, Section 5: Helping Honors Students Bring Focus to Multiple Talents (page 115)

- Unit Three, Section 7: Building Bridges With Students of Color Through Effective Communication (page 123)

Establish Student Intentions and Expectations

Establish student intentions as quickly as possible.

Student retention has a lot to do with student intentions. To help students and your institution, it's important for advisors to ask students questions about their intentions upon enrolling. Is the student planning to attend full or part time? Is the student enrolling with the intention of getting a degree or enrolling only to take a few courses for personal or professional interest? Is the student planning to get a degree from your institution or planning to transfer into a degree program at another institution?

Establish student expectations as quickly as possible.

Student retention has a lot to do with student expectations. To help students and your institution, it's important for advisors to ask students questions about their expectations upon enrolling. How difficult is the student expecting classes to be?

How much personal attention and contact does the student expect to have with faculty? How much does the student plan to study? How large does the student expect classes to be?

If student answers to questions like these do not fit the realities of the institution, the student will likely be more prone to dropping out. The advisor can greatly promote retention by identifying and discussing student expectations.

Conversation Starters

To start a conversation with a student, try some of these questions. What other questions can you add to the list?

1. What are some "hot buttons" of yours—things you can talk about forever?

2. What things can you do for hours at a time?

3. What would you get up to do at 5 a.m.?

4. What makes you feel great?

5. What are two successes you've had in the past six months?

6. What are some of your goals for the next six months?

7. How do you see yourself living five years from now?

8   Tell me about a turning point in your life?

9. What things do you dread doing?

10. What two or three areas of study are you considering? How are they similar? How are they different?

11. _____

12. _____

13. _____

14. _____

15. _____

END OF SECTION 4

Taking the First Step: Reaching Out to Students

Participant Note. For more information about intrusive advising, see the resource article by Margaret C. "Peggy" King, "Communication Skills," on page 195 in the appendix of the Participant Book.

Key Learning Points

1. Effective advisors recognize that students are often hesitant to seek help. Sometimes it's up to advisors to be proactive and to take the first step in the advising relationship.

2. The goal of informed advising is to prompt students to make critical decisions for themselves. Sometimes that's not possible. Advisors often need to walk a thin line between empowering students to act for themselves and providing direct assistance.

3. The goal is to move students toward more and more independence. Many times they do not have an understanding of these expectations at first, and part of the advising process is to correct that perception.

4. Advisors play a crucial role as advocates for students. Sometimes that can involve actually intervening on the student's behalf. Sometimes it's just encouraging the student to take that action, and showing how to go and talk with a professor and to try and get things resolved.

5. The decision of how much direct assistance to give students falls to the advisor and depends upon the immediacy of the student's need, the personality of the individual advisee and that of any other people involved.

Discussion Questions

Participant Note. Intrusiveness is defined as actions on the part of advisors or advising programs to reach out to students and to build relationships so that as problems or issues come up, students will know whom to contact. It is particularly important when working with at-risk students, first generation students and entering freshmen in general.

Question 1. Intrusive advising means reaching out to the student—having the advisor make the first step. Can anyone share a time when you reached out to a student and the effect this reaching out had on the student?

Question 2. Some faculty and staff reject the notion of intrusive advising because they take the position that students are adults and need to take responsibility for their own actions. If students need help they should to ask for it. In contrast, other faculty and staff maintain that advisors sometimes need to reach out to students because students "don't know what they don't know." They don't understand expectations and consequences of postsecondary education well enough to make consistently responsible decisions.

What are the advantages to students of an intrusive advising approach?

Question 3. What are the advantages to your institution of an intrusive advising approach?

Question 4. Identify several ways you can reach out to your advisees.

Question 5. An intrusive approach can take many forms. For instance, if you are notified that one of your advisees is doing very poorly in a math course, you could—

1. Invite the student to come to your office to talk about the course to determine the reasons for the poor performance.

2. Encourage the student to take advantage of the math lab and/or available math tutors.

3. Contact the student's math teacher to discuss the student's performance.

4. Have the student call the math lab to make an appointment from your office.

5. Walk the student over to the math lab to make an appointment.

6. Ask the student to come to talk with you to discuss his or her first visit to the math lab.

What are the advantages of each of the above approaches? Describe an advising situation in which you might take each of the above steps.

Question 6. How can you encourage students to take action on their own?

Question 7. What are ways you as an advisor reach out to students?

Question 8. What are ways your office or the institution can reach out to students?

Question 9. Telling is not necessarily communicating. Can you think of examples from your work when students aren't getting the messages you're communicating?

What do you or could you do to promote better communication?

Question 10. College can be very confusing to new students. Sometimes students don't know what they don't know, and advisors need to:

- Anticipate problems and bring them to a student's attention.

- Bring up issues that a student may not have thought of or wouldn't know to ask about.

Can you think of examples from your work with students when you had to anticipate problems or bring up issues students wouldn't think to ask about?

Activities

Role Plays

Situation. A first-year female student comes in very upset and says she was just sexually harassed by one of her teaching assistants.

Situation. A pre-medical student reports that everyone in principles of chemistry failed the first exam.

Situation. A student reports to you that he can't study because his roommate is selling drugs from their room.

Helping Students Identify and Reach Academic, Personal and Career Goals

Directions. Working in small groups or as a large group, discuss the tools portion of Section 5, Helping Students Identify and Reach Academic, Personal and Career Goals, on page 72. This segment describes how advisors can help students identify and reach goals. You may wish to consider the following questions in your discussion:

1. At your institution, what is the advisor's role and responsibility in helping students identify and reach academic, personal and career goals?

2. What assessment resources are available on your campus to help students identify and reach goals?

3. What other offices on campus do or could play a role in helping students identify and reach goals? Such offices might include academic support, career planning and placement, etc.

4. At your institution, what course-based options exist (such as freshman seminars) to help students identify and reach academic, personal and career goals?

5. If other offices and programs are used to help students identify and reach goals, how can advisors be involved in facilitating that process and in using the results of the goal-setting process when working with students?

Institution-Specific Issues

Identifying and Changing Student Behavior

Directions. Working in small groups or as a large group, identify and discuss student behaviors at your institution that have negative consequences for both students and the institution. Here are some examples:

- Continuing students who miss financial aid deadlines

- New students who choose not to attend pre-enrollment orientation and registration sessions and then don't get schedules they want and need

- Continuing students who don't pre-register for the next term

- Higher than normal drop rates in certain courses

After identifying these behaviors, discuss ways they could be addressed through advising.

Intrusiveness: Determining When and How to Respond

Directions. The concepts of intrusiveness and advocacy take on more definition and clarity when they are applied to actual student situations. The following situations concern both teaching and advising. Read the following statements and then discuss how you would respond to the situation. Options could include doing nothing, calling the student, writing a note or letter to the student, making a referral to another person or office or advocating on behalf of the student.

1. You're teaching a course to about 30 first-term freshmen that meets three days a week. About the third week of class one student who had been doing above average work suddenly stops coming to class. Five class periods go by and you don't hear from the student or get any drop slip.

2. One of your advisees whom you've had for three terms does not come in to pre-register for the next term.

3. One of your advisees is a first-term freshman. In your first advising meeting, the student seemed excited about school and looked forward to graduating from your institution. At the fifth week of the term you receive notice from the registrar's office that the student has dropped all but one of her classes.

4. As an advisor you usually expect that new students meet with you at least three times during the first term. One of your students misses the second scheduled meeting, and doesn't call to explain or reschedule.

5. You receive notification from the registrar's office that one of your advisees got a D and an F for mid-term grades in two of her four classes.

6. You notice in the student newspaper that one of your advisees won a scholarship from a local business.

7. You notice in the local paper that one of your advisees has been arrested for public intoxication twice in the past month.

8. One of your second-year student advisees is applying to be accepted into a school of business. The student is hard-working and motivated but her grade point average is slightly below the cutoff point because she has been going home most weekends the past year to help with a sick grandparent.

9. A first-term advisee is consistently working below his ability level in all his classes.

Background Discussion: The Issue of Intrusiveness

The issues of advocacy and intrusiveness bring up immediate philosophical arguments. Some faculty and advisors hold that college students are adults and ought to be treated that way. Students need to understand institutional rules, policies and regulations and be held accountable for them. Students shouldn't have to be reminded of deadlines, etc. If students need help they need to ask for it. Others hold that no one wins when students fail. When students make mistakes and suffer for them, the institution often suffers as well. Worst of all, when students make bad decisions through lack of knowledge or immaturity, they may suffer the consequences for years to come.

In a nutshell, the question that confronts all faculty, advisors and institutions is this: to what extent do students have a right to fail?

To get at the implications of that question, perhaps an analogy is helpful: consider mountain climbing—specifically, the difference between skilled mountain climbers and novices. Every year dozens of people are seriously injured and die in climbing accidents in the United States. Even considering that, very few people would advocate outlawing mountain climbing because of the potential dangers. On the other hand, most reasonable people likely would make a distinction between the right to fail (that is, to be injured or die) of experienced, highly skilled mountain climbers versus the right to fail of inexperienced novices who either don't have the skills to succeed or the experience and judgment to understand the risks of climbing. In other words an example of an intrusive approach to climbing would be someone saying, "You have to be at least this competent to climb this particular mountain."

Using this analogy, most beginning college students are closer to inexperienced novices than they are to skilled climbers.

Imagine a continuum of levels of intrusiveness. At one end is a completely hands-off approach in which students are free to take whatever courses they want and take them whenever they wish. At this end there are few institutional rules and policies, and advisors do not take an active role in influencing student decisions. At the other end of the continuum are institutions and advisors that take an active role in what students take and when. At this end are many course prerequisites and co-requisites, considerable use of placement tests and other assessments to control course placement and levels. At this end advisors take an active and sometimes prescriptive role in student behavior.

Although one doesn't usually apply the term "intrusive" to institutions, that is exactly what happens, for instance, when institutions specify general education requirements. In that case, an institution is saying in effect that in the absence of requirements some students might not take courses that the institution feels it is important for students to take. Similarly, an advisor who practices an intrusive approach by requiring new students to come in for a specified number of advising sessions in the first term is saying that in the absence of that expectation, many students who need advising the most might not come in at all.

In reality, most institutions and advisors fall somewhere between the two ends of the continuum. As an advisor it is worth spending time thinking about these issues and determining your position on them. However, all advisors can practice the kind of intrusiveness that involves reaching out to students and showing an active interest in them, taking the lead in setting up appointments, being proactive with information, and recognizing that students often don't know what they don't know.

Advising Issues and Implications

What are some situations for which many students don't realize the implications of their actions? Here are some starters:

- A student stops attending class but doesn't drop the course because he doesn't know he has to or doesn't think it's important.

- A student fails most of his first-year courses and doesn't realize his record will follow him to another institution.

What are the implications for advising in these situations?

Tools

Helping Students Identify and Reach Academic, Personal and Career Goals

Helping students identify and reach goals is a key function of advising. Advisors can help students identify behaviors and then tie the behaviors to goals that students are trying to achieve. Whatever the topic—time management, study skills, career awareness, test-preparation behaviors—the goal is to make students aware of current behaviors and then to identify behaviors to change or strengths to build upon. Anything advisors can do to help students see the connection between behavior and outcomes is valuable.

There are many resources available to help students analyze behaviors, particularly academic behaviors. For instance, one common tool is the Learning and Study Skills Inventory (LASSI).

Whatever tools are used, advisors can help students with this process by:

- Encouraging students to use whatever tools are available to analyze behaviors and set goals.

- Helping students see connections between current behaviors and short-term and long-term goals.

- Discussing and making sense of the results.

- Helping students set goals and determine a path to meet them.

- Pushing students to commit to reaching the goals they have set.

- Identifying and activating other campus resources that can help students change behaviors.

- Monitoring student progress toward reaching goals.

As an example, the following "Inventory of Out-of-Class Study Habits and Behaviors" is reprinted from *Planning for Success in Athletics, Academics and Careers* (USA Group Noel-Levitz, 1996, page 68). Notice especially the two key elements that make such inventories useful: (1) identifying behaviors to change, and (2) making a commitment to change specific behaviors within a fixed time period.

Inventory of Out-of-Class Study Habits and Behaviors

Directions. Complete the following Inventory of Out-of-Class Study Habits and Behavior. After you complete the inventory, take a careful look at your responses. Choose five items that represent habits and behaviors that you would most benefit by improving. List these five items in order of importance to you on the five lines under the "Personal Goal Statement."

The goal is for you to become aware of, and then continuously improve, your habits and behaviors. There are not necessarily right or wrong answers. For instance, look at item #15, "I study alone." For some student-athletes, studying alone might be very positive, especially if they have difficulty concentrating or are easily distracted by other people. In contrast, other student-athletes might benefit from the motivation and support that can come from focused study in pairs or small groups. The real question is this: how well are your current behaviors and attitudes helping you to achieve the academic goals you have set?

	Always		Sometimes		Never
1. I study when I am fresh and alert.	5	4	3	2	1
2. I concentrate well when I study.	5	4	3	2	1
3. I study in the library.	5	4	3	2	1
4. I study in a study lounge or study area.	5	4	3	2	1
5. I take notes when I read class materials.	5	4	3	2	1
6. I study with a partner who is serious about learning.	5	4	3	2	1
7. I study with a group that is serious about learning.	5	4	3	2	1
8. I study in the same place.	5	4	3	2	1
9. I study the same times of day.	5	4	3	2	1
10. I read material for the class period for which it is assigned.	5	4	3	2	1
11. I begin working on papers more than one day before they are due.	5	4	3	2	1
12. I review my class notes within a few hours of taking them.	5	4	3	2	1
13. I use my notes to quiz myself about course content.	5	4	3	2	1
14. I study in my room.	5	4	3	2	1
15. I study alone.	5	4	3	2	1
16. I am easily distracted when I study.	5	4	3	2	1
17. I study with my boyfriend/girlfriend.	5	4	3	2	1
18. I study with food.	5	4	3	2	1
19. I study while listening to music.	5	4	3	2	1
20. I study/read while lying down.	5	4	3	2	1
21. I often have difficulty reading or interpreting my notes.	5	4	3	2	1

Personal Goal Statement. In the next several weeks, I will improve some of my out-of-class study habits and behaviors. (From the inventory items above, list the top five in order of importance.)

1. _____

2. _____

3. _____

4. _____

5. _____

Helping Students Reach Short-term Academic Goals

Helping students achieve the course grades they want or need is a practical and useful activity for advisors. At the beginning of every term, ask students to do the following:

1. Make a list of current courses being taken.

2. Write down next to the course title the grade the student wants to or needs to earn.

3. Identify what resources or support (if any) the student will need to achieve each course grade.

4. Make a commitment to do what is necessary to achieve the goal.

Ten Positive Ways to Practice Intrusive Advising and Be a Student Advocate

Here are some ways to practice intrusive advising and to be a student advocate. What others can you add to the list?

1. Put yourself in the student's place. Take the lead in anticipating problems students may not know to expect and questions students may not know to ask.

2. Don't wait for students to volunteer information. They may not tell you when they are confused or having problems. You need to ask.

3. Don't assume that students will follow through on recommendations and referrals. Follow up to show your interest.

4. _____

5. _____

6. _____

7. _____

8. _____

9. _____

10. _____

END OF SECTION 5

Challenging Students to Clarify Attitudes and Actions

Key Learning Points

1. Sometimes it's appropriate to confront or challenge students.

2. Sometimes challenging takes the form of asking students questions that get them to think something through.

3. Sometimes challenging involves prodding students to move their thinking to the next level.

4. Sometimes challenging takes the form of asking students questions to defend their position or their choices.

5. It is much easier to talk openly and challenge after you have established a relationship with a student. To move students down that developmental road requires a relationship in which the student trusts you to have the knowledge, experience, care and interest in them to be their guide.

6. The goal is to challenge advisees to achieve more than they thought possible and to open for discussion and consideration contradictions or discrepancies between what the student says and what the student does.

7. Another goal is to help the student look at both sides of an issue.

Discussion Questions

Question 1. Why is challenging or confronting a student important to the advising process?

Question 2. What are some situations in which confrontation might be appropriate?

Question 3. How can confrontation be helpful in those situations?

Question 4. What questions have you found it helpful to ask students to get them to defend their choice of courses?

Question 5. What will likely happen if you confront or challenge a student before a relationship is established?

Question 6. Are there ways you could challenge a student before you have had time to establish a relationship?

Activities

Role Plays

Situation. A student comes in with a completed course schedule for the next term. He has chosen specific courses that fit right into the curriculum, but rather than just accepting that, the advisor challenges and says, "Why did you choose this course rather than any of the six other courses that fulfill the same requirement?"

Situation. A student has had her heart set on being a physician since she was in junior high. She is taking all the required science courses, but after three terms she has not gotten above a B in any of them. She maintains she will be able to be admitted to some medical school and won't consider your suggestion that she make some alternate plans just in case.

Situation. A student comes in for pre-registration advising with a full set of courses in which he isn't interested.

Situation. A new student who took only two years of math in high school wants to take Accounting I. Studies at your institution show that 75 percent of students with less than three years of high school math fail or drop out of Accounting I. The student says, "I know I can do it. I wasn't motivated in high school but now I am. I just need a chance."

Taking Action: What Advisors Can and Can't Do at Your Institution

Directions. Working in small groups or as a large group, discuss what authority advisors at your institution have for making commitments to students, for making exceptions to stated policies and for taking action to promote student success.

In your discussion, consider the following questions and issues:

1. What leeway, if any, do advisors have in making exceptions to institutional rules, regulations or policies for individual students?

2. Can advisors waive course prerequisites or co-requisites?

3. Can advisors make binding decisions regarding the use of transfer courses to satisfy institutional and program requirements?

4. Can advisors refuse to let a student do something not covered by institutional rules and policy? For instance, if a student who was struggling academically

wanted to work 35 hours a week and take a full course schedule, could an advisor refuse to sign a registration form?

5. Can advisors in individual circumstances require students to sign learning contracts or take any similar steps to promote student success?

6. Any other questions or issues specific to your institution.

Case Studies

Directions. The concepts of challenging and confrontation take on more definition and clarity when they are applied to actual student situations. Read the following situations and then discuss how you would respond.

Situation. Bob is a 19-year-old, first-term student at Oceanside Community College who hopes to get a degree in accounting. With only two years of high school math, Bob tests into a developmental math course. Because he wants to get a degree in accounting, he also plans to take Accounting I at the same time as the developmental math course. Even though the institution has no specific math prerequisite for accounting, you know that Bob will stand little chance of succeeding in the accounting course.

Sam is a 33-year-old first-term student at Oceanside Community College with no prior college experience. For the past nine years he has owned and run a small restaurant where he employs three people and keeps all the books himself. Like Bob, he also only has two years of high school math and tested into a developmental math course. He wants to enroll in Accounting I to help him in his business and to see if he might have an interest in pursuing a degree in the field.

How would you advise these students? Here are some things that the advisor in this situation might want to take into consideration:

1. What is the student demand for the Accounting I course? Does the course normally fill with students with an adequate math background?

2. What is the level of motivation of the student? You know the preparation is not good, but motivation and time may be more important.

3. What is the student's receptivity to help?

4. What is the fit between this course and the student's available time and energy?

Situation. A student you've advised for three terms has made no progress toward choosing a major. You have repeatedly encouraged the student to talk with the staff in the career planning office but the student has not done so.

Situation. A student comes in to discuss his course schedule for the next term and get a signature. The student's record is only average. During the course of the conversation, the student tells you he plans to work 35 hours a week the next term while taking a full load of 16 hours.

Tools

Challenging and Confronting Students

Challenging and confronting students can be effective when advisors and advisees have a relationship based on respect and understanding. Mild confrontation is appropriate when you want to:

1. Challenge students to achieve more than they might think possible.

2. Open up for consideration discrepancies in the student's behavior (on the one hand you say, on the other hand you do...), discrepancies in what a person says and how he appears (you say you're feeling good yet you look exhausted), and how the student is versus how she wants to be (you're not sure you can make it through college, yet your record indicates you can).

3. Help the student look at both sides of an issue (I understand what you feel your teacher does wrong, but what do you think your teacher thinks you do wrong? What would he say about you?).

Positive Ways to Challenge Students

Directions. Working in small groups or as a large group, build a list of positive ways to challenge students.

1. Ask students to explain why they choose to take individual courses.

2. Ask students what they expect out of the advising relationship.

3. Ask students who aren't involved in any campus activities to commit to joining at least one group.

4. _____

5. _____

6. _____

7. _____

8. _____

END OF SECTION 6

Helping Students Evaluate Alternatives and Make Decisions

Key Learning Points

1. Many new students do not arrive at college knowing how to make sound judgments.

2. Developing good decision-making skills in students is one of the most important goals of informed academic advising.

3. In many cases advisors will be more heavily involved with students at the onset of the advising relationship. Developmental advisors provide concentrated advising in the first term to help students understand expectations for college students.

4. An advising relationship needs to be an ongoing relationship, and it needs to progress in a certain direction.

5. Advisors need to both model and teach decision-making skills. By teaching them these skills, students then can apply them elsewhere in the future.

6. There are five steps that can help make teaching and modeling this process easier and more effective: (1) define the problem and clarify the situation; (2) collect information from the student and use that information to help steer the student toward alternatives and solutions; (3) evaluate the alternatives available; (4) assess the risks involved in each alternative plan; and (5) help the student develop a plan of action and a timetable to follow through on that plan.

7. Students are responsible for their own educations. They are responsible for their course selection decisions and every aspect of the college experience. As long as the advisor keeps that process going without inserting his or her own bias into that, then it's a healthy interaction.

Discussion Questions

Modeling and Teaching Decision-Making Skills

Students frequently come to advisors seeking a solution for a problem. Advisors can best help the student by modeling and teaching skills to use not just in that situation but in others they will face. The following are steps to use in the decision-making process:

1. Define the problem and clarify the situation.

2. Collect and use information relevant to a decision and search for alternatives.

3. Evaluate the alternatives against identified criteria.

4. Assess the risks involved with the decision.

5. Develop a plan of action and follow through.

Question 1. Think of an advising situation where a student has come to you with a problem. Describe that situation. Apply the five steps in the decision-making process to that problem.

Question 2. As an advisor, how can you model the steps of decision making as a way of teaching students how to make decisions for themselves?

Question 3. The video segment highlights the importance of front-loading advising so that students get more concentrated advising help in the first term and first year. What are some of the implications of this front-loading for both advisors and students?

Question 4. As an advisor, how do you help students learn to be responsible for their own educations?

Question 5. Who can share examples of advising assignments you give students to complete between advising sessions?

Question 6. How does effective advising move students from dependence to independence?

Activities

Role Plays

Situation. A second-year communications major comes in with questions. He would very much like to spend his junior year studying in Spain, but he is worried that he won't be able to graduate on time because he won't be able to take any of his required major courses at the university in Spain.

Situation. A student is in the middle of his third term at a community college studying auto mechanics. He has a problem. A local mechanic has offered him a job if he can begin immediately. The student is very eager to get out working and needs the money, but he also wants to finish his degree.

Situation. A student is trying to decide what to major in. She likes math and science, but is also good at art. And she has always thought about being a doctor someday.

Tools

Helpful Advising Assignments to Use

Directions. In discussion question 5 in this section, you discussed advising assignments to give students to complete between advising sessions. Working in small groups or as a large group, build a list of helpful advising assignments you could use.

1. _____

2. _____

3. _____

4. _____

5. _____

6. _____

7. _____

8. _____

9. _____

10. _____

Questions to Ask Students

Use the space below to build a list of helpful questions to ask students about decision making.

1. Do you ever have trouble making decisions? Little ones? Important ones?

2. How do you generally go about making a decision? Describe the process.

3. What specific strategies do you use?

4. Do you use the same method for all types of decisions?

5. Would you describe yourself as a spontaneous or a systematic decision maker?

6. Do you make decisions by yourself, or do you need other people's opinions first?

7. Are you feeling anxious about deciding on a major? Pressured?

8. How long does it take you to make a decision? How long do you want it to take?

9. _____

10. _____

11. _____

12. _____

13. _____

14. _____

15. _____

END OF SECTION 7

Accessing and Activating Campus Resources

Participant Note. For more information about campus resources, see the article by Thomas J. Kerr, "Advisor Resources," on page 183 in the appendix of the Participant Book. For more information about advising and referrals, see the resource article by Faye Vowell, "Referral Skills," on page 191 in the appendix.

Key Learning Points

1. Academic advising is a process that involves the entire campus. A key element of informed advising is helping students discover and access the wide array of resources and support services available on your campus.

2. The advisor is a resource person who can direct students to the campus experts—and not someone who has all the right answers.

3. Many students have difficulty dealing with referrals. Students think advisors are supposed to have the answers, and they feel they are being shuffled around when referred.

4. Part of the referral process is getting students to be comfortable operating on your campus. Sending them off with a list of tasks to do and report back to you is an important part of their educational process.

5. Students have certain responsibilities. One is to get the best possible information so that they can make the best possible decisions.

6. Referrals are important resources in helping students achieve their goals. In order to use referrals for this purpose, it's important for advisors to know what is available on campus.

7. Because the issues students must deal with are so complex, it's important to establish a process for referring students. That includes your best judgment about when or when not to refer students to other sources of help.

8. Advisors will not feel comfortable or competent to deal with some student issues that arise. At this point referrals become necessary.

9. Sometimes advisors need to contact the referral source directly and facilitate the student's use of that resource.

10. Follow-up is critical in the referral process. At the end of the session, schedule an appointment for a return visit. The referral and what is to be accomplished in that session sets the agenda for your next session with the student. Follow-up communicates to the student that the referral is important.

Discussion Questions

Question 1. How do you respond when students ask you what they should do?

Question 2. When is it proper or productive for you to express opinions or give advice to students?

Question 3. How do you refer students to other people and offices without making students feel they are being shuffled or brushed off?

Question 4. What techniques do you use (or could you use) to assure that students follow through on your referrals?

Question 5. Why is follow-up so important to the referral process?

Question 6. What do you need to know to be a good referral agent?

Question 7. What information and/or training do you need about campus resources to assure that you are an effective referral agent?

Question 8. Can anyone share examples of students with *personal* problems or situations for which you felt it necessary to refer students to other individuals or offices?

Question 9. Can anyone share examples of students with *academic* problems or situations for which you felt it necessary to refer students to other individuals or offices?

Question 10. What areas are you personally not comfortable with when working with students?

Question 11. How is the Family Educational Rights and Privacy Act of 1974 (The Buckley Amendment) interpreted at your institution? How does this interpretation affect information given out by advisors in on-campus and off-campus referrals?

Question 12. Can anyone share record-keeping approaches you use to keep track of student referrals?

Activities

Role Plays

Situation. A first-term student is having difficulty getting along with his roommate in the residence hall. He is so unhappy that he is thinking of transferring to an institution closer to home if he can't change roommates. He has already talked to his resident assistant, who told him that they want new students to learn to work out their problems rather than just switching roommates.

Situation. The advisor is discussing a student's poor performance in a course. Upon probing, the advisor finds a deeper-seated problem involving alcohol.

Situation. A student comes in to report that at least half the class cheated on the recent calculus exam.

Know Your Forms

Directions. Gather a comprehensive collection of all standard forms used on your campus that advisors might need to use or at least to know about. These might include such items as drop/add forms, change of major forms, requirement waiver forms, residency forms, degree analysis, etc. Make sure that each advisor has a complete set of forms. As a group, go over all forms so that advisors understand their use.

Develop a Referral Resource Grid

Directions. Often referrals are not made because faculty and advisors lack basic information on possible referral sources. If your institution does not have one, develop a referral resource grid. You may want to use the following sample grid as a starting point:

OFFICE	Dean of Students Office	Academic Support Center	Career Development Office	Health Center	Counseling Center
CONTACTS	Contact person/s	Contact person/s	Contact person/s	Contact person/s	Contact person/s
ISSUES ADDRESSED	Repeated absences General counseling information Programming complaints Withdrawals Financial aid problems Interpersonal conflicts Academic dishonesty Residence hall problems Roommate problems	Testing Tutoring Time management Study skills Peer counseling/advising Learning disabilities Audible testing	Career planning Career counseling Graduate school problems Career library Career testing GRE/GMAT/LSAT tests Placement service Résumé preparation	Health-related absences Health needs Health complaints Nutritional counseling Stress management Alcohol education Immunizations	Personal counseling Psychological problems Psychological testing Learning disabilities
HOURS PHONE LOCATION	8:30-4:30 M–F Ext 555 225 Johnson/dormitories	8:30-5 M–F; T, TH evenings Ext 456 35 Whittenberg Hall	8:30-4:30 M–F; W evening Ext 315 443 Smith Court	8:30-4:30 M–F Ext 281 860 Terry Street	8:30-4:30 M–F; evenings Ext 300 12 Howard Building
USE OF SERVICES	Drop-in and appointment	Drop-in and appointment	Drop-in and appointment	Drop-in and appointment	Drop-in and appointment

Tools

Some Guidelines for Referral

Use the following information to help you decide when and how to make referrals.

Refer when:

- The problem is beyond your level of competence.

- The problem is personal and the student is a friend or neighbor.

- Personality differences exist between you and the student.

- You are not being effective.

Refer to:

- A specific person in an appropriate office or agency.

How to refer:

- Assist the student in making an appointment.

- Do not transmit confidential information about the student in front of him or her.

- Ask whether or not the student kept the appointment, but do not "pump" the student for information after the referral.

- Respect the student's right to work out problems in his or her own way.

END OF SECTION 8

UNIT THREE
Advising Special Populations

JACK LEVIN

VIRGINIA GORDON

MARIO RIVAS

*"It's a tremendously satisfying achievement when
I can help a student, push a student, somehow inspire
a student to maximize his or her potential, get that
late bloomer to bloom, to shine, to do things that he
or she never thought were possible."*

JACK LEVIN, NORTHEASTERN UNIVERSITY

*"I think the majority of undecided students are just
developmentally not ready to make that choice, and
need some time and freedom to explore the many
alternatives that are available to them."*

VIRGINIA GORDON, THE OHIO STATE UNIVERSITY

*"We can help the student define the skills he or she
needs, break up the skills into component parts that
the student clearly understands, and then get the
student into the right class and the right learning
experience."*

MARIO RIVAS, SAN FRANCISCO STATE UNIVERSITY

Making the Connection With Adult Students

Participant Note. For more information about advising adult students, see the resource article by Cheryl J. Polson, "Advising Adult Learners," on page 235 in the appendix of the Participant Book.

Participant Note. All eight sections of Unit Three concern special populations or groups of students. The intent is not to stereotype groups of students but to help advisors think about how best to meet the needs of students who may fall within one of several identifiable groups. A particular student might fall under several of these special populations. For instance, a student could be adult, a student of color, an honors student and a student who is undecided.

Key Learning Points

1. One thing that sets adult students apart is the experience base they bring to campus. Advisors can help adult students build on this experience base and relate it to their classwork.

2. Adults bring special needs to the campus that the advisor must address if the student is to be retained.

3. Adults have multiple role commitments that may conflict with their educational experiences.

4. Adults bring varied life experiences that should be acknowledged within and outside the classroom. These experiences are a double-edged sword. They can be an asset to learning (provide a foundation for new learning) or they can be a deterrent to learning (students come with pre-conceived ideas).

5. Adults tend not to identify very closely with the institution. They are often off-campus directed and don't take advantage of available resources. Frequently they utilize resources and services available off campus.

6. Adults frequently have clear goals and a consumer orientation. They have set high standards for themselves and the institution.

7. Adults often return to campus as a result of a major life transition that in itself may impact the success of their return.

8. Adult students sometimes don't like to ask for help. Advisors may need to be more proactive when working with adults.

9. Adults sometimes bring "baggage" with them from past negative experiences in formal education. The resulting lack of self-confidence may prevent them from persisting through degree completion.

10. Adults want to expedite their degree completion and get frustrated when they are required to take courses that they think they may not need. Their prior learning must be assessed.

11. Adults frequently return to campus without support from spouses, family, co-workers and friends. This opposition must be balanced by institutional support.

12. Adult students often lack confidence in their ability to succeed.

13. The accessibility of advisors is critical to adult students.

14. Advisors need to help adult students remain open and flexible to new views.

Discussion Questions

Question 1. In what ways are you different now as an adult from the way you were as a late adolescent (18-22)?

Question 2. What implications might these differences have for what you would seek from your academic advisor?

Question 3. What are some strengths older students bring to their classes?

Question 4. What are some strengths older students bring to advising interactions and advising sessions?

Question 5. Do you think that involvement on campus is as important in the success and retention of adult students as it is with traditional-age students?

Question 6. The video suggests that often dramatic life changes trigger a decision to return to school. What are some of these changes and how do these changes impact student success?

Question 7. Adult students bring a lot of experience to campus. In what ways is their experience positive for their education? What opportunities does this create for you as an advisor?

Question 8. In what ways is their experience negative for their education? What challenges does this create for you as an advisor?

Question 9. The video suggests that adult learners often don't like to ask for help. In your experience have you found this to be true? How can you as an advisor get these students connected to help when they are reluctant to seek it?

Question 10. What are some retention issues concerning adult students at your institution? What is or could be the role of advising in addressing each issue?

Question 11. Everyone knows someone—perhaps a spouse, neighbor or relative—who returned to school as an adult. What are some of the issues they had to confront?

Question 12. Involvement in the campus is important to student retention. How can advisors do a better job of getting adult commuting students connected to the campus and involved in campus life?

Question 13. Do you find that you treat adult students differently from the way you treat traditional-age students? If so, in what ways?

Activities

Role Plays

Situation. An adult student comes to his advisor and says, "My teacher doesn't know anything about this subject. I've worked in this field for 15 years."

Situation. An adult student is returning to school after her husband died. She had very good grades in school 20 years ago but is very unsure and insecure about her ability to succeed and to compete with other students.

Situation. An adult student is returning to school after 10 years in the navy. He had a very poor record in high school, but 10 successful years in the service. Now he's married and returning to school to get a teaching degree. However, after being placed into several developmental courses based on his previous record, he is very discouraged and unsure.

Situation. An adult student is returning to school after a recent divorce. She has two young children at home and needs to work at least 30 hours a week to make ends meet at home. She is having difficulty balancing the demands of home, work and family.

Situation. An adult student is taking classes three evenings a week and is discouraged by all the bureaucratic hoops he has to jump through. He is also frustrated at the lack of availability of administrative offices and services during the evening.

Institution-Specific Issues

Directions. Discuss the characteristics and needs of adult students on your campus. For instance, you may want to look at:

- Numbers of adult students

- Their most frequently chosen academic programs

- Retention and graduation rates

- Adult student satisfaction with advising and other services

- Special retention issues or retention goals

Question 1. What are the key retention issues and retention goals concerning adult students at your institution? What role can advisors play in addressing these retention issues and goals?

Question 2. What institutional policies or procedures present barriers or inhibit the success of adult students? What are solutions to these problems? What role can advisors play in addressing these issues?

Identifying Adult Student Characteristics and Needs

Directions. To help identify adult student needs and characteristics, complete the following sentences.

1. Adults who return to college want....

2. Adults who return to college are....

3. Adults who return to college may have....

4. Adults who return to college need....

5. Adults who return to college may lack....

Helping Adult Students Connect With Institutional Resources

Directions. If your institution does not have one, develop a guide that identifies resources at your institution that might be of special value to adult students. You may want to consider some of the following:

- Scholarships

- Clubs, organizations, special interest groups

- Peer advising, mentoring or support groups

- Lists of child care providers

- On-campus study facilities for commuting students

- Stress and time-management workshops

- On-campus jobs

Tools

Helpful Questions to Ask Adult Students

Here are a few helpful questions to ask adult students. What other questions can you add to the list?

1. What made you decide to enroll (or re-enroll) in school?

2. Are you enrolling in school as the result of a big change in your life?

3. How do you think your transition to school will alter your life? How prepared do you feel for the changes this transition will create?

4. What past personal experiences do you feel will help you most in school?

5. What past work experiences do you feel will help you most in school?

6. How do your friends and family feel about your return to school?

7. _____

8. _____

9. _____

10. _____

END OF SECTION 1

SECTION 2

Building Schedules That Fit Adult Student Priorities

Key Learning Points

1. Because they feel the pressure of time or life circumstances, course selection is critical for adult students.

2. Fitting courses into adult lives can be complicated.

3. Adult students often come to advising with fully developed course schedules.

4. Many people assume that adult learners enroll with clearer educational goals than traditional age students. This is not necessarily true. They often come with short-term goals related to the issues in their lives. These issues sometimes cloud their real long-term education needs. Advisors need to help students assess these short-term goals to see if they are going to help them reach their long-term goals.

5. Advisors need to provide encouragement and support for adult learners.

6. Advisors need to focus on motivation, preparation and the way courses will fit into an adult student's life.

Discussion Questions

Question 1. The video suggests that course selection is even more critical for adult students than for traditional-age students. Do you agree and why?

Question 2. The video suggests that adult learners often come with short-term goals related to issues in their lives and that these short-term goals can cloud their real long-term educational needs. Can anyone share any examples of this from your work with adult students?

Question 3. As an advisor, how can you help adult students balance long-term educational needs with short-term goals?

Question 4. Traditional-age students often come to advising with no scheduling ideas and nontraditional-age students often come with too many. What are the problems with laying out a schedule too early, or prematurely?

Question 5. What are some issues for nontraditional-age students that often arise on your campus? How can advisors help adult students address these issues?

Question 6. Who can share some techniques or strategies for working with adult students you have found particularly successful?

Activities

Role Plays

Situation. A working mother is attending a community college to get an A.A. degree. She can only take courses on Tuesday and Wednesday evenings, and none of the required courses she needs are offered on those nights.

Situation. An adult student wants to complete a degree as quickly and easily as possible. He plans to take three courses while working nearly full time. He wants to know the required classes that will take the least amount of time and work.

Situation. A new adult student comes in for his first advising session. He is very motivated to finish a program. After studying the catalog extensively, he has filled out a complete degree plan with the courses he plans to take each term.

Situation. A new adult student comes in and says, "I need a bachelor's degree to get a promotion. I have 76 credit hours from four different institutions. What's the quickest way for me to get a degree here?"

Situation. An adult student comes in and says, "My company just went through a downsizing, and I've been laid off. I need to get into an area where I can just about be guaranteed a job. I need some education so this doesn't happen to me again. Tell me what I should take."

Helping Students Identify Credit Opportunities for Life Experience

Directions. Working in small groups or as a large group, discuss the opportunities that are available at your institution for students to receive credit for life experience. You may wish to consider the following questions in your discussion:

1. Can students receive any academic credit for life experience? If so, what is the process for doing so?

2. If students can receive credit for life experience, how can the credit be used to satisfy institutional, program or elective requirements?

3. Can life experience be used to waive course requirements or prerequisites?

4. Can life experience be used to waive any requirements such as internships, etc.?

5. Which academic departments have provisions for students to receive credit or waive requirements for life experience?

6. Can students take challenge exams in place of major courses?

Helping Students Identify Academic Programs That Fit the Time Demands of Adult Students

> **Directions.** Many adult students are not free to go to school full time or to take classes only during the day. Working in small groups or as a large group, identify academic programs at your institution that fit the time demands of adult students. You may wish to consider the following questions in your discussion:

1. Are there any programs at your institution that a student can complete exclusively by taking courses evenings and/or weekends?

2. Are there any programs at your institution that offer few if any required courses in the evening or on weekends?

3. Are there any programs at your institution that require students to attend full time during all or part of the program?

4. Does your institution offer any kind of "external degree" that provides adult students a more flexible path to degree completion?

Tools

Helpful Questions to Ask Adult Students Regarding Course Schedules

Here are a few helpful questions to ask adult students regarding course schedules. What other questions can you add to the list?

1. In what areas are you expecting to want or need help?

2. How would you describe your past experiences with school?

3. In addition to taking courses, what other obligations do you have that will take your time and energy?

4. How many hours a day are you planning to spend on campus in class, studying, in labs, doing research, etc.?

5. How much urgency do you feel to complete a degree?

6. _____

7. _____

8. _____

9. _____

10. _____

END OF SECTION 2

Motivating Underprepared Students by Building on Strengths

Key Learning Points

1. Underprepared students are at risk to give up and leave school.

2. Underprepared students need to be encouraged to focus on their strengths. Advisors can help students identify the skills they come with and can encourage students to build on those skills.

3. Many students have multiple deficiencies. If advisors try to attack the deficiencies all at once it can destroy student self-confidence and destroy the advising relationship.

4. Try to structure at least half a student's program to play to strengths and set the stage for success.

5. Students are capable of profound change. Advisors can inspire students to shine and to do things they didn't think were possible.

6. Advisors can help underprepared students learn how to study, how to get connected to the academic community and how to get involved.

7. Advisors can provide the spark to motivate unmotivated students.

Discussion Questions

Question 1. What are some of the characteristics of underprepared students at your institution?

Question 2. What questions have you found it helpful to ask underprepared students to assess their level of motivation?

Question 3. With underprepared students who are motivated (what the video terms late bloomers), the advisor can help to get students connected to success strategies. What are some ways advisors do this?

Question 4. With underprepared students who are also unmotivated, how can the advisor help to inspire the student to find the connections and tap into strengths that will lead to motivation?

Question 5. The video suggests that when students have multiple deficiencies, it can be a mistake to address them all at the same time. How do you determine when and how to address each deficiency?

Question 6. How do you help underprepared students play to their strengths?

Question 7. What's the relationship between motivation and skills? To what extent does motivation make up for a lack of skills?

Question 8. People tend to apply the term "underprepared" only to academic skills. In what other areas can students also be underprepared? How can advisors help students with these other areas of underpreparation?

Question 9. What are some retention issues concerning underprepared students at your institution? What is or could be the role of advising in addressing each issue?

Activities

Institution-Specific Issues

Directions. Discuss the characteristics and needs of underprepared students on your campus. For instance, you may want to look at:

- Numbers of underprepared students
- Their most frequently chosen academic programs
- Retention rates, course pass rates, course drop rates, graduation rates, etc.
- Special retention issues or retention goals

Question 1. What are the key retention issues and retention goals concerning underprepared students at your institution? What role can advisors play in addressing these retention issues and goals?

Question 2. What institutional policies or procedures present barriers or inhibit the success of underprepared students? What are solutions to these problems? What role can advisors play in addressing these issues?

Helping Connect Underprepared Students to Institutional Resources

Directions. If your institution does not have one, develop an academic support resource grid that advisors can use to help students get connected with sources of help. You may want to use the following sample grids as starting points. The first grid concerns various forms of course-based support. The second grid concerns non-course-based support.

Course-based Academic Support	Institutional Options Available	Guidelines, Requirements, Cut-off Scores for Entry, etc.
Developmental courses	_____	_____
Freshman seminars/student success courses	_____	_____
Course-based tutoring	_____	_____
Course-based supplemental instruction	_____	_____
Courses in personal development	_____	_____
Courses in career planning or development	_____	_____
Courses in academic success, learning strategies, etc.	_____	_____
Other	_____	_____

Non-Course-based Academic Support	Institutional Resources Available	Contact Person/s Hours, Phone, etc.	Referral Policies and Procedures
Skill-based tutoring	_____	_____	_____
Writing lab/s	_____	_____	_____
Math lab/s	_____	_____	_____
Workshops on personal success strategies	_____	_____	_____
Workshops on time management	_____	_____	_____
Workshops on career planning	_____	_____	_____
Workshops on effective study strategies	_____	_____	_____
Workshops on library skills	_____	_____	_____
Assessment and management of learning disabilities	_____	_____	_____
Other	_____	_____	_____

In addition to these institutional resources, advisors can help individual students do the following:

- Review and adjust use of time

- Review and adjust study habits

- Review and adjust in-class behaviors

- Review and adjust test-preparation behaviors

- Review and adjust test-taking strategies

- Review and adjust personal priorities

Role Plays

Situation. Conduct a first advising interview with a student with multiple skill and performance deficiencies. The student is aware of many of the deficiencies and is receptive to help.

Situation. Conduct a first advising interview with a student with multiple skill and performance deficiencies. The student is unwilling to acknowledge the deficiencies and is defensive about the need for help.

Tools

Helpful Questions to Ask Underprepared Students

Here are a few helpful questions to ask underprepared students. What other questions can you add to the list?

1. What subjects did you enjoy in high school? In what subjects were your best grades?

2. Name the highest point in your life so far or your greatest accomplishment? What about the experience made it special?

3. If you have a spare hour, what do you do?

4. What will a college degree mean for you?

5. What are your best personal qualities? What do your friends like the most about you?

6. What have your employers valued about you?

7. _____

8. _____

9. _____

10. _____

END OF SECTION 3

Moving Toward Informed Decisions With Undecided Students

Participant Note. For more information about advising undecided students, see the resource article by Virginia Gordon, "Advising Undecided/Exploratory Students," on page 201 in the appendix of the Participant Book.

Key Learning Points

1. Undecided students are often the rule rather than the exception. Many students are not ready or able to commit to a major when they enroll.

2. Students can be unable, unwilling or unready to make a decision about a major or program. The first task an advisor faces is to determine the source of the indecision.

3. Many students mistakenly equate educational decisions with career decisions.

4. Many decided students have not made informed decisions. They make decisions based on job trends, parent influence, etc.

5. Undecided students are at risk because of their confusion. Advisors need to help students clarify their values, beliefs and concerns.

6. Undecided students can feel pressure to make choices from a variety of outside sources.

7. Course selection is the key challenge with undecided students.

8. Advisors need to see students as unique individuals with different patterns of interests and abilities.

9. Advisors help students make sense of all the fragmented pieces of information they have.

10. An informed career choice frees the energy and drive students need to complete the education and training required for that career.

11. Some undecided students are truly undecided and may be open to many possibilities. Other students are undecided because they haven't been able to decide among two or three majors that they find appealing.

12. The more able the student, the harder the decision—because more options are available.

Discussion Questions

Question 1. How does your institution define undecided student? Is this adequate?

Question 2. What types of undecided students have you encountered in your advising experiences? Why were these students undecided?

Question 3. Can you name some specific characteristics of these students?

Question 4. What were these students' greatest needs? How did you address these needs in your advising sessions?

Question 5. What knowledge and skills do you think advisors of undecided students need?

Question 6. What specific resources do you need to advise undecided students most effectively (e.g., materials, information, campus offices, computer systems)?

Question 7. What advising approaches have you used with undecided students in the past? How does it differ from the approaches you use with "decided" students?

Question 8. How many of you ended up majoring in the major or program you indicated on your college application?

Question 9. How many students enter your campus undecided?

Question 10. How many students who specify a major at your institution do you feel are really undecided?

Question 11. How do you probe for indecision with students who say they are planning on a particular major or career?

Question 12. New students direct from high school who declare a major or program do so for a variety of reasons, some of which are listed below. Rank the items from 1 to 9 (with 1 being high) in degree of influence for the students you work with and/or the students at your institution:

_____   Recommendations from parents

_____   Recommendations from teachers

_____   Recommendations from peers

_____   Students read or hear there are good job prospects for the field

_____   Informed decision based on careful examination of personal
                    strengths and interests

_____   Success in related courses in high school

_____   Work experience in the field

_____   Family member, relative or friend works in the field

_____   Personal interest in the field

Based on your responses, what are the implications for advising?

Question 13. In what ways do students equate (or confuse) educational decisions
with career decisions? How can you help clarify this for students?

Question 14. In what areas at your institution are educational decisions largely the
same as career decisions? In what areas are they not?

Question 15. What are some common mistakes students make with educational
and career decisions?

Question 16. Is the problem the fact that students are undecided or that they are
undecided for too long?

Question 17. What are some of the positives and negatives about students
being undecided?

Question 18. What are some helpful questions you could ask students to get at the
source of their indecision?

Question 19. What are examples of typical course selection problems or issues that
affect undecided students at your institution?

Question 20. What are some retention issues concerning undecided students or
students changing majors at your institution? What is or could be the role of
advising in addressing each issue?

Question 21. What is the procedure for changing majors or programs at your institution?

Question 22. At your institution, when are students required to make a decision about a major or program?

Question 23. At your institution, which majors or programs require an early commitment, especially if students plan to graduate on schedule?

Activities

Role Plays

Situation. A student is undecided and hasn't considered any options.

Situation. A student is undecided but has several active possibilities.

Situation. A student has declared a major that he doesn't seem to know a great deal about.

Situation. A student is interested in two disparate areas, such as engineering and art, that have different general education requirements.

Situation. A student has been planning for many years on an area such as pre-med or engineering, and all of a sudden it's clear that that isn't going to work out and she has never thought of anything else.

Situation. A new student at a community college is having difficulty deciding between college transfer and vocational-technical business programs.

Situation. An undecided student has interests in both business and psychology and is not ready to choose between them.

Situation. A first-term student has absolutely no idea where to begin searching for a major.

Situation. A student insists on majoring in pre-med but has C's and D's in chemistry.

Situation. A junior has not decided on a major and is getting very anxious about it.

Situation. A student is in the process of changing out of an engineering major but doesn't know what other majors interest her.

Situation. A second-year student cannot make a commitment to a sociology major even though he has pretty much decided on it.

Situation. A freshman is feeling pressure from his parents to major in business but really wants to major in nursing.

Institution-Specific Issues

Directions. Discuss the characteristics and needs of undecided students on your campus. For instance, you may want to look at:

- Numbers of undecided students

- Average length of time undecided

- Retention rates, graduation rates, average number of major changes, etc.

- Special retention issues or retention goals

Question 1. What are the key retention issues and retention goals concerning undecided students at your institution? What role can advisors play in addressing these retention issues and goals?

Question 2. What institutional policies or procedures present barriers or inhibit the success of undecided students? What are solutions to these problems? What role can advisors play in addressing these issues?

Identifying and Addressing the Causes of Student Indecision

Students can be undecided for a variety of reasons. Advisors may want to use different strategies when working with students depending on the cause of indecision.

Directions. Working in small groups or as a large group, discuss the common causes for student indecision listed on the chart below and identify advisor strategies that are effective with each.

Cause of Indecision   **Advisor Strategies**

1. Student unable to make decision   _____

2. Student unwilling to make decision   _____

3. Student unready to make decision   _____

4. Student choosing between disparate majors   _____

5. Student choosing between disparate careers

_____
_____

6. Student genuinely undecided and open to many possibilities

_____
_____

7. Incompatibility between major and career plans

_____
_____

8. Incompatibility between major and academic preparation

_____
_____

9. Academically able student with multiple interests

_____
_____

Helping Students Manage Their Indecision

Being undecided can be positive or negative, depending on the circumstances. For instance, being undecided may be positive for a new student with many interests to explore. It can become negative when students are undecided too long or when they have no apparent academic interests.

Directions. Working in small groups or as a large group, discuss the positives of students being undecided and the advisor role in promoting these positives. Also discuss the negatives of being undecided and the advisor role in addressing these negatives.

Positives of Student Being Undecided   **Advisor Role in Promoting**

1. _____   _____

2. _____   _____

3. _____   _____

4. _____   _____

5. _____   _____

Negatives of Student Being Undecided   **Advisor Role in Addressing**

1. _____   _____

2. _____   _____

3. _____   _____

4. _____   _____

5. _____   _____

Identifying the Characteristics of Undecided Students at Your Institution

Directions. Write answers to the following questions and then discuss in small groups or as a large group.

1. Write three adjectives that describe undecided students at your institution:

    _____

2. List five reasons students have given you for being undecided:

    _____

    _____

3. Of the reasons for being undecided listed above, which have been the most difficult for you to address in an advising session? Why?

    _____

    _____

4. In what areas do you think undecided students need help? Be specific.

    _____

    _____

5. What characteristics set undecided students apart from the "decided" ones you have advised?

    _____

    _____

6. Overall, what are the most important characteristics of undecided students that influence your current advising approaches with them?

    _____

    _____

Identifying Strategies for Working With Undecided Students

Directions. Write answers to the following questions and then discuss in small groups or as a large group.

1. What special traits do you think advisors of undecided students need? Why are these traits important?

   _____

   _____

2. How are these different from the traits needed to advise decided students?

   _____

   _____

3. What special knowledge do advisors of undecided students need? How is this knowledge used in an advising session?

   _____

   _____

4. What special skills do advisors need to use when advising undecided students?

   _____

   _____

5. Describe how you help an undecided student select a major over an extended period of time. What are the most important tasks to move the student toward this goal?

   _____

   _____

6. Describe how you help students who are in a transition period and are changing their mind about a major.

   _____

   _____

Tools

Helpful Questions to Ask Undecided Students

Here are a few helpful questions to ask undecided students. What other questions can you add to the list?

1. How is each course you're taking now helping you decide your educational and career plans?

2. What is something you learned about yourself from taking this course that will help you to decide your major and career?

3. What courses would you take here if there were no requirements?

4. Looking at a list of required courses, which courses are you most excited about taking?

5. Which courses wouldn't you take unless they were requirements?

6. _____

7. _____

8. _____

9. _____

10. _____

END OF SECTION 4

Helping Honors Students Bring Focus to Multiple Talents

Key Learning Points

1. The best and brightest students can also be at risk.

2. Many high-ability students have difficulty making educational and career decisions because they have so many areas of strength and interest. Advisors can help students bring focus to multiple talents.

3. Academic boredom is a problem for some high-ability students. Advisors can help students identify challenging opportunities.

4. Institutions sometimes have rules and policies that inhibit high-ability students from exploring and finding the connections among majors, careers and courses.

5. High-ability students sometimes find it hard to make connections between what seem to them to be disparate areas of interest.

6. Some high-ability students are reluctant to seek out academic challenges.

Discussion Questions

Question 1. How can high-ability students be challenged and what is the advisor's role in that?

Question 2. What are some of the characteristics of high-ability students at your institution?

Question 3. What special needs do high-ability students have at your institution?

Question 4. What are some of the retention challenges in working with high-ability students at your institution?

Question 5. What special opportunities exist for high-ability students at your institution?

Question 6. Is it sometimes better for high-ability students to be undecided, or be undecided for a longer period of time than less academically able students?

Question 7. The advisor in the video segment says that Brian, the student she was working with, went through a two-year decision process that she felt was very valuable for him. When would that process of exploration stop being valuable for Brian? What is the advisor's role in bringing the exploration process to closure?

Question 8. How do you get students to see beyond course requirements? What questions could you ask?

Question 9. What are some retention issues concerning high-ability students at your institution? What is or could be the role of advising in addressing each issue?

Question 10. How do you deal with students who are overconfident about their academic abilities?

Activities

Role Plays

Situation: A very bright entering student tells you he got good grades by doing almost no homework in high school.

Situation. A second-year student comes in for pre-registration advising. He is hard-working and very academically successful. He was a high school valedictorian and has a 4.00 GPA after one year of college. Since he enrolled, you have been encouraging him to take honors sections of required courses. Even though he is slightly bored with his classes, the student resists taking honors sections because he doesn't want to risk his perfect grade point average.

Situation: A high-ability student requests your approval for an independent study option that is not listed in the catalog.

Situation: An honors student asks you to review study abroad programs she is considering.

Situation: A high-ability student comes to you with a complaint. He is taking freshman composition and he feels he's being ripped off because he never gets any useful feedback on his papers. He says, "We hand in papers. We get them back, but there's nothing on them but a grade."

Situation: A student who entered college with a perfect 4.00 high school GPA is earning C's and D's at mid-term.

Situation: An entering honors student tells you he wants to take Russian, Japanese, computer programming, calculus and chemistry—all in the first term.

Institution-Specific Issues

Directions. Discuss the characteristics and needs of high-ability students on your campus. For instance, you may want to look at:

- Numbers of high-ability students

- Their most frequently chosen academic programs

- Retention and graduation rates

- Student satisfaction surveys

- Special retention issues or retention goals

Question 1. What are the key retention issues and retention goals concerning high-ability students at your institution? What role can advisors play in addressing these retention issues and goals?

Question 2. Are there any institutional barriers that discourage high-ability students from exploring? What are solutions to these problems? What role can advisors play in addressing these issues?

Helping Connect High-Ability Students to Institutional Opportunities

Directions. If your institution does not have one, develop a resource guide that identifies special opportunities at your institution designed to challenge the best and brightest students. You may want to include the following:

- Courses or sections of courses

- Honors programs or organizations

- Interdisciplinary or multidisciplinary programs

- Internships and practical experience

- Exchange programs with other institutions

- Study abroad programs

- Collaborative research with faculty

Tools

Helpful Questions to Ask High-Ability Students

Here are a few helpful questions to ask high-ability students. What other questions can you add to the list?

1. What connections do you see among the courses you are considering taking? Why are those important connections for you?

2. What connections do you see among the majors or programs you are considering? Why are those important connections for you?

3. What faculty have you met that you'd like to get to know better?

4. If you had the opportunity to collaborate with a faculty member on research, in what area would you want to work?

5. What's the most exciting or interesting thing you've learned in a class this term?

6. _____

7. _____

8. _____

9. _____

10. _____

END OF SECTION 5

SECTION 6
Understanding and Meeting the Needs of Students of Color

Participant Note. For more information about advising students of color, see the resource article by Thomas Brown and Mario Rivas, "Advising Students of Color," on page 223 in the appendix of the Participant Book.

Key Learning Points

1. Ethnically diverse populations bring opportunities and challenges to advisors and institutions.

2. The key issue is helping students of color achieve success, not just simply persist.

3. It is important for advisors to recognize there is a great deal of diversity within diversity. Advisors need to avoid making generalizations and assumptions about students.

4. Students of color often must overcome numerous obstacles, including prejudice, in order to achieve academic success. This includes perceptions that they are unqualified or underprepared. If faculty members have low expectations, students may feel insulted or may begin to doubt their own abilities.

Discussion Questions

Question 1. What are some of the factors that could lead an individual advisor, educational institution or program to focus specific efforts on advising students of color?

Question 2. Identify as many subgroups as you can of the following populations:

- Asian Pacific Islander

- Black/African-American

- Hispanic/Latino

- Native American

In what ways are the experiences and individual needs of members of these groups and subgroups similar? In what ways are they different?

Question 3. What are some of the issues to consider when differentiating within broad categories (e.g., language, socioeconomic status, gender, citizenship and so forth)?

© USA GROUP NOEL-LEVITZ, INC.   119

Question 4. What are some of the characteristics of students of color at your institution?

Question 5. What are some retention issues concerning students of color at your institution? What is or could be the role of advising in addressing each issue?

Question 6. What special needs do students of color have at your institution (e.g., focusing on strengths such as academic performance, resilience, persistence, optimism, and so forth)?

Question 7. What special opportunities exist for students of color at your institution?

Question 8. What are some of the retention challenges in working with students of color at your institution?

Question 9. How can advisors use the strengths-based approach to promote the success of students of color?

Question 10. What questions can advisors ask to get at issues of academic and personal self-esteem?

Question 11. What special resources are available to help students of color at your institution?

Question 12. The video suggests that it is damaging for students of color to be automatically seen as underprepared and at risk. On the other hand, many retention programs and intrusive advising strategies are built on assumptions and historical data. When working with students of color, how can advisors anticipate problems without making negative assumptions?

Activities

Role Plays

Situation: An entering African-American student is attending a predominantly white institution in a town with few people of color. The student feels very out of place and is not sure he made the right decision to enroll.

Situation. A Native American student with high grades from a suburban community feels he is being negatively stereotyped with other "minority" students.

Situation. A Latino student comes in to drop his psychology class. He says the professor is racist because the professor singles him out in class by asking his opinion on "Latino issues."

Situation. A student is in the middle of her toughest term in pre-nursing. She tells her advisor she's worried about study time. She has pledged a black sorority and doesn't know how she'll find the time for all the pledge activities she very much wants to do.

Institution-Specific Issues

Directions. Discuss the characteristics and needs of students of color on your campus. For instance, you may want to look at:

- Numbers of students of color

- Their most frequently chosen academic programs

- Retention and graduation rates

- Student satisfaction with advising and other services

- Special retention issues or retention goals

Question 1. What are the enrollment trends for students of color on your campus in the last five years? In what ways have you adapted your advising to respond to these trends?

Question 2. What are the key retention issues and retention goals concerning students of color at your institution? What role can advisors play in addressing these retention issues and goals?

Question 3. What institutional policies or procedures present barriers or inhibit the success of students of color? What are solutions to these problems? What role can advisors play in addressing these issues?

Helping Students of Color Connect With Institutional Resources

Directions. If your institution does not have one, develop a guide that identifies resources at your institution that might be of special value to students of color. You may want to consider some of the following:

- Scholarships

- Clubs, organizations, special interest groups

- Mentoring programs

- Exchange programs with other institutions

END OF SECTION 6

Building Bridges With Students of Color Through Effective Communication

Key Learning Points

1. Students of color from disadvantaged backgrounds who have made it to college frequently are successful because they have overcome educational and social obstacles.

2. Establishing rapport with students of color is especially important because they may have previous negative experiences with people outside their ethnic group—especially people in positions of authority.

3. Establishing rapport requires openness, empathy and a genuine caring attitude.

4. Communication is critical in establishing and developing a relationship with students of color.

5. Advisors need to establish credibility in early interaction with students of color.

6. The racial match between advisor and students is not always as important as sensitivity, genuine care and support.

7. Advisors need to understand how the student's background might affect the advising relationship.

8. Many students of color come from traditional cultural backgrounds and are accustomed to hierarchical relationships. So an advising relationship that calls for the student to take a great deal of responsibility may be new.

Discussion Questions

Question 1. Are there any ethnic or international groups of students at your institution who because of their cultural backgrounds have certain expectations of advisors or the advising process?

Question 2. How can advisors help students of color succeed academically?

Question 3. How can advisors help students of color succeed socially?

Question 4. How does one go about developing sensitivity about the needs of students of color?

Question 5. The video segment suggests that many students of color have a history of problematic experiences with people in positions of authority. How can you show students of color that you genuinely care about them and their success?

Question 6. One of the advisors on the video suggests that the racial match between advisors and students of color is not important. Do you agree?

Question 7. As an advisor, how can you determine whether or not you are demonstrating sensitivity and a caring attitude to students of color? What evidence can you gather about how these students perceive you?

Question 8. Are there questions you find it difficult to ask students who come from ethnic backgrounds different from yours?

Activities

Role Plays

Situation. A Native American student comes to you upset because he and several other Native American students have been accused of cheating on an academic project on which they were collaborating.

Situation. A Hispanic student tells you she is sure that chemistry and calculus will not be too much for her in the same term, but you are reluctant, given her test scores, to allow her to take both. She brings her older brother to the next advising session, and he tells you that the family has decided she will take these courses. She is the family member who is going to become a doctor.

Situation. A Vietnamese student comes to register for summer school. He can't go home, he says, because of gang violence. He knows he will be in danger if he returns home.

Situation: You're working with an international student from Germany who doesn't speak until he is spoken to.

Tools

Helpful Questions to Ask Students of Color

Here are a few helpful questions to ask students of color. What other questions can you add to the list?

1. What attracted you to this school?

2. In your experience so far, how is the institution different from what you expected it to be?

3. How do your friends and family feel about your being here in school?

4. Of the faculty or staff you've met here, who are some you'd like to get to know better?

5. How does it feel to interact with students here, compared to your last educational experience?

6. _____

7. _____

8. _____

9. _____

10. _____

END OF SECTION 7

Building Success Plans With Students of Color

Key Learning Points

1. Advising relationships with students of color are an opportunity to put all of the skills you develop as an informed advisor to work.

2. Students of color tend to see advisors as experts and are coming to advisors with concrete problems they want help with. Advisors need to help resolve these issues in a nondirective style.

3. Advisors need to demonstrate that they have something to offer: they have skills, they are interested in the student and they are committed to the student's success.

4. Advisors need to help students take the long view—progress, not perfection. Advisors need to help students define the small steps necessary to attain goals.

5. Peers are important to the success of students of color.

6. Group interactions may be extremely positive. Advisors need to help students integrate their academic and social selves.

Discussion Questions

Question 1. How can advisors promote the benefits of group study and group interaction?

Question 2. How can advisors help students of color integrate their academic and personal lives?

Question 3. How can advisors of student organizations facilitate the success of students of color?

Question 4. What are examples of *academic* success strategies you have found to be particularly successful with students of color at your institution?

Question 5. What are examples of *personal* success strategies you have found to be particularly successful with students of color at your institution?

Activities

Role Plays

Situation. The president of the Black Student Union comes in and asks for ideas for service projects the group can undertake.

Situation. A Native American student confides that she is not doing well academically.

Situation. A Native American student is concerned about his biology mid-term. The bookstore had run out of textbooks, and he did not know they would order one for him so he didn't ask. He borrowed books from his friends to do the reading, but now the test is coming, and his friends have reclaimed their books. Can you help?

Situation. An Asian-American student is having difficulty in an upper-level math course. Her parents do not understand her problem. The student thinks that she should drop the course rather than get a C, but she is afraid of what her parents will say.

Situation. An African-American honors student wants to take chemistry, even though her math placement score is below the cutoff. When you say that you'd rather see her strengthen her math skills before she starts chemistry she becomes very defensive and angry.

Situation. An international student from Taiwan is having trouble with the reading in her general education courses. Even though she spends many hours studying with groups of Chinese-speaking friends, there doesn't seem to be enough time for her to read and comprehend the assignments fully.

Helpful Questions to Ask Students of Color

Here are a few helpful questions to ask students of color. What other questions can you add to the list?

1.   Do you do your most effective studying by yourself or with other students?

2.   If you need help in one of your classes, where do you usually turn—your friends, your classmates, the teacher, academic support offices on campus?

3.   How do your friends let off steam?

4.   What offices on campus seem to have the students' best interest at heart?

5.   What people are most supportive about your being in college?

6.   _____

7.   _____

8.   _____

9.   _____

10. _____

END OF SECTION 8

UNIT FOUR

Key Issues in Advising

THOMAS GRITES

MARGARET C. "PEGGY" KING

THOMAS J. KERR

"Any time that there is a human interaction, ethics are involved, particularly in a situation where one party in that human interaction has some position of power, of dominance, of influence over the other."

THOMAS GRITES, RICHARD STOCKTON COLLEGE OF NEW JERSEY

"If we have a bias…it's important that we recognize those feelings in ourselves, and also that we not impose our feelings on the student."

MARGARET C. "PEGGY" KING, SCHENECTADY COMMUNITY COLLEGE

"It's important that you know what kind of advice was given, what kind of action items were recommended…so if it ever does get into a situation where legal action is going to be taken, you at least know and are well-documented on what went on previously."

THOMAS J. KERR, ROWAN COLLEGE OF NEW JERSEY

Building on Your Strengths as an Advisor

Key Learning Points

1. Advising is similar to teaching in many ways. Effective teachers promote active learning. The same is true of effective advisors.

2. The root meaning of educate is to "draw out." Advisors help students recognize what their strengths are and to draw them out.

3. Effective teachers and advisors are good communicators. Listening and questioning skills are effective in the classroom and in advising sessions. They are the principal ways to draw out students.

4. It is also important for advisors to recognize and draw out their own strengths.

5. Teaching strengths are transferable to advising. The challenge for faculty advisors is to move from one arena to the other.

6. Effective teachers and advisors are enthusiastic about what they are teaching.

7. Effective teachers and advisors have a solid grasp of their subject matter.

Discussion Questions

Question 1. Thinking back to your *undergraduate* experience, who was the advisor who had the most positive effect on you? What are examples of things he or she did that made them so effective?

Question 2. Thinking about your *graduate school* experience, who was the advisor/mentor who had the most positive effect on you? What are examples of things he or she did that made them so effective?

Question 3. What are some of the most effective questions you use in advising?

Question 4. Which of your strengths as an educator are most useful in advising?

Question 5. In what ways is effective advising similar to effective teaching?

Question 6. If students learn from advisors, then advisors learn from one another. Write down the name of one person at your institution whom you feel is an excellent advisor. What makes that person a good advisor? What can you learn from him or her that would make you a better advisor?

Question 7. What aspects of your work as an advisor do you feel the best about and look forward to the most?

Question 8. What aspects of your work as an advisor do you look forward to the least? What could you do to change that?

Question 9. How have your views of academic advising changed after going through this program?

Question 10. What follow-up activities to this training program would be beneficial?

Activities

Teaching Self-Assessment

Directions. The following self-assessment will give you an opportunity to review your teaching skills and attitudes and to identify areas for improvement.

Teaching Skills and Attitudes	How I Would Rate Myself	How Students Would Rate Me
1. I motivate students to be interested in the subject.	6 5 4 3 2 1	6 5 4 3 2 1
2. I can present complex ideas simply through analogies and other means.	6 5 4 3 2 1	6 5 4 3 2 1
3. I inspire students to seek excellence.	6 5 4 3 2 1	6 5 4 3 2 1
4. I design effective learning situations.	6 5 4 3 2 1	6 5 4 3 2 1
5. I effectively assess student learning and progress.	6 5 4 3 2 1	6 5 4 3 2 1
6. I customize material to individual student needs.	6 5 4 3 2 1	6 5 4 3 2 1

Teaching Skills and Attitudes

		How I Would Rate Myself	How Students Would Rate Me
7.	I devise written tests and assignments that promote student learning.	6 5 4 3 2 1	6 5 4 3 2 1
8.	I know my subject matter well.	6 5 4 3 2 1	6 5 4 3 2 1
9.	I help students become independent learners.	6 5 4 3 2 1	6 5 4 3 2 1
10.	I encourage students to seek academic help when they need it.	6 5 4 3 2 1	6 5 4 3 2 1
11.	I don't let my opinions and beliefs get in the way of effective teaching or stifle student comment.	6 5 4 3 2 1	6 5 4 3 2 1
12.	I ask questions that are worth answering.	6 5 4 3 2 1	6 5 4 3 2 1
13.	I frequently elicit feedback and questions from students.	6 5 4 3 2 1	6 5 4 3 2 1
14.	I use student feedback and questions to change class pace and content.	6 5 4 3 2 1	6 5 4 3 2 1
15.	I respect the opinions of students in class.	6 5 4 3 2 1	6 5 4 3 2 1
16.	I carefully respond to student work.	6 5 4 3 2 1	6 5 4 3 2 1
17.	I stimulate and draw out student curiosity.	6 5 4 3 2 1	6 5 4 3 2 1
18.	I help students see a course in the context of their personal, academic and career interests.	6 5 4 3 2 1	6 5 4 3 2 1
19.	I listen to students to discern their questions— what they need to know.	6 5 4 3 2 1	6 5 4 3 2 1
20.	I listen for the questions students ask and the questions they don't quite ask.	6 5 4 3 2 1	6 5 4 3 2 1

Personal Goal Statement. In the next several weeks, I will improve some of my teaching skills. (From the inventory items above, list the top five in order of importance.)

1. _____

2. _____

3. _____

4. _____

5. _____

Advising Self-Assessment

Directions. The following self-assessment will give you an opportunity to review your advising skills and attitudes and to identify areas for improvement.

Advising Skills and Attitudes	How I Would Rate Myself	How Students Would Rate Me
1. I listen carefully and concentrate on what students are saying.	6 5 4 3 2 1	6 5 4 3 2 1
2. I take every student and his or her concerns seriously.	6 5 4 3 2 1	6 5 4 3 2 1
3. I motivate students to be interested in school.	6 5 4 3 2 1	6 5 4 3 2 1
4. I help students understand the mission and goals of the institution.	6 5 4 3 2 1	6 5 4 3 2 1
5. I motivate students to get involved with and connected to the institution.	6 5 4 3 2 1	6 5 4 3 2 1
6. I help students see the connection between educational programs and future careers.	6 5 4 3 2 1	6 5 4 3 2 1
7. I help students identify and build on their strengths.	6 5 4 3 2 1	6 5 4 3 2 1
8. I know the resources on campus when students need referrals.	6 5 4 3 2 1	6 5 4 3 2 1
9. I am knowledgeable and up-to-date concerning institution policies, procedures, general education and degree requirements, etc.	6 5 4 3 2 1	6 5 4 3 2 1
10. I use questions effectively to understand student needs and concerns.	6 5 4 3 2 1	6 5 4 3 2 1
11. I don't let strong personal beliefs and opinions get in the way of effective advising.	6 5 4 3 2 1	6 5 4 3 2 1
12. I effectively monitor student progress.	6 5 4 3 2 1	6 5 4 3 2 1
13. I care about students and their success.	6 5 4 3 2 1	6 5 4 3 2 1
14. I show students I can help them as an advisor.	6 5 4 3 2 1	6 5 4 3 2 1
15. I reach out to student advisees who don't seek help.	6 5 4 3 2 1	6 5 4 3 2 1
16. I make students' interests and curiosities a major focus of advising.	6 5 4 3 2 1	6 5 4 3 2 1

Personal Goal Statement. In the next several weeks, I will improve some of my advising skills. (From the inventory items above, list the top five in order of importance.)

1. _____

2. _____

3. _____

4. _____

5. _____

Advisor Strengths Action Planning

Throughout the program, you have been encouraged to help students identify and build on their strengths. As an advisor, it is equally important for you to look at your attitudes and behaviors as an advisor and to build on your strengths.

Directions. If you have not done so already, complete the self-assessments in Units Two and Four:

1. Personal Goals for Student Advising Sessions (Participant Book, page 47)

2. Looking at Yourself Through the Eyes of Others (Participant Book, page 56)

3. Communication (Participant Book, page 63)

4. Teaching Self-Assessment (Participant Book, page 132)

5. Advising Self-Assessment (Participant Book, page 134)

Based on the strengths and weaknesses you have identified, use the grids below to identify action steps you could take to build on your strengths and develop areas that are not strengths. Consider the following categories when developing your plan:

1. Ability to Motivate Students to Excellence

   - Tapping into students' intellectual interests and curiosities

   - Helping students identify and build on academic and personal strengths

2. Interpersonal Skills

   - Listening and questioning skills

   - Referral skills

3. Ability to Understand and Meet the Needs of Special Populations

4. Knowledge of the Institution

- Rules, policies and procedures

- Referral resources inside and outside the institution

My Strengths as an Advisor

1. _____
2. _____
3. _____
4. _____
5. _____
6. _____
7. _____
8. _____
9. _____
10. _____

Actions I Could Take to Build on These Strengths

1. _____
2. _____
3. _____
4. _____
5. _____
6. _____
7. _____
8. _____
9. _____
10. _____

My Weaknesses as an Advisor

1. _____
2. _____
3. _____
4. _____
5. _____
6. _____
7. _____
8. _____
9. _____
10. _____

Actions I Could Take to Minimize These Weaknesses

1. _____
2. _____
3. _____
4. _____
5. _____
6. _____
7. _____
8. _____
9. _____
10. _____

Overcoming Obstacles to Success

To be successful, both advisors and institutions sometimes have to overcome obstacles.

Directions. Many obstacles can get in the way of careful, informed advising. Some of these are listed below. In the first column, put a check by the items that you feel are major obstacles on your campus. In the second column, put a check by any items that are obstacles to you personally.

Campus Obstacles		**Personal Obstacles**
_____	Advisors don't have the time to devote to careful advising.	_____
_____	Advisors lack the information they need.	_____
_____	Advisors lack training.	_____
_____	Advisors lack interest in advising.	_____
_____	Advisors aren't rewarded for advising.	_____
_____	Advising isn't mandatory.	_____
_____	No one is in charge of advising.	_____
_____	Other _____	_____

Institutional Recommendations. Given some of the barriers listed above, what policy recommendations might you make about improving advising on your campus?

Question 1. What is the most difficult situation you have faced as an advisor? How did you handle it?

Question 2. What factors inhibit or limit your ability as an academic advisor?

Tools

Short-term Strategies to Enhance Success as an Advisor

1. List two things you'd like to learn that would make your work as an advisor easier.

2. List two listening skills you'd like to improve to make your advising sessions more effective.

3. List two questioning skills you'd like to improve to make your advising sessions more effective.

4. List one thing you could do to make your advising work space more conducive to effective advising.

5. List two academic programs at your institution you'd like to learn more about to help you be a more effective advisor.

6. List two careers you'd like to learn more about to help you be a more effective advisor.

7. List three positive changes in your department that would improve the delivery of advising to students.

Find an Advising Mentor

If students learn from advisors, then advisors can learn from one another.

1. Write down the name of one person at your institution whom you feel is an excellent advisor. What makes that person a good advisor? What can you learn from them that would make you a better advisor?

2. Find an advising mentor to: (1) talk with about advising questions and challenges, (2) observe your advising sessions and whom you can observe doing advising, and (3) help you identify and build on your strengths as an advisor.

END OF SECTION 1

SECTION 2

Ethical Implications and Practices of Advising

Participant Note. For more information about ethics and values, see the resource article by Marc Lowenstein, "Ethics and Values in Academic Advising," on page 247 in the appendix of the Participant Book. Parts of this section have been adapted from M. Lowenstein and T. Grites, (1993, Spring), "Ethics in academic advising," *NACADA Journal, 13*(1), 53-61. Used with permission.

Key Learning Points

1. Academic advising is a powerful activity. The potential to do good for students is great. So is the potential to do harm.

2. Ethics is involved in every human interaction, especially when one person has power over another.

3. Ethical violations are sometimes unintentional.

4. More than doing good or doing harm, advisors need to be concerned with how their decisions affect others down the road.

5. Equal time is not necessarily equal treatment. Try to make any time with students count.

6. Key ethical responsibilities: not to do things for students that students need to learn to do themselves, teach students how to assume responsibility for their own academic lives, keep detailed records, monitor the progress of students and look out for students.

Discussion Questions

Question 1. One could say that a person behaves ethically when he or she approaches a situation from a disinterested rather than a selfish perspective, asking not just what is best *for me* but what is, simply, best. What are examples of behaviors by an academic advisor that would *fail* to exemplify an ethical point of view?

Question 2. If you are a teacher, what are some key ethical responsibilities or issues you face in teaching?

Question 3. As an advisor, what are some key ethical responsibilities or issues you face in advising?

Question 4. What are examples of inadvertent ethical problems advisors need to be aware of?

Question 5. List all the reasons you can think of why you might want to advise a student against taking a class with a particular professor. In each case, do you think it might be unethical to tell the student? Might there be an ethical and an unethical way of doing it?

Question 6. What are examples of advising situations or issues that pose ethical considerations or issues that you have encountered at your institution? How did you handle them?

Question 7. What policies at your institution reinforce ethical advising behavior?

Question 8. What problems can arise when an advisor is also the teacher of a student?

Activities

Role Plays

Situation. A student comes to you for pre-registration advising. He is interested in taking a class that is taught by a professor you know to be "putting in his time" before retirement. The course is relatively popular with students because so little is demanded of them. You would much rather see the student take other courses to satisfy the requirement that would provide a more stimulating and demanding learning experience.

Situation. A student comes to you for pre-registration advising. She is interested in taking a class that is taught by a professor who has on prior occasions been accused of sexual harassment of female students. The student is aware of the accusations and asks your opinion of the situation.

Situation. A student comes to you and asks if she can switch from her advisor to you. Her official advisor is also the teacher of one of her classes she doesn't like and isn't doing well in.

Situation. A new student comes to you for pre-registration advising. He works full time for a local company that he likes and he has no plans of moving or changing jobs. He completed two and one-half years of college several years earlier. If he earns a baccalaureate degree, he gets an automatic promotion. He doesn't care what program he's in. He wants you to help him find the easiest program he can complete in the shortest time.

Situation. You are the advisor of a student who also is in one of the classes you teach. Because of the situation, you aren't sure the student is being honest and open with you about how his classes are going.

Situation. A student tells you he wants to go into teaching, but his parents are urging him very strongly to go into engineering. The student asks your advice in dealing with the situation. Do you encourage the student to pursue his interest when you know that will likely result in more conflict with his parents?

Situation. Use one or more of the situations in the Case Studies below for role plays.

Institution-Specific Issues

Directions. Discuss issues related to ethical advising on your campus. For instance, you may want to look at:

- Any institutional policy statements or similar documents that address ethics or ethical treatment of students.

- Any institutional policy statements or similar documents that address expected standards of professional conduct.

You may want to share with participants and discuss the "Statement of Core Values" from NACADA.

Case Studies

Directions. Working in small groups or as a large group, discuss the case studies in this section. To guide your discussion, use the Decision-Making Questions below. The *ethical ideals* and *ethical principles* for advising that are referred to in the Decision-Making Questions are listed in the Tools portion of this section, on page 145. More in-depth presentation of the ethical ideals and ethical principles are included in the resource article, "Ethics and Values in Academic Advising," (Participant Book, page 247).

Decision-Making Questions

1. What are your principal options in this situation?

2. Do you have any personal stake or feelings that might limit your ability to take an ethical point of view in this situation?

3. Identify each *ethical ideal* and each *ethical principle* for academic advising that has a bearing on the situation. What course of action does it call for?

4. Does a best course of action emerge from these considerations? If not, what are the principles supporting each side?

5. What additional information, if any, would you like to have in order to weigh the alternatives?

6. If there is a conflict, is there a way to honor each of the conflicting principles to some extent?

7. If not, does comparing this case to other cases help you decide which principles might be more "acceptable" to disobey?

8. If it seems inevitable that you will violate at least one principle, is there one such violation that would be of a lesser magnitude than the others?

The Case of Sally O'Mally

Your advisee Sally O'Mally has just come to see you. She has learned that she is deficient in a specific graduation requirement and is asking for help. She claims that her previous advisor failed to inform her of this requirement, though she also acknowledges that she has not been very conscientious in taking responsibility for knowing and meeting her requirements.

In this case, you are aware that Sally has the right to appeal to the dean who has jurisdiction. You also know that this dean has in the past granted appeals when they were based on allegations of procedural error—even when those allegations were dubiously documented. Another student of your acquaintance, Robby Robinson, was successful in such an appeal just recently. Thus you estimate that were Sally to appeal, she would have a very good chance of being excused from the requirement.

On the other hand, your professional judgment is that Sally would benefit educationally from taking the course that she is trying to avoid. You feel obliged to advise her of her right to appeal, though you know that if she appeals she likely will escape the requirement, which you don't want to see happen. What should you do?

The Case of Louis Lane

Louis Lane is one of your new advisees. During your meeting he describes his new, positive attitude toward school, indicating that he had never really taken education seriously at his previous colleges. Since you have only one transcript for him, you inquire about these "other" experiences. He informs you that he never bothered to indicate his first school because he got all F's and W's and wouldn't get any credit anyway.

You realize that your institution's admissions application calls for information about, and transcripts from, all previously attended colleges, and a signed pledge that all information supplied is complete and accurate. You also are aware that Louis would probably have been denied admission if the weakness of his previous record had been known. The campus conduct code permits dismissal for falsifying an admissions application. What should you do?

The Case of Phil Phorge

You have just received the registrar's copy of a course withdrawal for Phil Phorge, your advisee. You notice that the signature on the form is not yours, and indeed you don't recall discussing this situation with Phil. This is not the first such incident with Phil, and the reputation on campus is that "students do it all the time." In fact, you disagree with the policy of the required signature because you think it distorts the purpose of advising.

You have to decide what to do with the information in your hands. You can ask the registrar to void the withdrawal, thereby almost ensuring an F in the course, since Phil could not likely make up the missed work. You can also refer his case to the Campus Hearing Board, which could choose from a variety of sanctions including expulsion and an "academic dishonesty" notation on Phil's permanent record. And of course you can choose both, or neither of these options. You may feel (especially since you disagree with the signature policy) that the consequences of turning Phil in are more harsh than his offense warrants, even though it is unquestionably an offense.

What should you do?

The Case of Mindy Martin and Stan Wright

Mindy Martin and Stan Wright have separately come to you for your signature to drop a course, and you have asked them to explain the reasons.

Mindy, whom you learn was raised in a fundamentalist and "creationist" environment, is uncomfortable with the discussion of evolution that is dominating her required general education science course. There simply is no way to avoid the concept of evolution in any aspect of the work for this course, including the exams and papers. In addition to the discomfort she feels, she is afraid that she will fail the course. As it happens, you are aware that Mindy could meet the general science requirement through other courses that would not confront her with evolution quite so forcefully, if at all.

Stan is also uncomfortable with a class: his political science teacher is an avowed Marxist who, Stan says, not only puts a Marxist slant on all the course material but is also constantly making remarks that disparage American society and values and America's role in world history. You know from your own contact that this instructor often overdoes his rhetoric and carries his political statements beyond what the evidence at hand will support. (As in Mindy's case, this course is not an absolute requirement for Stan's economics curriculum; it satisfies a requirement that he study subjects related to his field, but other courses would do so as well.)

You have urged both students to stick with their courses on the grounds that involvement with ideas they don't like will benefit them, but they insist that their situations are too unpleasant to bear any longer. You must finally decide whether to sign the drop forms.

The Case of Willie Williams

Your advisee Willie Williams has asked for your signature to OK his adding a course. Willie is not a top student, and in fact he's on probation. You think this particular course is not a good one for him to take at this point, and you tell him so. To your surprise, he says he agrees. But he doesn't actually intend to take the course.

Right now, Willie tells you, he isn't registered for enough credits to be eligible for financial aid or for campus housing. He can't afford to attend even with a reduced load without a loan, and he knows from past experience that if he doesn't live on campus he won't focus on academics and he won't do well. (Since he's on probation, another term of bad grades could result in his dismissal.) His plan is to stay in this class far enough into the term to be considered "full time" and thus avoid losing his loan and his dorm room, and then drop it just in time to get a partial refund.

Should you sign?

The Case of Lee Roberts and Sandy Kelly

Lee Roberts and Sandy Kelly have come to seek your permission to drop a certain course because they say they are being sexually harassed by their professor, whom you know to be a distinguished, tenured full professor in your department. The students realize it is too late to enroll in another course, but they are so uncomfortable in class that they are willing to carry a reduced load for the term, even though this will create problems in their progress toward graduation.

When questioned about the nature of the harassment, Lee and Sandy say that there is a lot of winking, "knowing smiles," and innuendo in class that creates an unpleasant atmosphere when the professor communicates with them in class. They have not met in the professor's office and there have not been any direct overtures, offers or requests for sexual involvement.

In addition to seeking to drop the class, the students ask you how to go about filing sexual harassment charges. (The answer is, one completes a complaint form at the affirmative action office, and this triggers an investigation.)

You happen to know, but the students do not, that this is the professor's last term before retirement.

What advice and information do you give the students?

Tools

Professional Aspects of Advising

A professional is a person who has an understanding of his or her profession sufficient to be self-monitoring. One outgrowth of this self-monitoring is that professionals have thought through ethical issues, principles and practices, including the following:

1. You understand the limits of your expertise.

2. You acknowledge what you do not know.

3. You take the initiative to seek consultation whenever there is a question.

4. You make referrals when necessary.

5. You are a continuous learner.

6. You avoid dual relationships.

These principles apply, as well, to every academic discipline.

Four Ethical Ideals of Advising

1. Beneficence (doing good). This means bringing about the most benefit and the least harm that one possibly can.

2. Justice (or fairness). Treat all individuals equally, granting no one rights or privileges that are not granted to all.

3. Respect for persons. Treat individuals as ends in themselves, never merely as means to your own ends.

4. Fidelity. Live up to commitments that you have made, whether explicitly or implicitly.

Ethical Principles of Advising

1. Maximize educational benefit to the advisee.

2. Treat all students equitably; don't play favorites or create special privileges.

3. Enhance the advisee's ability to make decisions.

4. Tell the advisee the truth about policies and procedures. Tell others the truth as well. But respect the confidentiality of advisee interactions.

5. Advocate for the advisee with other offices when warranted.

6. Support the educational philosophy and policies of the institution.

7. Maintain the credibility of the advising program.

8. Accord colleagues appropriate professional courtesy and respect.

Minimum Standards of Conduct

1. Do not exploit your unequal relationship with the advisee.

2. Be available to your advisees. Keep office hours and keep appointments. Be on time.

3. Know the information that you need in order to give useful advice.

4. Meet deadlines.

5. Do not discriminate against students.

6. Do not limit advising to the quick signature.

7. Do not malign colleagues.

END OF SECTION 2

Avoiding Bias in Advising

Key Learning Points

1. Good advising relationships are those that treat each student individually and help advisees down the road of personal development.

2. Personal feelings and points of view can get in the way of good advising relationships. Advisors need to recognize those feelings and not impose their feelings on students.

3. Biases can result from religious, moral, cultural or political beliefs. They can put up roadblocks in any advising relationship.

4. If you have biases you think will make it difficult or impossible to work with a student, then help the student find a person who will be more effective.

Discussion Questions

Question 1. Why is it important that you not try to impose your values on others?

Question 2. What are areas of unintentional or intentional bias in advising you have encountered at your institution?

Question 3. What should you do in a situation where you find it difficult to be genuine and non-judgmental with an advisee?

Question 4. Students are just as prone to bias as advisors. How can you help students identify and deal with their own biases?

Question 5. What could/should you do when you hear a colleague giving a student advice that you consider sexist?

Question 6. Identify examples of racist advising.

Question 7. Identify some stereotypic assumptions faculty and staff may have about "older" students.

Activities

Role Plays

Situation. A student comes to you to switch from economics to journalism. Your personal bias is that "content majors" are better paths to journalism than the journalism major.

Situation. A student comes to you who wants to attend law school. Like many students he assumes he should major in political science or history. Your personal bias is that many other majors such as science, English or business are often better preparation for law school.

Situation. A new student at a community college plans to enroll in a vocational-technical business program that is not transferable to a four-year institution. The student is very academically able, but wants to get out working as soon as she can. Your personal bias is that she should enroll in a college-transfer business curriculum so she has that option later if she chooses.

Situation. A student comes to you to discuss his plans to take off a year to make some money and then return to school. You know that stop-outs at your institution very frequently become dropouts. The student has been doing good academic work, and you don't want to see the student get off track. Your personal bias is that the student should remain in school.

Situation. A student wants to complete pre-chiropractic requirements at your institution and then transfer to chiropractic school. You view chiropractors as quacks who should be prosecuted for malpractice.

Situation. A pre-law student tells you he wants to become a lawyer to help his family's construction firm evade ordinances and regulations that just "get in the way."

Self-Assessment: Areas of Personal Bias That Could Affect Your Advising

A person without opinions would be a dreadful bore and probably not a very helpful advisor. A continuum of advising behaviors might have on one end advisors who express no opinions or preferences at all. On the other end would be advisors whose strong opinions and preferences get in the way of effective advising. Effective advisors operate somewhere between these extremes.

One could make an analogy to drinking alcohol. One end of the continuum is abstention, the other is drinking to excess. The phrase "responsible drinking" refers to the area in between, in which people ask the question, "Does my drinking interfere with my life in ways that keep me from achieving my goals or that are unhealthy for me and those around me?" For advisors, a parallel question concerning bias might be, "Do I have prejudices, beliefs, opinions or preferences that get in the way of effective advising or that have a negative effect on my advisees?"

Having biases is natural and to be expected. The problem comes when biases are hidden. Advisors should make an effort to make biases known to advisees and to freely discuss the reasons behind them.

> **Directions.** For each of the following 11 areas of potential bias, identify any areas that could have a negative effect on your advisees. After taking this self-assessment, you may wish to discuss the results in pairs or small groups.

1. Educational programs

   Are there majors or educational programs I steer students toward or away from because of my preferences and opinions?

   _____

   _____

2. Careers, graduate school, other post-educational plans

   Are there particular careers or post-educational plans I steer students toward or away from because of my preferences and opinions?

   _____

   _____

3. Student activities

   Are there student activities on- or off-campus I steer students toward or away from because of my preferences and opinions?

   _____

   _____

4. Student employment

   Do I have strong opinions about students working in school that I express to students?

   _____

   _____

5. Gender issues

   Are there educational programs or careers I steer students toward or away from because of gender-based opinions?

   _____

   _____

6. Racial or ethnic issues

    Are there educational programs or careers I steer students toward or away from because of racial- or ethnic-based opinions?

    _____

    _____

7. Age

    Are there educational programs or careers I steer students toward or away from because of age-based opinions?

    _____

    _____

8. Religion

    Do any of my religious and/or moral opinions and preferences have a negative effect on my advising?

    _____

    _____

9. Politics

    Do any of my political opinions and preferences have a negative effect on my advising?

    _____

    _____

10. Student academic preparation

    Do I have strong opinions about academic preparation that I express to students in advising?

    _____

    _____

11. Students with disabilities

    Do any of my opinions about students with disabilities have a negative effect on my advising?

    _____

    _____

END OF SECTION 3

Meeting Challenging Legal Issues in Advising

Participant Note. For more information about legal issues in advising, see the resource article by Susan J. Daniell, "Legal Issues in Academic Advising," on page 251 in the appendix of the Participant Book.

Key Learning Points

1. Advisors today have many legal responsibilities.

2. All advisors need a basic awareness of legal issues related to academic advising.

3. There is a growing body of case law on inaccurate, misguided or inaccessible advising.

4. Institutions have a legal obligation to provide accurate and accessible advising to students.

5. When a student pays for an education, that forms a contract between the institution and the student.

6. To avoid legal difficulties, know what kind of advice was given, what action items were recommended and whether the student followed up.

7. It's important to take notes during advising sessions about any actual or proposed actions. This also helps you prepare for follow-up sessions with students.

Discussion Questions

Question 1. What kinds of legal problems, if any, have advisors had at your institution?

Question 2. Who can share record-keeping ideas that are effective but not overly time consuming?

Question 3. Advisors and students both need good information. As an advisor, what information would you like to have about institutional requirements, policies or procedures that you don't currently have?

Question 4. As an advisor, what training would you like to have about institutional requirements, policies or procedures that you have not had or that you don't feel is offered by the institution?

Question 5. As an advisor, what information would you like to have about your student advisees that you don't currently have?

Question 6. As an advisor, what training would you like to have about working with student information that you have not had or that you don't feel is offered by the institution?

Question 7. What are the salient points to remember about the contractual, statutory and constitutional relationships students have with their colleges and universities?

Question 8. How are faculty kept apprised of institutional changes in curriculum, requirements, policies, procedures, etc.? How are students informed of the same changes?

Question 9. Specifically, what is the institution's policy regarding the Family Educational Rights and Privacy Act? How is the policy interpreted and applied on your campus? What information may be released without a student's permission? What information is protected from release by FERPA?

Question 10. What is the most appropriate and effective way to deal with a parent (or other individual) who is requesting or "demanding" information about his or her child? What if the request seems very legitimate?

Question 11. How much latitude do faculty advisors have in making exceptions to academic requirements, policies, procedures, etc.? Who can make such exceptions?

Question 12. What is the "grievance chain" on campus? What kinds of grievances do different offices or administrators on campus handle?

Question 13. What types of situations do you feel uncomfortable dealing with or ill-prepared to handle accurately or effectively?

Question 14. Should faculty advisors consider purchasing personal professional liability insurance?

Activities

Role Plays

Situation. A faculty advisor receives a telephone call from a parent requesting/demanding information on his or her child's academic progress and performance.

Situation. A student contacts her faculty advisor alleging "academic malpractice." She states she was not advised in a manner that will facilitate a smooth transition to a transfer institution.

Situation. A faculty advisor receives a request for a recommendation (job, graduate school, etc.) for a student. The advisor has firsthand knowledge of significant personal problems encountered by the student that may possibly affect the student's suitability for the job, graduate school, etc.

Situation. In an advising appointment a student confides to his faculty advisor his thoughts of suicide or his intentions to harm himself or others. The student emphatically states he is talking confidentially with his advisor.

Situation. In an advising situation a student expresses an interest in a major or program of study and the advisor openly discourages the student from considering that program of study based on the student's gender, ethnicity, disability, or other "protected" classification.

Institution-Specific Issues

Directions. Discuss the legal issues in advising at your campus. For instance, you may want to look at:

- Past or pending legal issues at your institution relative to advising

- Potential legal issues that have already been identified

- Potential legal issues that have *not* already been identified

- Policies on sexual harassment at your campus

- Policies on racial or ethnic discrimination on your campus

- Interpretation of the Family Educational Rights and Privacy Act of 1974 (the Buckley Amendment) at your institution

- Policies regarding information given out by advisors in on-campus and off-campus referrals

- Institutional expectations that advisors are expected to follow to avoid legal difficulties

Keeping Track of Commitments to Reduce Problems

Six simple words usually precede student complaints about poor advising: "But my advisor told me that..." My advisor told me that the credits would transfer. My advisor told me I could take the same course at a community college during the summer. My advisor told me I could take an extra course for the same amount of money. My advisor told me that a semester of study abroad would count towards my degree.

Both advisors and students can be the cause of advising problems and potential legal issues. Advisors can and do make mistakes through carelessness or lack of information and training. Students, in turn, sometimes don't understand rules, policies and procedures that are explained to them. Students sometimes choose to hear what they want to hear.

While problems can never totally be eliminated, they can be dramatically reduced by keeping a written record of information given to and commitments made to students by advisors. Here is an example.

A new student tests into a developmental math course that is offered for institutional credit, but not degree credit. That is, the student receives credit hours for taking the class, but these hours do not count towards the total required for a degree. Two years later, a very angry student complains that he has three fewer hours than he thought. In this example, both the advisor and the student would have been well served had the student signed a short statement that he was informed about and understood that the developmental math course would not count toward his degree.

Directions. Working in small groups or as a large group, discuss how advisors could use written records to reduce student complaints about advising and to reduce legal issues and problems. In particular, you may want to look at:

- Common areas of student complaints about advising
- Common causes of student misunderstanding
- Common mistakes made by students
- Common mistakes made by advisors
- Institutional approaches to promote effective record keeping, i.e., standardized forms to record advisor commitments, etc.

Exceptions to Rules, Policies and Procedures

At every college and university students are subject to numerous rules, policies and procedures. And, every day, exceptions are made to those rules, policies and procedures. Exceptions can easily lead to complaints and legal problems for a variety of reasons:

- No record is kept of the exception or the reason for it.

- The exception is not transmitted to the proper office or individual for action.

- The person who made the exception did so incorrectly.

- The person who made the exception did not have the authority.

- The person who made the exception left the institution before the problem arose.

> **Directions.** Working in small groups or as a large group discuss the use of and problems associated with exceptions on your campus. In particular, focus on the following:

- What common exceptions to rules, policies and procedures are made on campus, and who has the authority to make them?

- What exceptions can be made by professional advisors?

- What exceptions can be made by faculty and/or faculty advisors?

- What exceptions can be made by academic administrators?

- What exceptions have led to problems in the past?

- What record-keeping strategies can reduce problems associated with exceptions?

Tools

Questions to Ask About Legal Issues at Your Institution

1. What is my institution's policy on the Family Educational Rights and Privacy Act (Buckley Amendment)? How is it interpreted and applied on this campus?

2. What information on a student am I permitted to release (and not permitted to release)? What is considered "directory information" at my institution?

3. Whom do I refer individuals to when I do not feel comfortable in dealing with their requests and demands for information?

4. Is there a form available for students to sign giving me permission to discuss their academic records with a third party?

5. As an advisor, what "authority" do I have to waive requirements, make exceptions to policies, substitute courses, and otherwise alter publicized institutional standards?

6. Whom do I refer students to for information regarding graduation requirements, exceptions to requirements, academic appeals, and other issues I feel are outside the scope of my responsibilities as a faculty advisor?

Other questions? Ask—don't assume!

Some Guidelines for Releasing Student Information

Permission to Release Information

In order to release student information protected by the Family Educational Rights and Privacy Act, *always* obtain *written* permission from the student. Written permission (or an institutionally designed form) should specify:

- Student name and ID number

- Type of information to be released—such as grade point average, courses taken, course grades, academic standing, credit hours earned, etc.—be very specific

- Name(s) of individual(s) to whom information may be released and purpose of release

- Student signature and date signed

Remember—

- This form should immediately be placed in the student's file and retained (even if later voided).

- The student may at any time void the permission granted to release information.

- Obtain *specific written* permission!

Information Generally Regarded as "Directory Information"

- Student name

- Student address and telephone number

- Dates of attendance

- Major

- Participation in officially recognized activities and athletics

- Degrees and awards received

- Date and place of birth

- Most recent institution attended

Remember, an institution's policy regarding FERPA specifies what information may be released without a student's consent. Students may restrict release of directory information by written request. Find out what is considered "directory information" at your institution.

Effective Ways to Reduce Problems and Complaints

Here are a few effective ways to reduce problems and complaints. What others can you add to the list?

1. Take good notes on advising sessions, especially concerning recommendations, commitments, exceptions and referrals.

2. In appropriate situations, ask students to sign statements that they understand and agree to actions that you are taking or that the student is taking.

3. Don't answer questions if you aren't sure of the correct answer. Instead, say you need to check or to look up the information.

4. When talking with students or explaining something, frequently ask them questions that probe for understanding.

5. When talking with students or explaining something, remind them to take notes and write down important information for their own records.

6. Remember that students should be able to rely on the accuracy of information provided by advisors and other institutional agents.

7. The advisor is an agent of the institution and cannot disclaim this responsibility. What is said may constitute an implied contract.

8. Ascertain your institution's interpretation of the Buckley Amendment—how it is applied locally.

9. Exercise care with student (peer advisors, student workers, etc.) access to confidential student files and records.

10. Require a written waiver from a student before releasing student information to a third party.

11. Keep anecdotal notes on advising contacts in students' files.

12. Any waivers of policy, degree requirements, etc., should be in writing and maintained in the student's file. Avoid oral permissions and waivers.

13. If or when requirements, policies, procedures, etc., change, make extraordinary efforts to inform students of the changes.

14. Review all institutional publications and other program/degree information. Make every effort to deliver what is "promised."

15. Include a disclaimer in institution publications ("... does not constitute a contract ... may be changed ..."). The institution may with good reason change requirements.

16. Stay abreast of policy and procedure changes. Participate in ongoing advisor training and communication.

17. Refer students to persons competent to give advice, and in some cases, persons officially recognized by the institution to disseminate information.

18. Be accessible to students—open lines of communication can avert many potential misunderstandings.

19. Refrain from voicing negative opinions regarding individuals, policies, courses, etc. to students (or anyone for that matter).

20. Do your best to provide sound, accurate information. Act in good faith and exercise your best professional judgment.

END OF SECTION 4

Appendix

Advising for Excellence (Edward "Chip" Anderson) 161

The Relationship Between Teaching and Advising (Carol Ryan) 169

Developmental Advising (Steven C. Ender) 171

Student Development Theory Into Practice: Implications for Advisors
    (Virginia Gordon) 177

Advisor Resources (Thomas J. Kerr) 183

Referral Skills (Faye Vowell) 191

Communication Skills (Margaret C. "Peggy" King) 195

Advising Undecided/Exploratory Students (Virginia Gordon) 201

Advising Graduate Students (Cheryl J. Polson) 207

Advising Transfer Students (Thomas J. Kerr and Margaret C. "Peggy" King) 215

Advising Students of Color (Thomas Brown and Mario Rivas) 223

Advising Adult Learners (Cheryl J. Polson) 235

Developing an Advising Portfolio (Faye Vowell) 241

Ethics and Values in Academic Advising (Marc Lowenstein) 247

Legal Issues in Academic Advising (Susan J. Daniell) 251

Advising for Excellence

Edward "Chip" Anderson, Ph.D.
Program Coordinator, Graduate School of Education and Information Studies, UCLA

Definitions and Methods of Defining Excellence

"Excellence" is a frequently used word in higher education. For some it represents an academic ideal. For others it is synonymous with scholarship, while for still others it represents a standard of performance at the highest levels.

Excellence has also been used to distinguish certain institutions of higher education. As John Gardner points out, "The word 'excellence' is all too often reserved for the dozen or two institutions which stand at the zenith of our higher education in terms of faculty distinction, selectivity of students and difficulty of curriculum" (Gardner, 1981, p. 99).

Unfortunately, using the term "excellence" to distinguish colleges and universities sometimes says little or nothing about what occurs in the lives of students as a result of attending these institutions. This point is supported by the research of Alexander Astin, who notes that the "hierarchy of institutions" that supposedly represent a "pecking order" of excellence is based upon a belief system, albeit a type of folklore, of assumptions that certain colleges and universities have "excellence" by virtue of some institutional attribute rather than because of what occurs in the lives of students.

Astin identifies three ways that excellence is usually attributed (Astin, 1983):

1. Excellence as reputation
Shared beliefs that excellence exists by virtue of the publication records of faculty members, graduate school ratings, undergraduate ratings and faculty/staff opinion polls.

2. Excellence as resources
Excellence is assumed based primarily on money or what money can buy: physical facilities, libraries and artistic holdings, endowments, grants, scholarships, funded research projects, and the salaries and status of faculty and staff. Sometimes students and their academic characteristics at admission are also given as examples of excellence, and thus some institutions attempt to lure national merit scholars and other achieving high-schoolers through special scholarships and incentives. But again, this does not speak to the issue of what students learn while in, or as a result of, the college environment.

3. Excellence as content
This approach defines the quality or excellence of an institution in terms of what it teaches. Thus, course offerings, majors, the structure of degree programs and requirements for graduation become the proxy for excellence. In most cases, the most prestigious institutions emphasize traditional liberal arts programs of study, with special emphases in literature and science.

There are two problems that these approaches present:

1. More than 3,000 colleges and universities are excluded from what is or can be considered "excellent."

2. These definitions do not emphasize students, either in terms of what they learn, how much they learn, or how they perform in college.

For many of us, it is hard to conceive of excellence without considering student learning, since learning is what we hold as the primary purpose of education. What is needed, therefore, is a way to conceptualize excellence in terms of the impact the college experience has on students. What is needed is a way of thinking about excellence in terms of:

- What do students learn in college?

- How do students change as a result of college experiences?

- What skills are acquired and developed—which abilities are refined and maximized as a result of the college experience?

- Which talents are developed and what gifts and talents are discovered in college?

- What new insights are made and what understandings are generated as a result of the college experience?

- What new self-understanding, awareness and what growth in confidence and self-efficacy result from the college experience?

- What substantive knowledge is gained, and what new appreciation for art, literature and culture have developed in college—because of college?

If our concept of excellence does not include students, student outcomes, student learning or student development, how can we call colleges and universities *educational* institutions? And until the definitions of excellence include student outcomes, student learning and student development, how can we call ourselves *educators*?

Excellence as the Development of Human Talent

In direct response to the limitations of the "reputation," "resource" and "content" methods of identifying supposed excellence, Astin proposes a way of viewing excellence from a more educational, learning, growing and developing perspective. He calls this approach "excellence as the development of human talent."

Astin's proposal of the development of human talent as the basis for defining excellence begins with an assertion about the most fundamental purposes of higher education. He asks questions such as:

- Isn't the purpose of a college or university to educate?

- If so, wouldn't it follow that definitions of excellence would emphasize the educational impacts of institutions of higher education?

- After all, if we are educators working in institutions of higher education, wouldn't it follow that definitions of excellence will emphasize the educational impacts of the college experience?

An aside, but critically important corollary, to Astin's proposal is an assumption that this view of excellence should emphasize the educational impact of the institution, not only on its students, but also on its faculty and professional staff members.

The proposition of excellence as the development of human talent can be summarized as follows:

- The talent development view of excellence emphasizes the educational impact of the institution on its students and faculty members, *i.e., on every member of the institutional community.*

- True excellence lies in an institution's ability to affect its students and faculty favorably, enhancing their intellectual and scholarly development and making a positive difference in their lives.

- The most excellent institutions are those that have the greatest impact on students' knowledge and personal development, and on the faculty's scholarly productivity and effectiveness in facilitating student learning and development.

In its simplest form, the talent development concept of excellence focuses on changes in the student from the beginning to the end of an educational program—changes that would likely include gains in substantive knowledge; the development of certain awarenesses, cognitive skills and intellectual abilities; and the development of important personal and affective attributes.

The Nature of Excellence—and Advising for Excellence

While it may seem that we are belaboring the process, a few more aspects of the notion of excellence need to be made clear.

The root "excel" means to raise, to raise oneself, to surpass, to project. Thus, the root meaning of excellence is highly personal. It speaks of positive movement. It involves positive progress and achievement in the sense of surpassing previous performance levels.

Excellence as a process of progressive movement to higher and higher levels of performance and achievement has much in common with the idea of development. Development too involves a positive and progressive process of surpassing previous levels and rising to higher levels of effectiveness. Another common bond exists between the process of excelling and the process of developing: both are dependent on learning.

But there is another way in which excellence is defined and used. Excellence often refers directly to a high performance level. And within higher education, one often hears references to "maintaining standards of excellence."

So our definition of excellence must involve not only surpassing our best, individual performance levels, but also surpassing some level of performance that is clearly above the minimum. In fact, most people would use the term excellence to denote a level of performance that is not only above minimum, but of the highest order; performance at a perfect or near perfect level.

Taking these two lines of thinking together and inserting the idea of "advising for excellence," it should be clear that we want to see students advised in a way that promotes their progressive, positive movement to higher and higher levels of performance and achievement, and that our standards and expectations of the advising process go far beyond minimum standards. The goal is for students to continually progress to the heights of their potential and abilities.

What Excellence Requires

Having sketched out the nature of excellence, let's think about what excellence demands. If we say that we want to promote excellence and can identify what excellence requires, then the next logical step is to think about what advising needs to do in order to help students fulfill the demands that excellence requires. These qualities fall into five key areas.

1. Understanding expectations for excellence

For those of us who have worked in higher education for some time, it is easy to forget that many people, and perhaps most students, don't know what excellence is or that it is expected.

This points to the twofold nature of the first requirement of excellence: (1) Students need to know that excellence is expected, and (2) they need to know what excellence is.

Helping students understand what excellence is, and that excellence is expected, can have a powerful effect on them, particularly during their first year. Clearly stated expectations greatly influence student motivation and help arrest ambiguity—one of the most difficult and troublesome human states.

To emphasize the importance of clear expectations, imagine that you are about to enter a graduate degree program. Now imagine that you have never seen or read a doctoral dissertation or a master's thesis. Also imagine that you have never read any original research or journal articles reporting research projects. However, in the application for the graduate program, you recall reading something about a requirement that each candidate complete an original research project and write a dissertation reporting on the project.

Can you imagine how overwhelming it would be to know that you are required to do original research and write a dissertation reporting on your research, but without knowing what either is? Let's take the example a step further. Imagine that no one explained what research is, no one described the attitudes and thought processes required in research, no one provided examples of research reports or journal articles, and you have never read a dissertation or received an explanation of what is expected in a dissertation! Does this sound outlandish? What about excellence? *Do we ever explain to students what excellence is or clearly present expectations regarding excellence?*

Certainly excellence is mentioned in virtually every institutional mission statement, and verbalized as a general expectation in every college catalog. But we cannot conclude that these citations are enough to ensure that students know what excellence means in terms of expectations for behavior and performance. And just because the school catalog and institutional mission statement mention excellence does not imply that students know what excellence looks like.

The importance of defining and communicating expectations can hardly be overstated. Consider this axiom of interpersonal relationships: *unexpressed and unclear expectations always lead to frustration and confusion, and demoralize those involved.*

Of course, we would hope that each professor provides examples of excellent papers, essays, test responses and projects from previous students, so that current students

can discover what "excellence" looks like, and so that expectations can be clearly and accurately defined.

But the issue here is advising. And the question becomes: what are the implications for advisors and the advising process in helping students: (1) understand that excellence is expected, and (2) understand what excellence is?

Take time to consider the nature of excellence at your institution, and reflect on how, when and by whom the institutional expectations for excellence are communicated to students.

2. Understanding how to meet excellence expectations

Even after expectations for excellence are clearly defined and communicated, much needs to be understood in terms of how to reach the standards of excellence. This understanding involves awareness of the *process dimension* of excellence, and a realization that progress and sequential movements are an integral part of that process. Gaining that understanding requires that students know not only what is expected, but when it is expected.

The process leading to performance at levels of excellence is related to the learning aspects of the entire college experience. *But what needs to be clear is that when the goal is excellence, a check list of required courses will not suffice.* For example, simply completing the English composition requirement by passing the class will not suffice. Even earning a high grade is not the issue when excellence is the goal. The issue becomes the types of writing skills and abilities that represent levels of excellence. To reach that level, more than just the required composition courses may be needed.

Of course, this creates many dilemmas for advising. In how many areas should we expect students to display excellence? What performance level represents excellence? Can we assume that passing certain classes or earning certain grades represents excellence? And if neither of these criteria is sufficient, how will we determine excellence?

The "how" or "process" dimensions of reaching standards of excellence includes other aspects as well. For example, what activities, what involvements, which courses, what sequences and/or combinations of courses and what types of involvements in campus or community service will most likely lead to levels of excellence?

An interesting exercise might be to consider that point in time when a person enters some profession or completes some major. We could then work backward to identify the ideal steps a person could take to achieve levels of excellence entering that profession. What would the person need to know, be able to do and/or have experienced in order for him or her to attain levels of excellence? And what types of activities, involvements, courses, extracurricular and cocurricular experiences would be most likely to produce levels of excellence?

One result of thinking in terms of process is the timely use of resources. Given goals of excellence, what are a student's best resources when considering that student's individual needs and particular characteristics? When should a student utilize each resource and become involved in specific activities in order to bring about their own excellence, meet standards of excellence, and make the most of the college experience?

When discussing these types of questions and the issue of understanding how to meet excellence expectations, we need to consider carefully the role of advisors and the advising process. Be aware that I am simply asking you to identify the implications for advising as a process, not implying that each advisor assume total responsibility for the outcomes of that process. Clearly, with the goal of excellence, new approaches, innovations and additional resources and staff may be required. However, before addressing the "how," we need to identify the "what."

3. Discovering and developing talents, strengths and abilities

Clearly, individuals who excel, who reach levels of excellence, must have the talents to do so. They also must have strengths and abilities that enable them to reach levels of excellence.

The topic of talents, strengths and abilities is a sensitive one because so many people have been held down or led to believe that they have only minimal talents, or perhaps none at all. Consequently, they may always question their abilities and fail to see their strengths. Of course, there are also people who display a facade of self-confidence or compulsively strive for perfection as a defense against the echoes of inner voices that tell them that they are not, nor can ever be, "good enough."

During my 30 years of working with college students from a broad spectrum of backgrounds and experiences, I've learned that the most significant issue is not whether a student has talents, strengths and abilities, but rather how to help the student discover and accept what his or her talents, strengths and abilities are.

Fortunately, the idea of "multiple intelligence" can help us understand that Intelligence Quotient (IQ) is not a unidimensional factor that one either possesses or lacks. In fact, what used to be called IQ is primarily determined by verbal abilities, verbal exposure and language. But the research on multiple intelligence has revealed at least seven or more distinct types of intelligence.

Important to the discussion of talents is the research conducted by Donald Clifton, who has studied highly effective individuals in a wide variety of professions. What Clifton has verified repeatedly is that individuals who dis-

play excellence in their chosen fields tend to build their lives around their strengths and talents. In fact, Clifton contends that people of excellence in particular fields achieve this status because they capitalize on their strengths and ignore, work around or enlist assistance from others to manage their weaknesses and deficiencies.

What are the advising implications of this line of thinking?

- Is it reasonable that students be expected to excel in everything?

- How should we advise students who are particularly talented in a specific area?

- How can we guide students who display little or no talent in an area?

- What courses should a student be encouraged to take—those that build upon his or her talents, or those that address areas in which he or she has little talent?

But perhaps even more importantly: who should help students discover, define and clarify their talents? Is this an appropriate part of an advisor's role? If not, are we to assume that students already know their talents, strengths and abilities, or that students will somehow discover them on their own?

Again, think first about the advising implications. Should advising help students identify their talents? If you believe that talents and awareness of strengths and abilities are important to achieving excellence, and if you find that some students are not aware of their talents, or need to become clearer about their strengths and abilities, then do you think the advising process has a responsibility to help students identify and clearly perceive their talents, strengths and abilities? And if not, who should?

4. Making a commitment to rigorous, sustained and high quality effort

The one thing that most people would agree about when identifying the requirements of excellence is that excellence demands rigorous, sustained and high quality effort in the face of almost certain discouragements. Simply stated, excellence doesn't come easily—it demands hard work.

This point was most graphically made by Thomas Edison, who responded to a compliment about his genius and his many innovations and inventions this way: "Genius is one percent inspiration, 99 percent perspiration."

Excellence requires, absolutely demands, rigorous effort. As a friend of mine once said, absolutely nothing gets better with neglect—and that includes talent. Most of us have encountered people who have enormous talent, people who have tremendous strengths and fabulous abilities. And yet, so many of these highly talented, capable people never developed or used even a small fraction of their abilities. What a tragedy!

Many of these individuals could have reached levels of excellence. They could have performed at the highest levels, achieved for themselves and others, and potentially made substantial contributions to society or some important cause. But they didn't. Not because they couldn't, but because they simply didn't invest the effort that excellence requires!

This line of thinking leads me to two of my firm contentions about college students (and anyone else who wishes to excel):

- Your most precious commodities are time and energy.

- Your most important decisions involve how you choose to invest your time and energy.

Many people believe that money is their most important commodity or resource. Not true. Time and energy are always your most precious and most important commodities. The perceived importance of money is, in fact, related to the significant amount of time and energy a person must commit to expend in earning it.

And when it comes to achieving in college, to reaching levels of excellence, time and energy invested in rigorous, sustained and quality effort are an absolute necessity.

Of course, this discussion must also consider the realities of the lives of college students: do they have the necessary time and energy to invest? Do they have sufficient time and energy to make excellence a personal reality? Is it a matter of having enough time and energy, or is it a matter of choosing to invest enough time and energy to make achievement and excellence a reality?

For some students, the demands and responsibilities of their lives so consume their time and energy that achieving to levels of excellence is virtually impossible—and for them "surviving" in college may be a real achievement. For some students, even persisting in college becomes impossible because they simply do not have the time and/or energy to do what college requires at a minimal level.

Other students could choose to invest the time and energy necessary to achieve at levels of excellence, but for them, such decisions may provoke conflict with other people and other roles and responsibilities. These situations involve issues of personal values. Where do students place excellence on their list of personal priorities?

Still other students don't choose to invest the time and energy because of priorities that are not so much imposed upon them as coming from their own immediate pleasures, desires and pursuits. So where does excellence stand in their priorities and values now? And where will their present priorities lead them?

One final group of students represents perhaps the most tragic case. These are individuals who have been broken down or abused to the extent that they don't believe that they can succeed even if they invested the necessary time and energy. These are students who have the desire, but whose lack of self-confidence leads them to conclude, "What's the use?"

This group of students can be further divided into two subgroups. The first includes students who don't believe they have the talents, skills or abilities necessary to achieve or excel, and so conclude that investing time and energy won't correct their inherent deficiencies.

The second subgroup is composed of students who have been victims of discrimination and who are convinced that they will always be victims of discrimination. Their "What's the use?" perspective is based on beliefs and experiences that lead them to conclude that no matter how well they perform, someone will prevent them from excelling. Thus, because excellence will ultimately be thwarted, "What's the use" trying or investing the time and effort that excellence demands?

It is a sad situation when students come to their "What's the use?" conclusion because they not only believe they don't have enough talent to achieve, but that no matter how hard they try, someone will somehow, someday, in some way snatch away their successes.

Assuming that you agree that rigorous effort, sustained effort and high quality effort are required for excellence, and assuming that you agree that advising should encourage students to excellence, the question becomes, "Exactly what should be the role of advising for excellence when it comes to students putting forth rigorous, sustained and high quality effort?"

Do advisors have a role in describing the type and quality of effort excellence requires? Should advisors try to assess students' willingness to put forth sustained effort? Should advisors attempt to influence students to put forth the necessary quality of effort? What about those students who are engaged in self-defeating thought and behavior patterns resulting in "What's the use?" attitudes? Do advisors have a role with students who are demoralized and who don't believe they can achieve, even after they invest time and energy?

Again, thinking in terms of the broader perspective of advising as a process (rather than the roles and/or responsibilities of specific advisors), do you think that the issues of rigorous, sustained and high quality effort should be addressed? What are the advising implications of this aspect of what excellence requires?

5. Developing motivation

Next we come to motivation, an extremely important aspect of excellence, possibly its most important prerequisite. But motivation is very difficult to talk about because it's complex.

The relationship between motivation and excellence stems from the essential role that hard work—rigorous, sustained and high quality effort—plays in producing excellence. But to understand the connection between motivation and quality effort, you must understand that effort involves energy, and motivation is the process by which energy is generated and directed and then applied as rigorous, sustained and high quality effort. Conversely, if there is no motivation, there will be no energy to invest in required effort, and there will be no progress, no achievement and no excellence. Simply stated, without the motivation to excel, there can be no excellence. No matter how many talents or how much understanding a person may have, without the desire or motivation to achieve and excel, excellence will not occur.

Seen from this perspective, it is little wonder that most educators consider motivation to be the most essential prerequisite and the most essential element in achievement.

Does advising have a role in helping students become motivated to achieve and excel? Does advising have a responsibility for helping students identify their motivations? Should advising be responsible for helping students correct motivational problems?

One approach to motivation within an educational environment focuses on the importance of personal curiosity. Clearly the questioning mind is the foundation for all inquiry, research and discovery. The human inclination to question is seemingly innate, as is obvious from observing children learning about the world. They are full of questions. Questions are natural, automatic and spontaneous. It is the questioning mind that also characterizes most advanced learners, the scholars and researchers. A primary motivation for the research scholar's pursuit of excellence is curiosity and the desire to discover better and more complete answers to questions. The child who questions everything, however, who enters elementary school with a spontaneous and active curiosity, is the same person who 12 years later responds with a blank expression when you ask, "What are your interests? What are you curious about? What would you like to learn?"

Some of us can identify personally with the destruction of curiosity and sense of wonderment that occurs when these aspects of our intelligence are ridiculed, ignored, devalued or stalled by schooling systems that do nothing to encourage them.

What a joyful experience it is to work with a student who has an active curiosity—who has questions he or she wants answered—who has interests and some clarity about learning goals. When we work with such a person, advising becomes significantly easier. The advising process becomes an adventure as we search for courses that address questions, programs of study that will refine curiosity, and a curriculum that will help develop the knowledge base and research skill to allow full pursuit of curiosity.

But the issue goes even deeper than the connection between curiosity as a motivation to learn and excellence, for questioning is the most fundamental component of the learning process. The forms of "higher learning" demand a questioning mind. For example, the process of analysis (an absolutely essential part of learning in every academic discipline) is a questioning process that attempts to understand "why" something happened—"what caused" something to occur—or "how" the component parts of something fit together. And the "something" could be a literary work, an artistic creation, a scientific theory or a technological breakthrough.

So, curiosity is not only a motivation for learning, it is an essential component of learning. And the curiosity/questioning process isn't just essential to analysis, it is also central to the processes of synthesis, problem solving, critical thinking and every form of research and inquiry.

What about other motivational issues? Some students excel for reasons other than their personal curiosities. Consider students who excel because of a goal they want to reach through college. For example, a student who has strong motivation for a career in medicine may have little interest or curiosity about required mathematics and chemistry courses. But he or she may be extremely motivated to excel in them because of the ultimate goal. In such cases there is a "reason," a "purpose," a "why" for achieving that is so motivating that the person will work until he or she reaches levels of excellence.

But again, what are the implications for the advising process? Is it the responsibility of advising or advisors to help students discover, clarify or affirm a personally meaningful reason for being in college? Does advising have a role for helping students become more motivated by helping them generate goals for their lives and then helping them connect the college experience to these life goals?

Student Concerns and Advising for Excellence

We began with a statement of values that featured excellence as both the hallmark and goal of higher education. Then we set forth a perspective on advising that lists educational outcomes and learning, growth and development as the most important defining characteristics of excellence in higher education.

In designing an approach to advising that targets excellence, however, we must be clear about what excellence requires and we must challenge ourselves to consider the advising implications of each factor.

Next, let's consider what students want and need from advising. But rather than focus on what students *expect* from advising and advisors (which may be distorted by lack of information, the influence of rumor and experiences with high school counselors), start from a broader perspective and attempt to identify general concerns. Challenge yourself once again to regard the advising implications of these student concerns.

From my experience there are five basic concerns that most undergraduates seem to have. These concerns can serve as a basis for forming an advising relationship with students, and may also hold the key to motivating students to meet with advisors in a timely way. I call these the "five C's":

1. Courses and course selection
One concern that seems universal among students is course selection. Choosing the right courses, in the right sequence, is a primary concern for virtually all new students, and it continues for most students even through their senior year. It is significantly more apparent and serious for students who are unclear about academic majors and/or career goals. For some students, concern about course selection may relate to other problems such as motivation, reasons for being in college, lack of understanding of the purpose of higher education, expectations of courses and instructors and/or the structure of degree requirements.

2. Connecting—getting connected
The college experience, particularly the transition from high school to college, stirs up every sort of insecurity and usually represents a turning point in the life of a student. It is a time when past attachments are severed and the availability of previous support systems may be reduced. There is a very real sense of disconnection and vulnerability when students enter college. Thus, students are often concerned about connecting and finding a place to fit in and belong. This concern goes beyond student organizations, peer acceptance, social safety and integration into groups or activities. As Vincent Tinto points out, the likelihood of student persistence is greatly enhanced when students become integrated within both the social and academic environments of an institution.

3. Careers—career selection
A third concern of virtually every college student is career choice. This is a difficult decision-making process, and the fact that students are in college seems to intensify career-related dilemmas and distress. Students want their college experience to be relevant to their future, and help them prepare for a career. They become very distressed when they haven't yet chosen a career, and those uncertainties trigger concerns about choosing a major, making the whole course selection process more difficult. Concern about careers also exacerbates doubts about being in college (or being in this college), as the student asks: "Why am I in college when I don't know where I'm going in my life?"

4. Confidence
The confidence levels of most college students are not uniformly high. Sometimes academic demands shake students' confidence. Sometimes students' self-confidence is shattered as they experience higher academic standards and are forced to realize they don't quite measure up or can't seem to catch up with assignments and other learning expectations. Of course, students' self-confidence is also diminished if they have difficulty connecting or feeling academically and socially integrated on campus. Confidence will also erode if students receive lower than expected grades and struggle with the demands of course selection and career decision making.

5. Confusion
With all the new requirements and expectations of college, with all the demands, the course selection and career decisions, and with the difficulty of trying to fit in while becoming independent, the most common experience of students is confusion.

Because excellence demands substantial commitments of time and energy, to the extent that students are preoccupied by these and other concerns, they will not be able to concentrate, focus or invest the time and energy necessary to excel. Therefore, advisors who are helping students aim for excellence must also consider how best to help students make plans, make adjustments and confront their concerns. •

Bibliography

Astin, A. W. (1983). *Achieving educational excellence.* San Francisco: Jossey-Bass.

Clifton, D. O., & Nelson, P. (1992). *Soar with your strengths.* New York: Delacorte Press.

Gardner, J. W. (1981). *Excellence.* New York: Harper and Row.

Advising for Student Success and Retention:
A Strengths-Based, Talent-Development Approach

Edward "Chip" Anderson, Ph.D., and William G. McGuire, Ph.D.

The Five C's of Student Concerns

Course Selection
- Which courses?
- When?

Connection
- Becoming part of campus, academic, and social community

Confusion
- What is expected?
- What is normal?
- What's happening in me?

Confidence
- Overcoming self-doubt
- Regaining optimism

Career Selection
- Which careers will fit and fulfill me?
- What factors need to be considered?

DOMAINS OF ADVISING

Course Selection	Adjusting	Career Planning
Strengths-based talent development approach to informed course selection	*Strengths-based talent approach to college adjustment*	*Strengths-based talent development approach to career planning*
Assessing and Affirming • Strengths and talents • Motivation • Preparation **Identifying Opportunities** • To build strengths • To develop talents • To pursue motives • To strengthen preparation **Matching and Fitting** • Assessments and opportunities to demands and requirements	**Understanding** • Forces and pressures • Time and energy demands • Developmental phases • Changing relationships **Using Strengths to Make Adjustment and to Grow**	**Extending Strengths and Talents From College to Careers** **Understanding Career Realities** **Using College to Develop Career-Relevant Skills**

What Excellence Requires

- Talents, strengths and abilities to excel
- Motivation and desire to excel
- Understanding what excellence is
- Understanding how to achieve excellence
- Investing rigorous, sustained and quality effort

The Relationship Between Teaching and Advising

Carol Ryan, Ph.D.
Dean, First College and Coordinator of Academic Advising, Metropolitan State University

Advising as an Extension of Teaching

Faculty have received little preparation or training either in graduate school or in our colleges and universities for our role as academic advisors. We need general knowledge of university programs, policies, procedures and student services in addition to our own major fields if we are to work effectively with advisees. Some understanding of student development is also useful. We should also consider ways in which, as faculty advisors, we can apply our teaching knowledge and skills to the advising relationship.

Academic advising gives faculty members an opportunity to extend our primary teaching role beyond the classroom to the one-to-one advising encounter. In the advising setting, a learning environment can be created that encourages and challenges individual students to develop educational plans and programs that are congruent with their personal and vocational goals, and with their skills, abilities and interests.

Effective Teaching Skills and Knowledge

Most of the effective teaching techniques we have practiced in the classroom can be transferred to individual or group work with advisees. Only the format (the small group or individual meeting in a more informal atmosphere) and the content are different. In the teaching/advising meeting, the content of our discussion centers on educational planning. Students want to discuss whole programs or majors with us or need assistance in understanding policies and procedures that may affect progress. As trust is created between the faculty advisor and the advisee, questions of values and life goals and their relationship to the student's educational goals will also be part of the teaching/advising exchange.

A 15-year review of the literature on teaching (Ryan, 1992) reveals 20 factors most commonly listed by faculty and students as exemplary. These were grouped into three categories. The first category is teaching skills and knowledge. Among the most commonly mentioned characteristics are:

- Mastery of subject area or material
- Encouragement of active student participation in the learning process
- Provision of regular feedback
- Reinforcement and encouragement to students
- Instruction in how to analyze, synthesize and evaluate information and express ideas clearly

Communication skills and knowledge is the second category under which a number of exemplary teaching characteristics were cited. Two that directly relate to effective advising are good questioning techniques and strong listening skills.

Attitudes toward students is the final category. Here the listing includes:

- Demonstration of positive regard, concern and respect for students
- Open, genuine presentation of one's self to students
- Exemplifying what a university community is, what is expected of students in the academy, and what one does after college in a professional or work role

Examples of Application of Teaching Skills and Knowledge in the Advising Meeting

Teaching

In the category of teaching skills and knowledge, the effective advisor can expand mastery of her subject area to include knowing what is required in a specific major or program as well as a general understanding of institutional resources and requirements. Students give high marks to advisors who know university programs and procedures and can provide them with specific and accurate information—just as they do for teachers who know their material.

Students also say their best classroom learning occurs when they are actively involved in the teaching-learning process. The same is true in the advising setting. Faculty advisors can engage students in the advising process by asking questions about their aims, concerns and possible educational goals or programs, and can work with students to develop academic plans to meet their goals.

An advisor should also monitor the student's progress and provide regular feedback to the advisee just as in the classroom, even if this simply means mailing a computer-generated letter with a print-out of course completions. A note from the advisor encouraging the student would also be welcomed.

Written or verbal encouragement similar to what we might say in the classroom or write on a student paper is also positive reinforcement when we see that an advisee has passed a difficult course or is engaged in significant co-curricular activity on campus. And if we are alerted to some academic difficulty the student is experiencing, we need to intervene and give timely warning of the difficulties and possible remedies—just as we would if the student were in one of our classes.

Faculty regularly teach students in their disciplines how to search for information and how to analyze and draw informed conclusions about issues or problems. Advisors can also give problem-solving and decision-making assignments. In this case, students are researching educational and career options including specific courses, internships or cooperative opportunities, and are trying to make good decisions about future directions. The teacher/advisor points the student toward university or community resources that will help her gather information and draw careful conclusions about best courses of action.

Communication

Faculty have honed their questioning skills in the classroom and can easily transfer these techniques to the advising meeting. Open-ended questions work best, especially when getting acquainted with the advisee and helping her reflect on future educational and life goals.

The advisor might ask the student to talk about what she would like to do after graduation. Does she wish to stay in the area? Move to a large or small community? What subjects in high school or college have interested her most? Does the advisee have concerns about the courses she is taking now or the experience she is having at the institution? Asking broad questions first, about life and career goals, and then focusing in on questions about majors, followed by specific course and scheduling discussions, gives the advisor and advisee a real opportunity to exchange ideas and information and to set goals or learning objectives for the next meeting.

Careful listening, or concentrating on what the student is actually trying to tell you, is as critical in the advising setting as it is in the classroom. Often, we can help the advisee communicate meaning more clearly by restating or clarifying his comments. This allows the student to move to a higher level of discussion or to more clearly articulate his position. It also helps the advisor reassess the advisee's learning needs or concerns.

Attitudes toward students

Students respond more favorably in the classroom when they sense that the instructor likes teaching and working with them. This is equally true in the advising relationship. Students do not expect the faculty advisor to be a best friend or even a counselor, but they do want an advisor to exhibit a personal and caring attitude toward them. Another transferable attitudinal trait is our ability or willingness to let students see us as we are—our interests and concerns in our subject area and our involvement in the university or external community.

Many of our students are first-generation college students. They look to us as examples or models of what a university is or can be. We may also model what they hope to become when they leave our institutions. Advisees often need assistance in determining just what it is one does with a degree in our field and how one gets started in the workplace.

Further, as academic advisors, we should show respect for all students and the issues and concerns they bring to us, just as we ought to do in the classroom. The students we see today are increasingly diverse in terms of age, ethnicity and academic preparation. This requires us to become reasonably knowledgeable about student differences based on gender and culture, so we can refer students to campus resources that will be most useful to them.

Outcomes of Application of Teaching Skills and Knowledge to the Faculty Advisor Role

Faculty have an opportunity as academic advisors to extend their teaching skills and knowledge to one-to-one or small-group encounters with advisees. Conscious application of such specific teaching skills as open-ended or probing questions, encouragement of active student participation in the advising process and assistance in helping students learn to problem solve and make sound educational decisions, will lead to a more satisfying teaching-learning experience for both the faculty member and the advisee.

The advisor has an opportunity to develop a teaching relationship with individual students that goes far beyond simple information exchanges. The faculty member and the advisee focus instead on the personal and career goals the student would like to achieve and ways in which she might do so. Such relationships with faculty encourage the student to persist and succeed at the institution which is important for both the student and the school.

A final reward for the faculty advisor is evidence of the student's social and intellectual development over time. This will be apparent to the advisor who has adopted a long-term teaching approach to the advising endeavor. •

Bibliography

Crookston, B. B. (1972). A developmental view of academic advising as teaching. *Journal of College Student Personnel, 13*, 12-17.

Kramer, H. C. (1983). Advising implications for faculty development. *NACADA Journal, 3* (2), 23-31.

Ryan, C. C. (1992). Advising as teaching. *NACADA Journal, 12*(1), 4-8.

Developmental Advising

Steven C. Ender, Ed.D.
Professor, Learning Center, Indiana University of Pennsylvania

Introduction

The goals of this article are to: (l) define developmental advising and identify three broad developmental themes related to it; (2) discuss requirements of the developmental advising relationship; (3) present an interview model that can facilitate advisee planning and problem solving; and (4) identify types of student requests and the developmental or remedial concerns they contain.

What Is Developmental Advising?

Developmental academic advising is a special advising relationship with students that both stimulates and supports their quest for an enriched educational experience. The relationship involves a systematic process of ongoing student-advisor interactions. It helps students achieve educational and personal goals by utilizing the full range of institutional and community resources.

Beyond course registration and scheduling, the specific themes of academic competence, personal involvement and developing or validating life purpose become the content that the developmental advising relationship frames. Educators who implement developmental advising recognize and acknowledge that the advisor is the institutional representative most responsible for assuring that advisees know how to seek out the greatest possible benefits from higher education.

Characteristics of a Developmental Advising Relationship

The relationship is process-oriented and intentional. The developmental advisor establishes a procedure to assist students as they define academic, personal and professional goals and objectives. The advisor and the advising relationship provide the context for the process to take place, and the advisee provides the content.

Developmental advisors are not experts on outcomes for individual students. They are, however, experts on the institution, curriculum, campus resources and planning processes that allow advisees to explore and change. Advisors structure the advising interview so that it will lead to specific and intentional outcomes. These outcomes parallel the three global themes of the developmental advising relationship: academic competence, personal involvement and life purpose.

Developmental advising is *ongoing* and *purposeful*. The advisor and student focus on the entire time span of enrollment — not just one term or one point in time. That is, developmental advising continues after course registration is complete. The relationship can be described as purposeful, continuing and cumulative. One advising session leads to another. Assignments for students to complete are specified and discussed, and follow-up sessions are scheduled to review results and develop further plans of action.

Developmental advisors challenge and support advisees to make the most of their higher education. Advisors encourage students to challenge themselves with regard to their academic potential, and to take advantage of the opportunities on and off campus. For example, when appropriate, the developmental advisor will propose and advocate that the student take challenging courses, rather than classes that repeat coursework from high school. Developmental advisors challenge students to select courses within the liberal studies area that are personally or professionally interesting, rather than with professors who are reputed to be "easy."

Developmental advisors encourage students to think about and discuss academic, career and personal issues within the context of the advising interview. Students should be active partners, not passive recipients, of the advisor's knowledge and expertise.

Developmental advising is goal-related. The advisor helps the advisee learn to think about and articulate academic, career and personal goals. Students should be challenged in these areas. Advisors ask, "What do you want to accomplish this term? —this year? —at this institution?"

"What do you hope to learn by taking these particular courses?"

"What do you want to accomplish within the context of university-sponsored activities, clubs, athletic participation?"

"How is your life purposeful?"

These are serious questions to ask advisees, because they can lead to meaningful goal-setting and purposeful living.

To be most effective, advisors should also be seen as role models of effective, purposeful academic planning. As advisors challenge students to be purposeful, set direction and accomplish goals, they may find it useful to refer to examples in their own lives. Selective and appropriate self-disclosure about the advisor's education or career experiences can help students understand the importance of goal-setting and accepting academic challenge. When suggesting that a student seek out a volunteer experience, for example, an advisor might appropriately mention the personal knowledge gained from volunteering in a human service agency. In the final analysis, our expectations of students should be no greater than those we set for ourselves, if credibility is to be a characteristic of the relationship.

The developmental advisor utilizes the full range of campus and community resources. Advisors should be knowledgeable about local resources and mechanisms for referral.

Examples of college-based resources to which students may be referred during the interview include the counseling center, learning center, tutoring services, student activities, health center, career services, housing office and many others. Most communities also have agencies to assist community members with life issues of health, safety, security and prevention. Advisors should, at the very minimum, have access to information that explains the available campus and community resources and referral procedures.

Acknowledging Individual Differences

Human beings tend to pass through similar developmental stages where they complete accompanying developmental tasks. But for a variety of reasons, individuals respond to the challenges of developmental task completion in unique and different ways. Where one student will eagerly approach the challenge of Calculus II, another will face the same classroom experience with feelings of high anxiety and dread. The same can be said for many interpersonal and cross-cultural experiences. Where some students feel stimulated, challenged and eager for opportunities to explore cultures different from their own, others may enter into these new situations with no appreciation of the wonderful learning opportunities they present.

Developmental Advising Themes

Traditionally, academic advising has been thought of as course registration and scheduling. The intentional introduction of three specific academic and life themes that are embedded within the context of the advising relationship distinguish developmental advising from traditional advising practices. These themes focus on issues within academic and human development areas and are intended to assist students as they strive to achieve the self-direction and responsibility essential for planned and purposeful living. The themes include:

- Assessing, achieving, and maintaining academic competence

- Planning and implementing active personal involvement in co-curricular offerings

- The validation or exploration and identification of an academic major that has meaningful regard to life goals and objectives

The intentional introduction and continued exploration of these three themes characterizes the developmental advising relationship.

Academic competence

At matriculation, especially in the freshman year, the advisor should assess the advisee's confidence, or lack thereof, about academic competence. If students feel inadequate in the classroom, they may have little chance of academic success. Students who worry constantly about academic competence may not have time to investigate and take advantage of co-curricular offerings.

Personal involvement

The second major theme advisors should intentionally investigate with advisees involves the student's overall feelings of personal well-being, compatibility and involvement in the environment of higher education. Within this theme area, the advisor should encourage advisee involvement in the co-curriculum and should assess the advisee's ability to adjust and react flexibly to change. In many cases this will require the developmental advisor to encourage advisees to learn and practice different types of behavioral responses to new situations. For instance, students may need to take personal risks to investigate people and events that are new and different. The advisor should help the advisee seek out the many opportunities for personal growth and maturation within the co-curriculum. Advisors should encourage advisees to take advantage of, and learn from, their out-of-classroom experiences.

Participation in these opportunities enables students to explore themselves in relation to others, learn to get along and work with others different from themselves, and learn to live and work as productive members of a democratic society.

Life purpose

The third broad theme area for investigation in the context of a developmental advising relationship involves the advisee's formulation of specific life plans. Here the advisor helps students make connections between the academic curriculum and life after the baccalaureate degree. If students have spent the first year exploring academic areas, then ideally, the theme of life plans begins to emerge as the student goes on to the second year. Unfortunately, some majors are so tightly packed with lockstep course requirements that students are forced to make critical decisions regarding the academic major when filling out admission applications. The challenge for the developmental advisor is to assist advisees as they validate initial academic major choices, or to facilitate a process that enables advisees to discover the academic major most compatible with interests, abilities and life goals after graduation.

These three global areas of student maturation provide the necessary context for a developmental advising relationship. It is the responsibility of the advisor to intentionally draw upon these concepts as appropriate and necessary within the context of academic advising.

The freshman year is critical for the first two themes of developmental advising—developing and maintaining academic competence and planning and implementing active personal involvement in co-curricular offerings. Freshmen are typically challenged academically and personally during their first year of college. What the individual student brings to the campus in the way of skills, competencies, attitude and aptitude will determine, to a large extent, the type of challenges the student should take on, and the amount of difficulty the student may encounter.

Assessment of students' readiness for various educational and out-of-class challenges is one of the developmental advisor's major tasks. Accurate assessment should lead to proper goal identification relative to coursework, extracurricular pursuits and meaningful life planning. New freshmen should be encouraged to develop goals in all three areas. The advisor and student determine the level of challenge through a realistic assessment of the skills the student brings to the environment. Assessment takes place within the context of a structured interview. Test scores, college placement records, high school courses and grades, as well as open and honest give-and-take between advisor and student, are all essential if assessment is to be accurate and constructive.

The more difficult the challenge the student faces in goal achievement, the more likely the need for ongoing support, encouragement and mentoring from the advisor—who must be sensitive about when to listen and when to lead. That is, the advisor should challenge the student to set goals that require an academic, personal or pre-professional stretch. But goals should also be realistic and attainable. Given students' various skills and competencies, sufficient effort should enable them to reach their goals. In order to assure that the stretch is realistic, the advisor should be sensitive to standardized, cognitive information and to the more subjective, personal information the student shares while assessing personal readiness to accept challenge.

The Structured Interview

Structured interviews seek to implement a problem-solving model as part of the interaction between advisor and advisee. The developmental advisor assumes the role of trusted guide or mentor supporting the student's self-inves-

tigation in the three theme areas. The interview moves through several distinct and identifiable stages. These stages include:

- Identification of the theme area to be investigated, solved or discussed
- Assessment of readiness to establish goals and take action
- Assessment of advisees' strengths and weaknesses relative to the theme area under investigation
- Articulation of goals and objectives to be completed
- Establishment of a timetable
- Identification of outcomes that signify goal completion

Stage One: Identification of theme area (starting the interview)

Ideally, developmental advisors have previously helped student advisees understand that their relationship will involve more than course registration and scheduling. In the best-case scenario, this message has been communicated through institutional publications and reinforced during the first advisor/advisee interaction. Once students understand that the advisor is a resource for the issues of academic competence, personal involvement and life goals, each scheduled or unscheduled visit should be purposeful. The role of the advisor is to seek clarification of the area in which the student wishes to work. This should occur through the natural give-and-take of the conversation. Because some advisee concerns within the three areas can be sensitive and anxiety-provoking, the advisor will need to listen actively, to be patient, or at times, to prod gently.

In most instances, freshmen will need more encouragement to develop goals within the three theme areas than upper-division students who are visiting to discuss progress towards goals established earlier. Questions that may help advisees begin thinking about the theme areas might include:

"Describe what you like and dislike about your courses this term."

"What course is the most interesting and why?"

"Assess your current performance in your classes."

"What activities are you pursuing outside of the classroom?"

"Have you made any friends with students from other cultures or ethnic groups?"

"Describe what you envision yourself doing 10 years from now."

These questions give advisees opportunities to reflect on the present and to think about the future. Regardless of the theme area ultimately decided upon, stage one concludes with the definition of the area to be explored or problem to be solved.

Stage Two: Assessment of readiness to establish goals and goal identification

This stage may seem a little puzzling to the advisor. Many times we take for granted that a person who can identify a concern or feel a need for personal action and problem solving also has the energy, commitment and desire to get down to the real work of goal accomplishment. Students say they want to achieve academically, but they may not be ready or willing to do the hard work required to make excellent grades. The advisor should carefully help advisees assess motivation and psychological and behavioral commitment to the work ahead. Advisees who lack motivation to change should be instructed to revisit the advisor when they are ready to work. One of the most frustrating situations of developmental advising is when the advisor has more energy and motivation for the tasks ahead than the advisee who must do the work.

Once convinced that the advisee has a serious intention to work, the interview can proceed. At this point a goal statement should be clarified and written down. Writing helps crystallize thought and helps develop the personal commitment required for action. Goal statements might include: "I will earn a 3.00 grade point average this term," or "I will investigate one ethnic minority group different from my own during my freshman year," or "I will decide whether to be a pre-med or biology major before I enroll in classes my sophomore year."

Stage Three: Assessment of strengths and weaknesses related to the goal to be accomplished

At this stage, the advisor helps the student identify and discuss strengths and weaknesses related to goal achievement. In order to identify appropriate objectives on the way to the goal, students need to understand their starting points. For example, let's say, within the theme of life purpose, that the student is attempting to determine an academic major appropriate to interests, abilities and aptitude. Discussion helps to clarify the amount of work required to reach the goal and select a major. The student who loves and excels in the sciences, but needs to choose between pre-med and biology will need to gather very different amounts and types of information than the student who is completely undecided about academic interests and majors.

Assessment may involve referring the student to the counseling center for the career inventories that will show how interests and abilities relate to occupations and professions. With this information, the advisor can link occupations to academic majors. Additional information includes

the student's interest in and aptitude for the major. Another piece of assessment data may be the student's past performance in academic courses offered by the major department.

Stage Four: Written objectives for goal accomplishment

As stage three indicates, the type of work to be completed by students depends on their distance from their goals. The undecided major has a completely different agenda than the science student deciding between chemistry and biology. In either case, the advisor and student should identify several objectives that will move the student toward the goal. As the attainment of most goals calls for informed decision making, the data gleaned by completing objectives should give the student more substantial knowledge. The role of developmental advisor is to help the student identify the objectives most likely to provide good information for decision making.

Stage Five: Establishing a timetable

Development of and adherence to a timetable are essential to goal accomplishment. As the student completes objectives, advisors should schedule appointments where the student can give periodic progress reports. The developmental advisor should insist on this interaction, because the role of the advisor is to be available as a sounding board when problems emerge or when information needs to be discussed. These can be wonderful and exciting sessions with advisees. Helping others take control of their lives is quite a rewarding experience.

Stage Six: Goal completion

How do students know they have reached a goal? There should be clear and identifiable evidence. Examples include: the major has been declared, the student has been removed from academic probation, or the volunteer experience has been completed. As one goal is completed, another should be established; this process continues throughout the period of enrollment.

Requests for Information, Action, Understanding and Involvement

Developmental advisors learn to discriminate between the types of requests the advisee brings into the office. The first two, information and action, are fairly straightforward. Deadlines in the college calendar, the location of the counseling center, or the number of hours required for junior standing are all examples of commonly requested information. Requests for action involve signature needs, letters of reference and other types of behavioral responses from the advisor.

Requests for understanding and involvement are more demanding and will occur often if the relationship between the advisor and advisee is trusting, secure and genuine. Typically, these requests occur when advisees are trying to make important personal decisions. Examples include conflicts with professors, friends and parents; decisions regarding various elective courses within the liberal studies area; or identification of a specific major within a department. These requests usually require the advisor to be an attentive listener and an active participant in the decision-making process. A student who sees the advisor as genuinely concerned will seek the advisor often for advice and counsel.

Advisee requests for understanding and personal involvement will challenge the advisor to use special listening and responding skills if true, meaningful assistance is to take place. Since the "presenting problem" may be different from the "real problem," active listening is required to really hear the concerns that are being communicated. Accurate responses can then demonstrate that the advisee has not only been heard, but has been understood.

Listening skills are more difficult to implement than we might imagine, because most of us tend to think when we should be listening. How many times do colleagues, students and family talk to us—and even though we look as though we are listening, in fact we are thinking of something else? It is critical, within the context of a developmental advising relationship, that advisors really listen to students. The daily routines of life must be forgotten during the time one listens and talks with advisees. Advisors unwilling to give advisees their undivided attention should not attempt to be developmental in their approach. It will not work. To facilitate another's development in college calls for genuineness on the part of the advisor. Advisees will quickly recognize who is really interested and who is not. Authenticity and genuineness are key human qualities of the developmental advisor.

Developmental vs. Remedial Issues

Within the context of active listening and the use of the problem-solving model for interviews, the advisor should determine whether the area under investigation by the advisee is a developmental concern or one that may be remedial in its origin. This means, from a simplistic point of view, "Is the advisee's concern typical for this stage of the person's life and at this point in the educational process?" For example, a returning adult, age 35, who worries about the inability to develop and sustain personal relationships, is dealing with a developmental task that should have been mastered at a much younger age. If this were a 19- or 20-

year-old, we might expect to encounter such a struggle, but the adult student should be referred to the counseling center for a thorough airing of the problem.

On the other hand, a young adult with the same concerns should establish goals to practice developing relationships. These could include objectives such as starting study groups with other students, joining a group that has a number of members, or asking a friend to dinner.

Advisors should not feel compelled or obligated within the developmental advising relationship to serve as personal counselors for their advisees. The developmental advisor's role is to help students formulate plans within the three theme areas. Personal and anxiety-producing problems that may emerge from the work within the areas should be referred to professionals who are trained to deal with concerns of a psychological nature. A hint: if you feel anxious as you listen to a student's concern, you are hearing something you should probably refer to a more qualified professional.

Summary

Developmental advising relationships are purposeful. The content for discussion within the advisor/student interaction should be focused on those outcomes the college is attempting to achieve with all enrolled students. Developmental advising provides the opportunity for colleges and universities to identify specific educational goals and outcomes, and to provide a context and process to help students achieve these outcomes. •

Bibliography

Ender, S. C. (1983). Assisting high academic risk athletes: Recommendations for the academic advisor. *National Academic Advising Journal, 3,* 1-10.

Ender, S. C. (1993). Peer counseling. In G. S. Blimbling (Ed.), *The experienced resident assistant: Readings, case studies, and structured group exercises for advanced training* (rev. ed.). Dubuque, IA: Kendall/Hunt.

Gazda, G. M. (1973). *Human relations development: A manual for educators.* Boston: Allyn and Bacon, Inc.

Winston, R. B., Ender, S. C., & Miller, T. K. (Eds.). (1982). *New directions for student services: Developmental approaches to academic advising, No.17.* San Francisco: Jossey-Bass.

Winston, R. B., Miller, T. K., Ender, S. C., & Grites, T. J. (Eds.). (1984). *Developmental academic advising: Addressing students' emotional, career, and personal needs.* San Francisco: Jossey-Bass.

Student Development Theory Into Practice: Implications for Advisors

Virginia Gordon, Ph.D.
Assistant Dean Emerita, The Ohio State University

Why Are Student Development Theories Useful in Advising?

1. Students are the primary focus of the advising process. Although theoretical in nature, many developmental theories have proved through research to be accurate in describing a broad spectrum of traditional student behavior.

2. Developmental theory helps to explain why students behave as they do at different ages and college years (i.e., why freshmen have different needs and ideas than seniors).

3. Theory can serve as a predictive function by helping us estimate what students may do under certain conditions.

4. A more thorough understanding of how students develop personally and socially during the college years can help advisors tailor their advice to the needs of the individual student.

5. The central questions asked by developmental theorists are:

    a. What are the developmental tasks and identity issues of college students?

    b. What is the effect of the college environment on these issues and tasks?

    c. How do students grow and increase in complexity? (Bradbury et al., 1976)

6. Advising techniques can be developed to take advantage of this knowledge.

7. These concepts can be demonstrated to be useful in academic advising by studying two particular theories, Arthur Chickering's student development theory and William Perry's cognitive development theory.

Discussion questions

1. What are some characteristics of advisees that you think are important for you to know in order to have a more effective relationship with them (e.g., academically, personally, socially)?

2. How can knowledge of student development theory help you understand students at different levels of their college experience?

Two Examples of Student Development Theory

Chickering's seven vectors of development

(Chickering & Reisser, 1993)

1. General concepts

    *   Students develop (change) gradually and incrementally, not suddenly.

    *   Seven vectors (or tasks) are proposed as "maps" to help determine where students are developmentally and where they are headed.

    *   "The journey is just as important as the destination" (p. 37).

    *   Students move along a vector at their own pace.

    *   Students' involvement in one vector may interact with another vector.

    *   As students progress through a vector (lower to higher), they exhibit more "awareness, skill, confidence, complexity, stability and integration" (p. 34).

    *   College students "live out recurring themes: gaining competence, learning control and flexibility, balancing intimacy with freedom, finding one's voice or vocation, refining beliefs and making commitments" (p. 35).

2. Concepts pertaining to the tasks themselves:

    a. The tasks are culturally related and take two to seven years to resolve.

    b. Each task has content and direction.

    c. Each task surfaces at different times in students' lives, is hopefully resolve, and continues to be with them.

    d. The need to revisit the task may resurface later in times of crises or when needed.

    e. How students resolve each of the tasks affects how future tasks are resolved.

Students move through the following seven vectors or developmental tasks during (and after) the college years.

1. Developing competence

Chickering describes competence as a "three-tined pitchfork": intellectual competence, physical and manual skills and interpersonal competence. Competence comes with the confidence that they (students) have the ability to cope with any situation and can successfully achieve what they set out to do. "Increasing competence leads to increasing readiness to take risks, to try new things, and to take one's place among peers..." (p. 82).

Intellectual competence

- Involves comprehending, reflecting, analyzing, synthesizing and interpreting information.
- Involves developing the ability to reason, solve problems, weigh evidence, think originally and engage in learning activity (pp. 53-54).
- There is a general and specific increase in knowledge as students move from college entrance to graduation.
- Cultural, aesthetic or intellectual attitudes and values are enhanced during the college years.
- Another category of intellectual development involves ways of knowing and reasoning.
- Intellectual competence must not be defined as skill in passing tests or mastering course content.
- "Skills in listening, questioning, reflecting and communicating can be built in any course that engages students in actively searching for valuable knowledge rather than passively receiving prepackaged material" (p. 63).

Physical and manual competence

- The prestige and recreational value of athletic skills or the creative value of arts and crafts are important to many college students.
- Athletic experiences not only develop a sense of competence but increase awareness of emotions and ability to manage them.
- Athletic prowess can lead to rising self-esteem.
- Experiences in athletics and arts and crafts interact with intellectual competence and the development of identity.
- "Development of physical and manual skills can foster development in other areas by permitting objects and events to be tied to symbols through action" (p. 71).
- An integrated system results when abstractions are "translated into tangible and visible products" (p. 71).

Interpersonal competence

- Involves broad abilities to work smoothly with a group, facilitate others' communication and to be sensitive and empathic with others.
- Develops through effort and efficacy in human interaction.
- Interpersonal skills are prerequisite for building successful friendships and intimate relationships.

- They are essential for career, family and citizen roles.
- They need to be balanced with the other two competencies.

2. Managing emotions

- "Development involves finding appropriate channels for releasing irritations before they explode, dealing with fears before they immobilize, counteracting pain and guilt and controlling impulses to exploit others or give in to unwanted pressures" (p. 87).
- Emotional development also involves the positive emotions of love, joy and hope.
- Need to find ways of balancing negative or painful feelings with positive, uplifting emotions and integrating feeling with thought and action.
- The challenge is to become aware of different feelings and to understand their legitimacy.
- Self-control and self-expression must come into balance.
- Two major impulses need to be managed: aggression and sex.
- Maturity implies students have found legitimate ways to express anger and hate.
- Sexual impulses are more insistent than ever before and issues of interpersonal relationships, of value and of identity are raised.

3. Moving through autonomy toward interdependence

- Three components of this vector are emotional independence, instrumental independence, and interdependence.
- Emotional independence involves "some level of separation from parents, increased reliance on peers, authorities, and institutional support systems and growing confidence in one's own self-sufficiency" (p. 117).
- Instrumental independence has two major components: the ability to be self-sufficient and to leave one place and function well in another.
- Emotional and instrumental independence are linked and mutually facilitating.
- Instrumental autonomy increases as students gain intellectual competence; learning to think objectively is an indicator of instrumental autonomy.
- Interdependence is the capstone of autonomy.

4. Developing mature interpersonal relationships

- This vector involves tolerance and appreciation of differences and the capacity for intimacy.

- This requires the ability to accept individuals for who they are, to appreciate and respect differences and to empathize.

- "Tolerance implies a willingness to suspend judgment, to refrain from condemnation and to attempt to understand an unfamiliar or unsettling way of thinking or acting rather than to ignore, attack or belittle it" (p. 146).

- It involves sensitivity to people from other cultures.

- There is increased capacity for intimacy.

- Healthy intimacy is expressed in both sexual and non-sexual ways.

- Tolerance involves both intercultural and interpersonal areas.

- It involves the understanding and the appreciation of differences.

- Relationships are "reciprocal and interdependent, with high levels of trust, openness and stability" (p. 172).

5. Establishing identity

- All developmental vectors could be classified under "identity formation."

- "Establishing identity involves growing awareness of competencies, emotions and values, confidence in standing alone and bonding with others, and moving beyond intolerance toward openness and self-esteem" (p. 173).

- By facing crises and making commitments, a strong ego is built and high self-esteem is gained.

- Identity is "a solid sense of self, an inner feeling of mastery and ownership that takes shape as the developmental tasks for competence, emotions, autonomy and relationships are undertaken with some success and as it becomes firmer, provides a framework for purpose and integrity..." (p. 181).

- Identity involves comfort with body and appearance, comfort with gender and sexual orientation and a sense of self in a social, historical and cultural context.

6. Developing purpose

- Developing purpose entails "increasing ability to be intentional, to assess interests and options, to clarify goals, to make plans and to persist despite obstacles" (p. 209).

- Interests tend to stabilize and various vocational alternatives are explored.

- A general orientation is achieved first and then more specific career decisions are made.

- Vocational plans and aspirations become increasingly clear.

- Vocational and lifestyle considerations are integrated.

- A strong commitment to value or belief can determine purpose; purpose and integrity are interrelated.

7. Developing integrity

- Involves clarifying a personally valid set of beliefs that have internal consistency.

- Core values and beliefs (e.g., right and wrong, good and bad, true or false, important and unimportant) acquired from many sources such as parents, church, school, media.

- Developing integrity involves reviewing personal values "in an inquiring environment that emphasizes diversity, critical thinking, the use of evidence and experimentation" (p. 235).

- Involves exploring links between values and behavior.

- Involves three sequential but overlapping stages: humanizing values, personalizing values and developing congruence.

- Humanizing values is the process of "shifting away from automatic application of uncompromising beliefs and using principled thinking in balancing one's own self-interest with interests of one's fellow human beings" (p. 236-237).

- Personalizing values means consciously affirming core values and beliefs while respecting other points of view.

- Developing congruence involves matching personal values with socially responsible behavior" (p. 237).

- "By tempering rigid beliefs, becoming open to other interpretations, weighing evidence and experience, and claiming ownership of a meaningful set of principles, students humanize and personalize values and thus develop integrity" (p. 264).

Perry's cognitive development theory

(Perry, 1970)

1. General concepts

   - Perry's scheme describes how students perceive knowledge and values during the college years.

   - This scheme concentrates on students' internal cognitive structure.

   - Cognitive structure is "a set of assumptions which acts as a filter dictating how the individual will perceive, organize and evaluate events in the environment and, though less directly, how he/she will behave in response to those events" (Widick, 1975).

   - Intellectual development is generally an irreversible series of stages "in which each stage represents a qualitatively different structure for perceiving the meaning of knowledge."

   - Students pass through nine major positions in their intellectual and ethical development.

   - Students move from a simplistic, categorical view of knowledge and values to a complex pluralistic perspective.

   - As students are capable of more complex reasoning, they are able to challenge and be challenged by new ideas and new ways of thinking.

   - The model comprises nine positions or stages, each representing a qualitatively different mode of thinking about the nature of knowledge.

   - These are the "lenses" through which students see their world.

2. Positions or stages of cognitive development

   Dualism: The first three positions present a dualistic perspective.

   - First, the student views the world in polar terms of "right or wrong" and right answers exist in the absolute; second, the student perceives diversity of opinion and uncertainty as unwarranted confusion of poorly qualified authorities; third, the student accepts diversity and uncertainty as legitimate but still temporary in areas where authorities haven't found the answer yet.

   - The three positions within dualism are differentiated based upon how one accounts for uncertainty.

   Relativism: Positions 4, 5 and 6 view questions of knowledge as contextual.

   - In position 4 (multiplicity) uncertainty is pervasive and legitimate and dualistic assumptions have been broken down; the notion of evidence or qualitative distinctions has not been integrated, however.

   - In position 5, all knowledge is perceived as contextual and relativistic; concern with the nature of knowledge intersects with the student's personal life in terms of identity questions.

   - In 6, students recognize that their identities, in particular their values, will not be given to them, but will emerge from their commitments.

   Commitment: In positions 7, 8 and 9, students attempt to define their identities through the act of choice.

   - "The student makes an initial commitment in some area; next the student experiences the implications of commitment and explores the issues of responsibility; in the last position, students experience the affirmation of identity among multiple responsibilities and realizes commitment as an ongoing, unfolding activity through which he expresses his lifestyle" (p. 10).

Other important concepts

- *Temporizing*. Student delays in a position for a year, exploring its implications or explicitly hesitates to take care of the next step.

- *Escape*. Student exploits the opportunity for detachment offered by the structures of positions 4 and 5 to deny responsibility through passive or opportunistic alienation.

- *Retreat*. Student entrenches in the dualistic, absolutistic structures of positions 2 and 3.

Discussion questions

1. What general concepts of Chickering's theory strike you as most helpful in advising students?

2. Name the seven developmental tasks that Chickering suggests students need to accomplish during the college years and briefly describe each.

3. Have any of your advisees been involved in these tasks? How has it affected their adjustment and attitude toward their college experiences?

4. Which general concepts of Perry's cognitive development theory strike you as most relevant to academic advising? To teaching?

5. Briefly describe the four general positions of cognitive development as outlined by Perry.

6. How do Perry's descriptions relate to your own experiences in advising and teaching?

Applying Developmental Theories to the Academic Advising Process

Application of Chickering for advising

- Advisors need time to establish a personal relationship with each of their advisees.

- Advisors can recognize the particular developmental tasks a student is working through and help them become more aware of the resources available to assist in mastering those tasks (e.g., a student who lacks social competence might be encouraged to join a campus club or activity in an area of his or her interest).

- Advisors can facilitate students' development by ensuring they live in an environment that will help them:

  - Develop intellectual competence through discipline and experience (e.g., referring students with poor academic preparation to writing labs, tutoring).

  - Develop emotional independence by helping them deal with authority figures (such as yourself).

  - Develop an ethical system as it relates to academic honesty.

  - Make mature educational plans; help analyze various academic disciplines and select an appropriate major.

  - Develop increased tolerance for people culturally different from themselves.

  - Find and use campus resources where they can assess their abilities and skills relating to a career.

  - Explore and clarify both personal and career values.

  - Experience opportunities for developing problem-solving skills.

  - Be exposed to effective role models and have significant relationships with faculty and staff.

- The Seven Principles for Good Practice in Undergraduate Education (Chickering & Gamson, 1987) apply to advising as well as teaching. Good practice:

  1. Encourages student-faculty contact
  2. Encourages cooperation among students
  3. Encourages active learning
  4. Gives prompt feedback
  5. Emphasizes time on task
  6. Communicates high expectations
  7. Respects diverse talents and ways of learning (p. 1).

Applications of Perry's theory to advising

- Advisors need to be prepared for dualistic students to view them as the authority with all the right answers.

- Advisors can help dualistic students learn to identify parts of a whole, compare and contrast, see multiple perspectives, learn how to use supportive evidence, provide structure, reinforce legitimate alternative views, challenge students to question authorities' opinions.

- Advisors can help multiplistic students generate alternative perspectives on issues, ask for supporting evidence, provide concrete experiences of ideas, encourage introspection on study techniques, help discriminate between choices, assist them to analyze and evaluate from their own perspective and experiences, loosen structure.

- Advisors can help relativistic students focus on narrowing down their choices, help them synthesize, encourage high degree of freedom to structure their own learning, encourage commitment.

- Advisors can help students in commitment to assume responsibility for themselves and establish identity by acts of commitment and developmental task resolution; students will be selecting a career, a set of values, a lifestyle; help students recognize personal themes within themselves; through reassessment, commitments might be changed; help them realize commitment is an ongoing activity.

- An important concept in Perry's scheme is that of "challenge and support"; advisors can challenge students by offering diversity of ideas and content and by providing the opportunity for experiences (readings, role play, field trips, interviews, etc.).

- Support can be given through structure and personalism.

The themes of academic competence, personal involvement and life purpose are incorporated into a developmental advising model. All of these have as their foundation, many of the tenets of the theories described above.

Discussion questions

1. How can knowledge of student development theory enhance the knowledge and techniques of advisors?

2. What general concepts from Chickering's theory have you encountered in the students you advise?

3. Which of Chickering's developmental tasks have you observed in your freshman advisees? In sophomores? In juniors? In seniors? In graduate students?

4. As an academic advisor, how can you help a student who is struggling with the following tasks?

- Developing intellectual competence (e.g., not understanding what is expected in a class)

- Managing emotions (e.g., having roommate problems)

- Developing autonomy (e.g., wants to withdraw because of homesickness)

- Developing mature interpersonal relationships (e.g., not tolerant of other students who are culturally different)

- Establishing identity (e.g., is facing a crisis but can't make a commitment; has not mastered the task of autonomy)

- Developing purpose (e.g., can't decide between two majors that hold equal interest)

- Developing integrity (e.g., holds a strong value but is struggling to act in accordance with that value)

5. What specific concepts from Chickering's theory are most useful to you in your advising role?

6. What general concepts from Perry's theory have you encountered in your advising role? In your teaching role?

7. How will you adjust your advising (and/or teaching) approaches to take into consideration the cognitive levels of your students?

8. Dualistic students are known to benefit from high structure, a personal atmosphere and experiential learning. How could you incorporate this knowledge in the way you approach these students in an advising situation?

   Relativistic students are known to benefit from lower structure, more freedom in the learning environment and display a more questioning attitude. How could you incorporate this knowledge in the way you approach these students in an advising situation?

9. Have you discovered any new information about college students in this discussion? If so, what?

10. Specifically, how will this information affect your advising practices?

Case Study

Dr. Ray is quite concerned about one of her advisees. John is in the second term of his first year. He barely made a C average in his first-term courses, and is struggling already during the first week of the new term with his current ones. He has indicated he feels lost in his classes and has trouble approaching his teachers for help. Dr. Ray does not think the problem is lack of ability since John placed second in his high school class and has excellent ACT scores. However, John seems to be distracted with many personal and social concerns in addition to his academic ones.

John has declared a business major but does not seem very enthusiastic about his choice. He has told Dr. Ray his father wants him to enter the family business when he graduates. He cannot articulate his career goals and seems to be drifting without a purpose. He says he is lonely and has difficulty making friends. He goes home almost every weekend. Dr. Ray senses he is not adjusting to the college environment in a positive way.

Over the year John has visited Dr. Ray several times and they have built a good relationship. Dr. Ray is now ready to be more assertive in her role of advisor.

Discussion questions

1. What developmental tasks as outlined by Chickering do you think John is struggling with?

2. Where do you think John is according to Perry's scheme? Why?

3. As his advisor, how would you broach the subject of John's lack of adjustment with him?

4. What steps would you recommend he take?

5. To what resources on campus would you refer him?

6. How would you follow up with John as the term progresses? •

Bibliography

Baxter, M. (1992). *Knowing and reasoning in college: Gender-related patterns in students' intellectual development.* San Francisco: Jossey-Bass.

Bradbury, J., Cornfeld, J., Wertheimer, L., & Harrison, K. (1976). *Career planning and decision making: A developmental approach.* Presented at the American Personnel and Guidance Association Annual Convention, Chicago.

Chickering, A. W., & Gamson, Z. F. (1987). Seven principles for good practice in undergraduate education. *American Association of Higher Education Bulletin, 39,* 3-7.

Chickering, A. W., & Reisser, L. (1993). *Education and identity* (2nd ed.). San Francisco: Jossey-Bass.

Knefelkamp, L., Widick, C., & Parker, C. (Eds.). (1978). Applying new developmental findings. *New Directions for Student Services, No. 4.* San Francisco: Jossey-Bass.

Parker, C. A. (Ed.). (1978). *Encouraging development in college students.* Minneapolis: University of Minnesota.

Thomas, R., & Chickering, A.W. (1984). Education and identity revisited. *Journal of College Student Personnel, 25,* 392-399.

Widick, C. (1975). *The Perry Scheme: A foundation for developmental practice.* Paper presented at the convention of the American Psychological Association.

Winston, R. B., Miller, T. K., Ender, S. C., Grites, T. J., & Associates. (1984). *Developmental academic advising.* San Francisco: Jossey-Bass.

Advisor Resources

Thomas J. Kerr, Ph.D.
Associate Provost, Rowan College of New Jersey

The Advisor "Library"

The advisor library consists of materials prepared by the college or university for marketing and recruitment purposes, those developed as internal documents that are generic across all academic disciplines, and those that are college or discipline specific. Each serves a very different purpose, but all are important resources with which the advisor needs to be familiar.

Recruitment and promotional documents

One might think that recruitment materials would not be important for the advisor. But because these materials are made to be used generically for an entire campus, they may confuse prospective students and parents. Suppose a recruitment brochure states that the faculty-student classroom ratio across campus averages 25-to-1. This may be accurate for juniors and seniors in your departments, but because some courses in the freshman and sophomore years are larger, the faculty-student ratio may be significantly higher.

The advisor unprepared to answer questions from parents or students about the data in recruitment materials may seem uninformed or a poor representative of the college. This will have a negative impact on the advising relationship, because trust between the advisor and advisee may not be readily developed.

Similarly, faculty advisors need to be aware of recruitment information that has become outdated. Have new faculty been added, or others retired or replaced? Have any degree programs been eliminated? There is nothing more embarrassing than to be corrected or find out something "new" from a prospective student or parent. The advisor needs to be prepared with the answers!

College/university documents

Internal documents that are generic across the campus include the university or college catalog, a student life book, the schedule of courses and documents prepared by specific units on campus. Academic advisors usually consider the catalog "the Bible" because it normally includes information about institutional policies, curricular requirements, registration dates, the academic calendar, etc. Much of this information may be duplicated in other documents.

Student life manuals are designed to provide students with important information about the institution and its resources. A great deal of this information is directly useful and important in the advising process, even though it is not academic. Residence life information, library, bookstore, campus ministries, health, dining, student organizations, intramural sports, extracurricular activities and tutoring services are just a few of the topics covered in such a document. By becoming familiar with the student life book and pointing out to students specific sections that relate to the topic under discussion in an advising session, the advisor will reinforce its value and promote its use.

Documents are often prepared by specific units within the college or university that describe their function resources, and give information about how to access those resources. These may include, but would not be limited to: financial aid, registrar's office, international student office, career planning and placement, learning resource center, study abroad, etc. The more information of this type that advisors can accumulate and have at their disposal, the better prepared they will be to advise their students. For those programs that do not publish their own resource document, the advisor needs, at a minimum, to establish a contact in these offices. Knowing when and how to refer a student to another resource is crucial to effective advising.

Discipline specific documents

The documents that are most commonly specific to a college within a university or an academic discipline within a small college are faculty handbooks and student handbooks. The student handbook may differ from the student life handbook if it restricts itself to academic policy and procedures, and the latter provides comprehensive coverage of such topic areas as an academic planner, position description and names of key personnel, academic policies and procedures, curriculum outlines, forms and special programs with samples, a college and university directory, academic conduct code, plagiarism policies and alcohol policies.

Even more important for the advisor than the college bulletin is a comprehensive faculty advising handbook. Ford and Ford (1990) suggest the following content for an advising handbook:

1. Philosophy and objectives of the advising program
2. Definitions of the advisor and the advising process
3. General and specific responsibilities of the advisor
4. Characteristics of a good advisor and strategies for effective advising
5. Academic policies and procedures
6. Scheduling and registration procedures
7. Legal responsibilities of the advisor

8. Advising procedures for special populations (e.g., those on academic probation, undecided students)

9. Listings of campus resources for referral purposes

10. Advising and scheduling calendar

11. Easily used table of contents

12. Appendices with test interpretation information, student assistance resources, and other pertinent material

A foreword written by the president, provost or dean should emphasize the important role of advising.

If an advising handbook is not available, advisors need to collect as much of the above material as they can to create their own advising handbook. Both the student handbook and the faculty handbook will only be effective if they are used frequently. The advisor must use these documents much as they would a dictionary or thesaurus when preparing a position or research paper—always keep them close at hand and refer to them when in doubt! Handbooks must be constantly updated to be effective, and they must be made easily accessible to the faculty advisor. A technique that has proven effective is to have a dean's staff person responsible for updating both the student and faculty handbook each summer. The revisions should be hand-delivered and inserted into the individual faculty member's handbook before the fall term begins. This ensures that the faculty advisor always works with current and accurate information.

Advisors who master efficient use of these documents are typically able to make more appropriate referrals. Because they are more knowledgeable and resourceful advisors, their students are likely to be more satisfied.

Student Advising Folder

To assist in developing personal advising relationships, every advisor should maintain an advising folder for each student. The portfolio serves as both a repository for student records, including advising notes, and as a rich resource of information useful in developmental advising. Included in the portfolio should be at least the following: high school transcript, college transcript, standardized test scores, placement exam results, academic status reports, preregistration information, class schedule, curriculum plan, admissions application including essays, non-institutional assessment instruments (ACT/SAT) and anecdotal records of advising sessions.

Pre-matriculation

The admissions application is an excellent document for the advisor to review in order to gain insight about students. Applications that contain an essay provide a sample of the student's writing ability, and convey something about the student. This information is useful as advisors begin to establish personal relationships with advisees. Of equal importance is the high school transcript, which also provides a wealth of information about the student.

Most importantly, advisors will be able to determine the student's academic strengths and weaknesses by reviewing high school grades. Are students prepared for the academic majors in which they are enrolled? Are the courses they have selected at the correct level? Properly reviewed transcripts serve as an advising tool that goes beyond the simple recording of previously completed coursework. The insightful advisor will use them to determine the student's potential, identify possible difficulties and establish whether the student has realistic educational goals.

In addition to the application essay and high school transcript, admissions applications usually contain parental information such as education, employment and marital status. Also included are recommendations from guidance counselors or teachers that comment on the student's abilities, academic potential and interests. This is supplemented by students self-reporting their activities and interests both within and outside the high school environment. All of this information is useful in the advising of freshmen.

Additional advising tools include institutional placement exams as well as standardized exams such as the American College Test (ACT) or the Scholastic Aptitude Test (SAT). Advisors need to be knowledgeable about standardized exams and placement tests, particularly what they are measuring and how to interpret the results. Care must be exercised about the importance placed on placement exams. While they can be a valuable tool for assessment of a student's current level of understanding of a subject area, they should be used with other instruments, i.e., transcripts, advanced standing credit (AP), prior college work, etc., as a measure of the student's past achievements. A combination of resources helps advisors to ensure that advisees are placed in courses appropriate to their level of understanding of the subject matter.

An often overlooked resource that is a part of both the ACT assessment and the SAT is the student profile. The ACT assessment includes an interest inventory that identifies potential college majors for the student and a listing of occupations that match the student's areas of interest. It also requests the student to list extracurricular activities in which they participated in high school, as well as those they intend to be a part of in college, special interests or needs, and educational and vocational plans.

In a similar manner, the SAT, as part of its student descriptive questionnaire, provides information about students on college choices, potential majors, careers, special assistance needs, activities and interests.

The high school transcript, admission application and essays, letters of recommendation, placement exams and standardized tests, when used in combination, provide the advisor with a powerful resource to initiate developmental advising.

Students new to your college, especially freshmen, are often unsure of themselves and anxious when beginning this new chapter of their lives. By referring to these documents, the advisor can establish a warm and friendly environment for students and can show a personal interest as well.

First year and beyond

Once your advisee has matriculated, a new set of documents must be collected to be used as an academic resource for providing developmental advising. These include the current college transcript, academic status reports, preregistration documents, class schedules, an up-to-date curriculum plan and mid-semester reports of grades, if available.

The college transcript, like the high school transcript, can provide a wealth of information, and not just a history of past performance. In the hands of a capable advisor, the transcript provides clues about the reasons for a student's performance, and is also a useful tool to predict future academic success or failure.

Advisors need more than the student's completed pre-registration materials (the courses they intend to take in the upcoming term). To practice true developmental advising, the advisor needs to analyze the student's complete transcript to determine factors that have led to past successes or failures. The goal is to duplicate success, while avoiding poor academic terms. (For example, a poor academic term in an otherwise good record could result from poor academic preparation, inadequate prerequisites, family problems, changes in career plans or focus, living arrangements, etc.)

Other common patterns are patterns of withdrawals, or "roller coaster" transcripts (good semesters alternating with poor semesters). This pattern could result from poor advising, students over-committing themselves with difficult courses, financial problems (students must work too many hours), seasonal participation in an extracurricular activity, inappropriate major advice and so forth.

In summary, advisors can only complete part of their advising tasks if they fail to examine the student's transcript looking for indicators of success or failure. The transcript indicates problems that the advisor and student can work to identify and solve. Grites (1984) provides an excellent summary of the importance of the transcript as a valuable tool for developmental advising: "Transcripts, then, serve as advising tools beyond the simple reflection of courses completed. The capable advisor will use them to analyze the

student's potential, determine possible difficulties and monitor the student's progress toward established educational goals" (Grites, p. 64).

Anecdotal records

Unless you are employed in one of those "rare" institutions where advisor to advisee ratios are low enough to permit advisors to truly know each of their advisees, you will be forced to rely on alternate methods to make personalized advising a consistent reality. A simple yet very effective procedure is to keep notes on each advising session. A quick review by the advisor before each advising session will tell you what has transpired in past sessions and what assignments and/or plans were made for the student to pursue. These notes could include such items as: future course selections, investigation of alternate educational options, i.e., internships, study abroad, double major, transfer course options, or other specific requirements the student was to complete to correct prior problems, such as missing documents, transcripts or placement exam scores.

Detailed notes alleviate several major problems or concerns. First, they provide a way for the advisor to know personal information about the advisee vital to a friendly and comfortable advising relationship.

Second, notes enable the advisor to cover more ground during each advising session. With good notes, the advisor and student can begin where they last left off, rather than always beginning anew.

Third, because you don't have to rely on memory, you will be more consistent in the information you are providing to the student. The better an advisor you become, the more students will want to become your advisee, and you will need to keep anecdotal records to remain "efficient" in advising.

Unfortunately, an important use of anecdotal records is to protect the advisor from legal actions taken by disgruntled students. When dealing with students in situations that are unpleasant, e.g., academic probation, academic misconduct, course deficiencies, etc., it is wise and prudent for the advisor to take accurate and comprehensive notes on each advising session. These should be shared with the advisee and included as a permanent component of the students' advising folder. If the student changes advisors or someone needs to fill in for you, the notes contain a documented record of what has been going on with the student in the advising sessions.

A final note on the use and development of a student advising folder. The advisor must maintain the confidentiality of records, including all information in the advising folder, at all times. The Family Educational Rights and Privacy Act of 1974 specifies that a student must provide written consent before educational records or information may be released to third parties. While exceptions are permitted for individuals who have legitimate educational interests on a "need to know" basis, the advisor needs to be cognizant of this act and be prudent in the release of student information.

Academic Curricula

To make advising a true developmental process, the advisor must first get beyond what Crookston (1972) describes as prescriptive advising or O'Banion's (1972) levels 4 and 5, course choice and scheduling courses. Crockett (1979) describes advising as a multifaceted activity, which provides accurate information about educational options, requirements, policies and procedures. The developmental advisor must first take care of the basics, by advising students on curriculum, course requirements and other practical matters. But the role of the advisor will change as the student proceeds through school. To meet the evolving needs of students, the advisor needs to be broadly informed and flexible.

Freshman advising

Advising first-year students on curriculum issues is not necessarily an easy task. The advisor must be knowledgeable about general education requirements, must review placement test results to place a student in the proper course level and must review high school transcripts to evaluate the student's preparation. When advising pre-major and undecided students, advisors may also need to communicate the academic mission and goals of the college/university, the purposes of general education and the organizational structure of the college/university.

A word of caution! Most students experience the first year as a time of personal and social adjustment—as well as a time of academic challenge. But it may be difficult for them to talk about these adjustment processes. For example, once a freshman has preregistered for the second semester, some students feel compelled to follow that schedule regardless of their performance in their first semester. It's wise to take a preventive approach and check grade reports against registrations, and to contact any student who may have done poorly in a prerequisite course.

Upper-class advising

As students move into their upper-class years, the advisor needs to be fully aware of the general education requirements of the university, the major and any requirements of the discipline. They also need to be knowledgeable about selective admissions criteria for restrictive majors, and about internships and career paths appropriate to the major.

Attention to detail is most important! Do you know where to find the answers to the following questions?

- Are there enrollment restrictions on particular courses?
- What is the prerequisite structure for courses in your major?
- When are required courses offered? Yearly? Every two years? Every term?
- How do students arrange to take a course during the summer at a different institution and transfer it back to the college?
- Are students able to have a minor within your discipline?

The list of questions is endless. What is important is to emphasize that the advisor needs to know the curriculum and related policies, or at a minimum, know where to find the answers to student questions during the advising session.

Advising students on curriculum concerns or course selection may seem a tedious task, but it is vitally important. If done improperly, it can have disastrous consequences for the student. There are a variety of tools available to make the task easier and more efficient.

Curriculum advising aids

Curriculum flow charts or curriculum guides are a very simple yet effective tool to help the advisor explain the rationale for various course requirements, the place of electives in the curriculum, and how advanced placement or transfer courses will affect the student. There are many ways in which the curriculum can be presented in these guides.

One of the most effective is the use of a curriculum flow chart. This presents the student with a visual picture of how the degree is organized, the prerequisite structure, and most importantly, the sequencing of courses. Requesting a student to fill out a curriculum flow chart with grades prior to a preregistration advising session enables the advisor and the student to monitor the student's progress effectively and efficiently.

A second powerful tool that is computer-assisted advising. This may range from basic—student grade records—to sophisticated—a complete graduation audit of degree requirements. Advantages of utilizing computer systems include: reduction of errors in information on courses, curriculum, graduation requirements and enrollments. The time saved searching for information in an advising session can then be used to deliver more substantial advising (Kramer & Megerian, 1985; Lawry & Grites, 1982; Peterson & Kramer, 1984). Although the computer is a powerful advising tool, it should never replace an advisor's commitment to the process of developmental advising.

The advisor as a generalist

A last word. The faculty advisor needs to be knowledgeable about curricula to be effective. However, it is not sufficient to know only your own academic discipline or even only the curricula options that are offered in your department or college. Advisors need to be knowledgeable about other academic curricula on campus and the resources on campus to which students may be referred. Although advisors are not expected to be experts in all disciplines, they do have an obligation to assist students in clarifying their career/vocational interests and settling into an appropriate academic major.

The beginning of the 21st century will represent a dramatic change in the type of student we have traditionally seen (Hodgkinson, 1985). The advising needs of students who approach the college experience from many nontraditional perspectives will be different. Some predictions indicate that the number of undecided students may increase—as a result of changes in majors because of an academic redirection or a change in career or vocational interest.

Related Advisor Responsibilities

Some bureaucracy ensures advising structure and consistency. Advisors must know, or at least have available, all policies and procedures that impact students. Student and faculty handbooks should contain all relevant rules and guidance. Advisors should also maintain and be able to provide instruction on completing all forms, paper or electronic.

No one likes bureaucratic red tape, but in institutions of higher learning, we have come to expect red tape as a way of life. On the positive side, it ensures consistency in the application of the rules and procedures that we expect our students to follow. However, we must work to ensure that bureaucratic procedures do not unnecessarily frustrate the students. Advisors can play a vital role in this process by knowing the academic policies that will affect their students, and the forms and procedures required to adhere to these policies. Essentially, advisors can teach students how to negotiate the university environment.

Academic policies

What policies do advisors need to know? The answer is "as many as possible." Any issue a student is attempting to resolve that requires an application of an academic policy is important and critical to that student. Advisors need to constantly try to place themselves in the position of the student when considering the "importance" of policy issues.

If possible, all policies should be included in at least two documents. The two most common documents are the student handbook and the faculty handbook. This will enable students and faculty to be knowledgeable about the policies that may impact the student's academic career. Progressive institutions take this one step further by providing the parents of incoming freshmen a copy of the student handbook. This provides a resource document to another set of "advisors" that are frequently used by our freshman students. It also tends to discourage the "they never told me" excuse heard from students at all levels of their academic careers.

Procedures and forms

Many academic policies and procedures require students to complete forms. Ideally, forms are developed to help students clarify what they are trying to do. Forms also document the history of what has been agreed upon. At a minimum, a copy of the approved form should be retained by the advisee, the advisor, registrar (the official keeper of the students' records) or other appropriate individuals. As more and more transactions are made on computer, however, forms are being replaced by computer records. Again, the intent of all policies, procedures and forms should be to protect the student from being subjected to arbitrary decisions.

An effective advising technique is to maintain a supply of these forms and have them at your disposal for advising sessions. If this is not practical, then the advisor needs to know who it is that maintains the inventory of these documents (so the student may be properly referred). It is very helpful to the advisee if you can show them a sample form that has been filled out. Advisors must constantly remind themselves that familiarity often breeds complacency, and familiar forms seem to be extremely routine and easy. For someone unfamiliar with the process, however, the process may seem intimidating or confusing. If a student handbook has been prepared, it is wise to include a section containing samples of completed forms.

Special Programs/Activities

Academic advising is a multifaceted activity. Grites (1979) defines advising as "assisting students to realize the maximum educational benefits available to them by helping them to better understand themselves and to learn to use the resources of an educational institution to meet their special educational needs and aspirations" (p. 1). Winston, Ender and Miller (1982) provide a more refined definition of the developmental advising process: "Developmental advising both stimulates and supports students in their quest for an enriched quality of life; it is a systematic process based on a close student-advisor relationship intended to aid students in achieving educational and personal goals through the utilization of the full range of institutional and community services" (p. 8).

It should be obvious that each institution must develop its own definition of academic advising with goals and objectives that reflect the unique character of the institution. There is, however, a common set of expectations that need to be fulfilled if developmental advising is to occur. In order to help students achieve their own educational and personal goals, the advisor needs to be knowledgeable about special programs, both campuswide as well as those in the academic departments.

Advisors will have to develop their own list of specialized programs that are unique to their college or department. As with policies and procedures, the advisor needs to be aware of specialized programs that not only assist students who are in need of academic support, but just as importantly, programs that provide enrichment for students who excel in their academic programs. Too often the focus is on the underprepared, academically "at-risk" student, only to ignore the needs of the best and brightest. Advisors need to work at providing the enriched environment necessary to challenge these students so they are retained at the institution.

Campus Resources

Advisors need to be aware of their limitations and understand what to do when confronted with a situation that is beyond their comfort level. It is an advisor's responsibility to be knowledgeable about the campus resources available to students because *referral agent* is one of the most critical roles of the developmental advisor. A listing of campus resources should be provided in faculty advising handbooks, training manuals and student handbooks.

When possible, the advisor needs to collect documents prepared by other campus offices that describe their function and purpose. These may be on paper or, increasingly, on World Wide Web pages. It is also important to establish who the contact personnel are in the specialty area to which students would be referred. These documents, updated on a yearly basis, become a part of the advisor resource library.

Campus resources divide into two distinct groupings— those that have direct influence on providing assistance to the delivery of developmental advising (learning resource center, career planning and placement, counseling and testing, tutoring office, off-campus programs) and those that provide a function or service designed to deliver a specific need for the student (registrar's office, financial aid, admissions, international study, minority affairs, adult affairs, disability services, veteran affairs, computer assistance office). It is important for the advisor to be aware that these offices exist on campus and to know who to contact

in each office to arrange a consultation or refer a student.

Campus resources expand and enhance the advising that individual advisors or offices provide. Gordon (1992) summarizes the four important components of referral: "When referring, advisors need to make it clear to the student (1) why they are being referred, (2) where they go for help and whom to contact, (3) what questions to ask and what tasks need to be completed, and (4) how to provide feedback to the advisor about the outcome of the referral when it is appropriate" (p. 58). In summary, it is the advisor's responsibility to know all of the resources available on campus and when appropriate to refer students to these resources. •

Bibliography

Abel, J. (1980). Academic advising: Goals and delivery system. *Journal of College Student Personnel, 21*, 151-154.

Aitken, C. E., & Conrad, C. F. (1977). Improving academic advising through computerization. *College and University, 53*, 115-123.

Astin, A. W. (1977). *Four critical years.* San Francisco: Jossey-Bass.

Barnett, L. (1982). Academic advising: ERIC as a resource. *NACADA Journal*, 1-13.

Beal, P. E., & Noel, L. (1980). *What works in student retention.* Iowa City, IA: American College Testing Program and National Center for Higher Education Management Systems. (ERIC Document Reproduction Service No. ED. 197 635)

Beasley-Fielstein, L. (1986). Student perceptions of the developmental advisor-advisee relationship. *NACADA Journal, 6*, 107-117.

Biggs, D. A., Brodie, J. S., & Barnhart, W. J. (1975). The dynamics of undergraduate academic advising. *Research in Higher Education, 3*, 345-357.

Borgard, J. H., Hornbuckle, P. A., & Mahoney, J. (1977). Faculty perceptions of academic advising. *NASPA Journal, 14*, 4-10.

Boyer, E. L. (1987). *College: The undergraduate experience in America. The Carnegie Foundation for the Advancement of Teaching.* New York: Harper & Row.

Carstenson, D. J., & Silberhorn, C. (1979). *A national survey of academic advising.* Iowa City, IA: American College Testing Program.

Chickering, A. W. (1969). *Education and identity.* San Francisco: Jossey-Bass.

Cohen, R. D. (Ed.). (1985). *Working with parents of college students. New Directions for Student Services, No. 32.* San Francisco: Jossey-Bass.

Council for the Advancement of Standards for Student Services/Development Programs. (1990). *NACADA Journal, 10*, 52-60.

Crockett, D. S. (Ed.). (1979). *Academic advising: A resource document.* Iowa City, IA: American College Testing Program.

Crockett, D. S. (1982). Academic advisement delivery systems. In R. B. Winston, S. C. Enders, & T. K. Miller (Eds.), *Developmental approaches to academic advising* (pp. 39-53). *New Directions for Student Services, No. 17.* San Francisco: Jossey-Bass.

Crockett, D. S., & Levitz, R. (1983). *A national survey of academic advising.* Iowa City, IA: American College Testing Program.

Crookston, B. B. (1972). A developmental view of academic advising as teaching. *Journal of College Student Personnel, 13*, 12-17.

Cross, K. P. (1974). *Beyond the open door: New students to higher education.* San Francisco: Jossey-Bass.

Dameron, J. D., & Wold, J. C. (1974). Academic advisement in higher education: A new model. *Journal of College Student Personnel, 15,* 470-473.

Dehn, S. (1987). Using faculty to advise new students. *NACADA Journal, 7,* 62-66.

Ender, S. C. Winston, R. B., & Miller, T. K. (1982). Academic advising as student development. In R. B. Winston, S. C. Ender, & T. K. Miller (Eds.), *Developmental approaches to academic advising* (pp. 3-18). San Francisco: Jossey-Bass.

Ford, J., & Ford, S. S. (1990). *Producing a comprehensive academic advising handbook.* Columbus, OH: The National Clearinghouse for Academic Advising.

Frank, C. P. (1988). The development of academic advising programs. *NACADA Journal, 8,* 11-28.

Fulfilling the promise of academic advising: New roles for faculty. (1994). Proceedings from National Conference in Higher Education (AAHE), Chicago, IL.

Gardner, J. N. (1985). The freshman year experience. *College and University, 61,* 261-274.

Gordon, V. (1990). *Handbook of academic advising.* Westport, CT: Greenwood Press.

Gordon, V. N., & Grites, T. J. (1984). The freshman seminar course: Helping students succeed. *Journal of College Student Personnel, 25,* 315-320.

Grites, T. J. (1977). Student development through academic advising: A 4x4 model. *NASPA Journal, 14,* 33-37.

Grites, T. J. (1979). *Academic advising: Getting us through the eighties.* Washington, DC: American Association of Higher Education. (AAHE-ERIC Higher Education Research Report, No. 7)

Grites, T. J. (1984). Techniques and tools for improving advising. *NACADA Journal,* 55-74.

Habley, W. P. (1981). Academic advising: The critical link in student retention. *NASPA Journal, 18,* 45-50.

Habley, W. R. (1983). Organizational structures for academic advising: Models and implications. *Journal of College Student Personnel, 24,* 535-540.

Habley, W. R. (1988). *The status and future of academic advising.* Iowa City, IA: American College Testing Program.

Hardee, M. D. (1970). *Faculty advising in colleges and universities.* Washington, DC: American Personnel and Guidance Association.

Hines, E. R. (1984). Delivery systems and the institutional context. In R. B. Winston, S. C. Ender, T. K. Miller, T. J. Grites, & Associates, *Developmental academic advising* (pp. 317-346). San Francisco: Jossey-Bass.

Hodgkinson, H. L. (1985). *All one system: Demographics of education, kindergarten through graduate school.* Washington, DC: Institute for Educational Leadership.

Hornbuckle, P., Mahoney, J., & Borgard, J. (1979). A structured analysis of student perceptions of faculty advising. *Journal of College Student Personnel, 20,* 296-300.

Johnson, J., & Sprandel, K. (1975). Centralized academic advising at the department level. *University College Quarterly, 21,* 17-19.

Juola, A. E., Winburne, J. W., & Whitmore, A. (1968). Computer-assisted academic advising. *Personnel and Guidance Journal, 2,* 59-60.

Kapraun, E. D., & Coldren, D. W. (1982). Academic advising to facilitate student retention. *NACADA Journal, 2,* 59-60.

Kerr, T. (1981) *Academic advising for continuing education: An assessment of the perceptions of students, faculty, advisors, and institutional commitment.* Dissertation, Boston College, Boston, MA.

Kohlberg, L. (1981). *The philosophy of moral development.* San Francisco: Harper & Row.

Kolb, D. A. (9181). Learning styles and disciplinary differences. In A. W. Chickering, *The modern American college* (pp. 232-255). San Francisco: Jossey-Bass.

Kramer, G. L. (1994). *Technology and academic advising: Oxymoron or allies?* Presentation made at Summer Institute on Academic Advising, Williamsburg, VA.

Kramer, G. L., & Megerian, A. (1985). Using computer technology to aid faculty advising. *NACADA Journal, 5,* 51-61.

Kramer, G. L., Arrington, N. R., & Chynoweth, B. (1985). The academic advising center and faculty advising: A comparison. *NASPA Journal, 23,* 24-35.

Kramer, H. C., & Gardner, R. E. (1983). *Advising by faculty.* Washington, DC: National Education Association.

Levine, A. (1989). Who are today's freshmen? In M. L. Upcraft & J. N. Gardner, *The freshman year experience* (pp. 15-24). San Francisco: Jossey-Bass.

Lowry, G. R., & Grites, T. J. (1982). The classroom as an institutional resource: An example of computer-assisted advising. *NACADA Journal, 4,* 33-40.

Lumpkins, B., & Hall, H. (1987). Advising college undergraduates—a neglected area. *College Student Journal, 21,* 98-100.

Mahoney, J., Borgard, J., & Hornbuckle, P. A. (1978). The relationship of faculty experience and advisee load to perceptions of academic advising. *Journal of College Student Personnel, 19,* 28-32.

McFarland, D., & Daniels, V. (1977). Academic advising with a personal plan and record book. *Journal of College Student Personnel, 18,* 243-244.

Moore, K. M. (1976). Faculty advising: Panacea or placebo? *Journal of College Student Personnel, 12,* 371-374.

Moore, L. V. (Ed.). (1990). *Evolving theoretical perspectives on college students. New Directions for Student Services, No. 51.* San Francisco: Jossey-Bass.

Noel, L., Levitz, R., & Saluri, D. (1985). *Increasing student retention.* San Francisco: Jossey-Bass.

O'Banion, T. (1972). An academic advising model. *Junior College Journal, 44,* 62-69.

Peterson, E. D., & Kramer, G. L. (1984). Computer-assisted advising: The next agenda item for computer development. *NACADA Journal, 4,* 33-40.

Peterson, E. D., & Kramer, G. L. (1981). *Landmark developments in academic advising.* Paper presented at annual meeting of National Academic Advising Association (NACADA), Archville, NC.

Sheffield, W., & Meskill, V. P. (1972). Faculty adviser and academic counselor: A pragmatic marriage. *Journal of College Student Personnel, 13,* 28-30.

Spencer, R. W., Peterson, E. D., & Kramer, G. L. (1983). Designing and implementing a computer-assisted academic advising program. *Journal of College Student Personnel, 24,* 513-518.

Spencer, R. W., Peterson, E. D., & Kramer, G. L. (1982). Utilizing college advising centers to Facilitate and revitalize academic advising. *NACADA Journal, 2,* 13-23.

Stickle, F. (1982). Faculty and student perceptions of faculty advising effectiveness. *Journal of College Student Personnel, 23,* 262-265.

Teague, G. V., & Grites, T. J. (1980). Faculty contracts and academic advising. *Journal of College Student Personnel, 21,* 40-44.

Thompson, R. G. (1980). Computer-assisted advising program. *Journal of College Student Personnel, 21,* 571-572.

Tinto, V. (1982). Limits of theory and practice in student attrition. *Journal of Higher Education, 53,* 687-700.

Vowell, F., & Karst, R. (1987). Student satisfaction with faculty advisors in an intrusive advising program. *NACADA Journal, 7,* 31-33.

Walsh, E. M. (1979). Revitalizing academic advisement. *Personnel and Guidance Journal, 57,* 446-449.

Winston, R., Ender, S., & Miller, T. (1982). *Developmental approaches to academic advising. New Directions for Student Services, No. 17.* San Francisco: Jossey-Bass.

Referral Skills

Faye Vowell, Ph.D.
Dean, School of Library and Information Management, Emporia State University

An advisor cannot be all things to all students, regardless of the strength and variety of his or her background and experience. Advising on any campus is inevitably a team effort. An advisor will therefore need to develop a network of referral sources to help advisees in a number of areas. The suggestions contained here will assist in that process.

Campus Resources

Most schools have a number of support services that offer help to students. In the academic area, your school most probably has a writing lab, a math lab and a reading lab as well as labs in subjects such as economics or biology—where many freshmen seem to need assistance.

Many schools maintain lists of students with expertise in certain areas who will tutor others for free or for a fee. Often these lists are maintained in the counseling center, the dean's office or the advising office.

Your school might also have a student support services program, a federally funded TRIO program that works with enrolled students from low-income, first-generation-college backgrounds and students with disabilities. Usually, this program will provide tutors or special classes for students who qualify for the program. Other programs of this type may be funded by state grants or by the institution.

Frequently a school will offer some kind of academic testing services to students. These may range from diagnostic testing to help with class placement, to credit by exam, to vocational counseling. Students who come with deficiencies of preparation or atypical backgrounds in certain areas may need diagnostic testing to know where to enter a required sequence of classes such as math or foreign language. Sometimes an institution will offer CLEP testing or locally developed examinations by which students may test out of courses.

Students may also need to be referred to the appropriate person to find out how advanced placement for courses taken in high school will be counted in course placement and for degree requirements. In terms of vocational testing, schools may offer a computerized program such as SIGI or the Discover program to help with major selection. These services may be found in your counseling center or in the placement office.

The counseling center is another good referral source for students with personal problems. Students who are adjusting to being away from home for the first time; having problems with roommates, dating relationships, alcohol or drugs; having problems dealing with parents who are divorcing, or who themselves are divorced, divorcing or separated, may need trained help working through their difficulties.

The counselors within a counseling center may specialize in certain problems, so a working knowledge of who does what within the counseling center is crucial for good referral. Counselors operate with stringent concerns for student privacy; if you wish to be updated on the student's progress in dealing with the problem for which you referred him or her, you need to ask that a consent form be signed.

If yours is a residential campus, the residence hall staff or the resident assistants are good referral sources for helping advisees learn to fit into the new environment and peer group. Campuses also often have nontraditional student organizations as well as single parent organizations within the student affairs areas, which are of great assistance to these constituent groups.

Other special interest groups to which you may wish to refer your advisees include the various social organizations attached to different disciplines such as PSI CHI for psychology students, fraternities and sororities, religious and political clubs and student governance organizations.

In addition, campuses often have such groups as the Black Student Union, the Hispanic American Leadership Organization, the Native American Student Association or others which provide support to members of various ethnic groups. Less frequently, organizations that support gay and lesbian awareness are also available. All of these groups may have faculty advisors and may be a part of a student organizations unit under student affairs.

Referral sources for student fiscal concerns include the financial aid office and the student employment office. Federal regulations concerning financial aid change so frequently and are so complex that students will often have specific questions that only a financial aid counselor can answer. Sample questions might be, "What kinds of material do I need to take with me when I am told I have been selected for financial aid verification?" or "By what date must I have my financial aid application in to receive a check when I register for classes?"

If scholarship information is not housed in financial aid, you may need to refer students to a separate office to find out what scholarships are available and how to apply. Often, students need to work to help pay their way through school. Much of the literature suggests that on-campus employment is better for the student than off-campus employment. Some students qualify for federal work-study

191

funds, which are usually administered through the student employment office.

Many schools have a Cooperative Education (COOP) program that will allow students to work and receive credit for a work experience that is an integral part of their academic major.

Transfer students make up a large part of the student body on many campuses. These students often need the help of a transcript analyst or someone who can give them the official verdict on what courses will transfer to fit specific requirements. Transfers often need many of the same services that new freshmen need, but at a different level; most schools are less likely to make these services as easily available since they are not perceived as needing the same kind of campus orientation as new freshmen.

International students are another group for which an advisor may need to develop a referral network. These students have special needs associated with visas, adjustment to a different culture, and acceptance of people from a variety of backgrounds. In addition, they may need language instruction to help them perform well in classes.

Students with disabilities are often advised by a designated person, but you may also advise students with disabilities, especially those not readily identifiable. Visually-impaired, hearing-impaired and mobility-impaired students have been on campuses for a number of years, so the procedures for dealing with their concerns are usually accessible in student and faculty handbooks.

Students who have learning disabilities or mental disabilities are enrolling in record numbers. The Americans with Disabilities Act (ADA) has caused many schools to rethink their accommodations in the classroom. Your advisees with needs in these areas will have more help than they might have in the past.

Finally, students may need referral in dealing with the issues of sexual harassment. Your institution will have a person whose responsibility is to deal with allegations of this kind and a written policy in place. Often this person is the affirmative action officer or someone in the human resources (personnel) area.

List of Contact People

In order to refer advisees efficiently and effectively, you need to become acquainted with the people who staff the various services described above. Often the director of advising on your campus will have created a list of referral sources in an advising handbook. This is a good starting place. If such a list does not exist, you can compile your own or work with colleagues to do so. To supplement a list of names, phone numbers, and hours of operation, a visit to the particular area is advisable.

When you actually visit the office where the service is housed, you can get a concrete sense of the atmosphere and level of service. You can discuss with providers the scope of the service they offer and the time frame in which they are able to provide the service. For instance, can the writing lab deal with students who drop in or do they need appointments? Is there a welcoming feeling to the office area, or will you need to warn your advisee not to be put off? Often, the service will have brochures or written material you can take away with you to share with your advisees. In addition, you will establish yourself as a known and caring person, so asking for help over the phone for your advisees will be easier.

While this seems like a great deal of effort, the personal touch pays dividends. Not only will your advisees benefit, but you will have established a network of friends across campus. You might also want to think of a systematic way to update your information bank on referral sources periodically—especially if you haven't contacted a service in some time. Like all relationships, the referral relationship takes some nurturing to keep it strong.

Examining Your Comfort Level in Referrals

As an individual with unique background and experience, you probably have a definite "comfort level" when discussing personal concerns advisees may bring up. Your school also has an institutional culture and set of traditions and expectations in this area. The interplay between these two factors and the needs of your advisees becomes important in a referral situation.

As you develop your list of referral sources, you may also want to begin to explore what your level of comfort is either by yourself or with a friend. You could do this exploration in a number of ways. First set aside some time to write down the referral areas mentioned above that make you uncomfortable or that you would have trouble discussing with a student.

You might also write down the areas in which you have a particular interest or strength. As you list these areas, jot down particular incidents from your past experience or experience with advisees that influence your feelings. This act of writing will give you concrete things to think about and will help objectify the areas to a certain extent. As you analyze your responses, you can ask yourself whether this is a response that is no longer valid for you or whether you want to work to change this response. You might also decide that your level of comfort is one that you're satisfied with.

Next, you might move on to consider what messages your institutional culture or environment gives you about referral expectations. Look carefully at written materials in the catalog, student handbook and faculty handbook. Examine the mission statement for your school as well as the advising mission statement for your department. Write down what these printed resources tell you about expectations. For example, if your school espouses developmental intrusive advising and refers to it in the advising mission statement, there will most likely be an expectation that you work with your advisees in certain specific ways. These expectations should be clearly conveyed in training sessions. You may be expected to seek out students who miss appointments with you or with people to whom you have referred them. You might be expected to model for your advisees problem-solving strategies that require referrals.

Different institutions have different cultures, and therefore different kinds and levels of expectations. For example, if your school is church-related, you may be expected to help students with questions of faith and with moral or ethical issues—which would not be expected in a research institution. You might also be expected to perform more of a counseling function and to address these issues in greater depth than if you were in a liberal arts college. A regional comprehensive school with a high need for retention of students might have yet a different kind of expectation.

Colleagues are good sources of information about institutional expectations, as are interviews with the director of advising or your department chairperson. Sometimes the referral expectations are not written down but are embedded in an attitude toward advising. A conversation with a friend or supervisor could help you elicit useful information.

Once you feel you have collected enough information about institutional expectations, then ask yourself if there is a conflict between your comfort level and institutional expectations. If there is, you will need to develop strategies for addressing these disparities. For example, your school might encourage advisors to help students address study skills issues or concerns dealing with roommates without referrals. But you might feel that students should not be in college if they do not possess the self-discipline, time management and study skills necessary to make good grades or sufficient maturity to deal with interpersonal situations.

Another kind of incongruity could arise if you feel that you want to do much more individual work with students in such areas as goal setting and problem solving, but your institution did not encourage or reward you for it. In both cases, you would need to visit with your supervisor or chairperson and work out an understanding. Untenured faculty members should probably consider the impact of such disparate expectations on prospects for tenure and promotion.

Experience will probably help you gauge the best timing of referrals within an ongoing discussion of a difficulty. You are likely to find that your comfort level will change as you work with advisees in certain areas. Using the example of a roommate difficulty, you may initially feel comfortable only asking how that relationship is going; if there are problems, you may refer the advisee to a resident assistant. After a time, you may begin to feel comfortable listening to the student describe the problem in detail and suggesting problem-solving strategies for the student to try out.

At the other end of the problem spectrum, if a student discloses that he or she is a victim of date rape or childhood sexual abuse, you would probably want to refer to the counseling center for therapy rather than dealing with the problem yourself. So, the severity of the problem will help you to find your comfort level and decide when to refer.

Referral and Student Development Theory

A knowledge of some components of student development theory is useful as you evolve your own philosophy and practice in regard to referrals. If you have a familiarity with one or more theories, you can use them to help you describe, explain, predict and direct student growth in appropriate areas.

Student development theories may be grouped into the following categories: psychosocial theories that address the relationship between the self and others such as those of Ericson and Chickering; cognitive-structural theories that address how students make meaning such as those of Kohlberg, Gilligan, Belenky, Piaget and Perry; topological models such as that found in the Myers-Briggs Type Inventory and in Jung; and person-environment interaction models like those proposed by Astin and Schlossberg.

In your interactions with students, you may need to know how to help them maximize the help in a referral. You will also evolve a philosophy addressing how much help you need to give particular students in following through on a referral. Knowledge of one or more of the above student development theories would assist you in describing a referral process appropriate to the situation. Although it is possible to outline a generic process (the section below will attempt to do just that), you will want to adapt that generic process to the particular student.

For example, William Perry's model of Intellectual and Ethical Development describes four categories containing nine stages of development through which students move: dualism, multiplicity, relativism and commitment in relativism. [*Editor's note: for further discussion of Perry's model, see Virginia Gordon's article, "Student Development Theory Into Practice: Implications for Advisors," on page 177 of the Participant Book.*]

In stage 2 (dualism), students view people, knowledge and values through absolute and concrete categories. The "right" answers are determined by authorities who are not to be questioned. Students do not acknowledge alternative perspectives.

In stage 3 (multiplicity), students defy or resist authority. They acknowledge multiple points of view, but believe that questions have multiple answers. All points of view are valid, and the process of challenging viewpoints is still avoided.

If you are working with a student who sees the world in dualistic terms, you would use a different referral strategy than you would with a student whose perspective was that of multiplicity. One difference might be that after you had helped the stage 2 student to make an appointment with the referral source, you might count on the student doing what you had suggested because you would be viewed as an authority figure. The person to whom you referred the advisee might also be seen as an authority. The stage 3 student might need to be persuaded that your advice or that of the referral source would be valid. Both students would have difficulty in making choices and would probably want you to make the choice for them.

If you practice developmental advising, knowledge of student development theory could help you devise strategies to encourage your advisees to grow and develop. This could apply to referral situations in the following way. You might decide that you would give your advisees the maximum help needed to profit from a first referral. This could include modeling the kinds of questions to ask, walking with them to the particular service area and following up with a phone call or meeting to process what happened during the referral. Subsequent referrals could be managed so that the students assume more responsibility in the process as they are able.

This process may sound overly protective and simplistic as described above, since much of what has been said is common sense. Let me urge you to adapt what works for you.

Suggested Procedure for Referral

This process was described first by Jack Roundy in the *NACADA Newsletter*.

1. Determine what the referral need is: sometimes students won't ask for help directly, or sometimes they ask for help in one area but you can see the problem is more basic or in another area.

2. Talk with the student about the purpose/goal of the referral (cognitive aspect of referral) and how success will be measured.

3. Reassure the student about his or her right to the service requested and the referral source's ability to provide it (affective aspect of referral).

4. Help the student outline the process (steps to be taken) and try to keep the referral chain as simple as possible.

5. Explore with the student crucial questions that he or she needs to ask and perhaps even role play a part of the process with the student.

6. Make the telephone call to set up the initial appointment with the referral source while the student is in your office. Perhaps you need to explain the situation or perhaps you can give the telephone to the student to do so. If the referral source is not accessible by telephone, agree with the student on a time frame within which he or she will contact the referral source.

7. Make an appointment with the student for a return advising session to follow up on the referral.

8. Summarize the referral goals/purposes and specific directions you want to follow up on with the student.

9. When the student returns for the next advising session, discuss results and how he or she feels the referral went. If the student did not follow through, discuss the reasons. Reexamine the problem again. Consider whether you need to take a more or less active role. Consider whether a different referral is necessary.

This process is perhaps most appropriate for students who have low levels of motivation and self-esteem. Many of the steps may be collapsed or rendered unnecessary with a student who has better skills and just needs to discuss the appropriate source to go to for help.

Evaluation

Evaluation is an essential component of any educational process. You can gauge the success of individual referrals by whether the student actually follows through on the process you work out together. You can also ask students to give you feedback on their satisfaction with the referral process.

An advising portfolio could also give you evidence on which to judge your success. A colleague or the staff in the faculty development or teaching and learning center of your school are additional sources for an evaluation on the processes that you have designed. Jack Roundy also suggests that you may want to examine your files periodically to look for patterns of referral needs. If a number of students need the same referrals, the solution may need to be systemic or curricular. You could then propose to the appropriate people that the information be presented in a campus newsletter, computer bulletin board, freshman seminar or another appropriate vehicle. •

Communication Skills

Margaret C. "Peggy" King, Ed.D.
Assistant Dean for Student Development, Schenectady County Community College

An advisor-advisee relationship is frequently a helping relationship, designed to meet the needs of the advisee, not those of the advisor. "The relationship is meant largely to enable helpees to assume responsibility for themselves and make their own decisions based on expanded alternatives and approaches. Therefore, helpers neither solve helpees' problems nor reassure them merely to make them feel better" (Okun, 1992, p. 20).

The prerequisite skill in any helping/advising relationship is effective, empathic communication. According to Webster's Dictionary, communication is defined as "an act or instance of transmitting; an exchange of information; a process by which meanings are exchanged between individuals through a common system of symbols."

Good communication skills are a key to developing a positive advisor-advisee relationship. When we think of communication, however, we frequently think of only verbal communication. Yet our nonverbal communication (gestures, appearance, expressions, environment) can be of equal or greater importance in terms of the messages we convey. Some would suggest that more than two-thirds of any communication occurs on a nonverbal level (Okun, 1992, pp. 47-48).

Nonverbal Communication

Nonverbal communication means smiling, frowning, laughing, crying, signing, standing close to others, being standoffish; the way you look; your handshake, postures, gestures, mannerisms; your voice; the environment you create (Adler & Towne, 1975).

Physical environment

The physical environment of an office can affect the kind of communication that takes place within it. Overall attractiveness, comfortable chairs, the location of the desk and chairs, brightness, etc., can convey positive or negative images, making students feel welcome and comfortable or vice versa.

Preparedness

When advisees come for scheduled appointments, our preparedness for those appointments can go a long way in conveying a message that we care about the student and that the student is important.

Things you can do to make the student aware that you are prepared for his or her visit:

- Be on time.
- Welcome the student by name.
- Have the advisee's file available.
- Recall previous conversations you may have had.
- Ask about some details of the student's life.

Body language/attending behavior

People express their feelings by their actions, by what they do, not just by what they say. In fact, it is probably safe to say you can't *not* communicate in that way. And nonverbal communication transmits feelings. At times, people can simultaneously express different and even contradictory messages through their verbal and nonverbal behavior.

Helping relationships such as an advisor-advisee relationship demand a physical presence, a certain kind of "attending" behavior. That behavior can be expressed by the following:

1. Face the other person squarely. This shows involvement with and interest in the student.
2. Maintain good eye contact. Look directly at the student. This demonstrates that your attention is focused on the student.
3. Maintain an "open" posture. Crossed arms and legs can signal less interest and involvement.
4. Lean toward the student. This also conveys interest and involvement.
5. Remain relatively relaxed. This conveys a feeling of comfortableness.

Verbal Communication

Verbal communication skills are essential in building rapport with advisees. While most people feel comfortable with their communication skills, it is helpful to review some specific aspects of communication that can be particularly important in an advising relationship. They include listening, questioning and reflecting/paraphrasing.

Listening

"Listening is (a) taking in information from speakers, other people or ourselves while remaining non-judgmental and empathic; (b) acknowledging the speaker in a way that invites the communication to continue; and (c) providing limited but encouraging input to the talker's response, carrying the person's idea one step forward" (Burley-Allen, 1982, pp. 2-3).

Each of us listens in different ways at different times. That listening can occur at several levels:

Level 3

Listening in spurts (tuning in and out; aware of the presence of others but mainly paying attention to oneself); half-listening (following the discussion only enough to get a chance to talk); quiet, passive listening (hearing but not responding, faking attention while thinking what one wants to say next).

Level 2

Hearing sounds and words but not really listening (listening at a surface level, hearing the words but not attempting to understand the intent of the feeling behind the words).

Level 1

Active listening (attempting to see things from the other's point of view and not evaluating the speaker's words; characteristics may include "taking in main ideas, acknowledging and responding, not letting one's self be distracted, paying attention to the speaker's total communication—including body language; not only attentive to the words being spoken but empathetic to the speaker's feelings and thoughts, suspending one's own thoughts and feelings to give attention solely to listening" (Burley-Allen, 1982, pp. 10-11).

Listening, then, is more than hearing what your advisee says. It is an active process that includes eye contact, body language, verbal response and tone of voice. The following checklist of do's and don'ts will be helpful:

DO—

- Listen with understanding, non-judgementally and non-critically
- Make eye contact
- Face the person in an open, relaxed position
- Acknowledge the speaker by—
  - Nodding the head
  - Brief expressions such as I see, oh, uh huh
  - Leaning forward
  - Making facial expressions that match the person's feelings
- Invite the speaker to say more

DO NOT—

- Interrupt
- Take the subject off in another direction
- Rehearse in your own head
- Interrogate
- Teach
- Give advice
- Use stock phrases such as "Oh well, it's not that bad," "Don't worry, things will get better," etc. (Burley-Allen, 1982, pp. 63, 101-102)

Questioning

Questioning is a tool that can open new areas for discussion, can help a student explore concerns, and can help identify issues in the discussion. There are four different types of questions:

Open questions

These are invitations to the student to talk about his or her concerns and to express him or herself. They put the advisor in a supporting, not directing position. Open questions can be questions that more actively draw the student into discussion (e.g., What would you like to talk about today?), questions that get the student to elaborate on needs, objectives, wants, goals and problems (e.g., Could you tell me more about that?), and questions that help the student focus on feelings (e.g., How do you feel about what happened in class today?).

Closed questions

These are questions that tend to emphasize factual information and can often be answered briefly or with a yes/no response. Closed questions can be used to obtain specific facts (e.g., What did your professor do?) or to direct the conversation to specific areas (e.g., What are your next steps?).

Clarifying questions

These are questions that can clarify your understanding of what the student has said. They can invite the student to expand or clarify an idea they previously expressed (e.g., Your interpretation of the professor's comment is that...), they can provide feedback of your understanding of what you thought the student meant (e.g., If I'm understanding you correctly, you believe that...), or they can help uncover what is really on the student's mind.

Continuing (key word) questions

These are questions that ask students for a more detailed explanation of what they were saying (e.g., Tell me more about the situation).

Reflecting/paraphrasing

Advisors need to hear as well as listen. And since it is often so difficult for students to say precisely what is on their minds and in their hearts, and since it is also hard for advisors to listen without distraction or distortion to what students are saying, we periodically need to check for accuracy in our conversation. One way of doing this is to reflect back, or paraphrase or restate, what the student has said. For example:

Student: "I am having a terrible time in my psychology class. The teacher demands so much work and time, and I can't seem to handle it."

Advisor: "You're feeling frustrated that you can't seem to handle the workload."

Reflective listening makes a great deal of sense when one considers the following:

1. Words have different meanings for different people.

2. People often "code" their messages.

3. People frequently talk about "presenting problems" when another topic is of greater concern to them.

4. The speaker may be blind to his or her emotions or blinded by them.

5. Listeners are often easily distracted.

6. Listeners hear through "filters" that distort much of what is being said (Bolton, 1979, p. 76).

Paraphrasing and reflecting provide a check for accuracy as well as a way to communicate warmth and concern. They also encourage the student to focus on what his or her feelings are, not on what the advisor thinks they are.

Advising Strategies

There are a variety of strategies that an advisor can use and teach the student to use that can enhance the advising relationship and can help the student develop skills beneficial throughout college and life. These strategies include:

1. Advocacy/intervention

2. Intrusiveness

3. Challenging/confrontation

4. Modeling and teaching decision-making skills

Advocacy/intervention

At times, the advisor will need to advocate for or intervene on behalf of a student. There is a delicate balance between empowering students to act for themselves or providing direct assistance in helping them negotiate the institutional bureaucracy. The decision to use one of the following methods will depend on the personalities of the student and others involved and the immediacy of the student need.

Choices:

1. Refer the student to the faculty/staff member directly involved

2. Make contact yourself

3. Refer the student to someone who can help the student develop the skills to deal with such issues

Intrusiveness

This includes actions on the part of advisors or advising programs to reach out to students and to build relationships so that as problems or issues come up, students know whom to contact. It is particularly important when working with at-risk students, first-generation students and entering freshmen in general.

Things you can do to reach out to your advisees:

• Send letters

• Talk after class

• Invite to a meeting

• Invite to lunch

• Schedule regular appointments

• Invite to group advising sessions

Challenging/confronting the student

This can be effective when you and your advisee have a relationship based on respect and understanding. Mild confrontation is appropriate when you want to:

1. Challenge students to achieve more than they might think possible.

2. Open up for consideration discrepancies in the student's behavior (on the one hand you say, on the other hand you do...), discrepancies in what a person says and how he appears (you say you're feeling good, yet you look exhausted), and how the student is vs. how she wants to be (you're not sure you can make it through college, yet your record indicates you can).

3. Help the student look at both sides of an issue (I understand what you feel your teacher does wrong, but what do you think your teacher thinks you do wrong? What would he say about you?).

Modeling/teaching decision-making skills

Students frequently come to advisors seeking a solution for a problem. Advisors can best help the student by modeling/teaching them skills to use not just in that situation but in others they will confront. The following are steps to use in the decision-making process:

1. Define the problem and clarify the situation.

2. Collect and use information relevant to a decision and search for alternatives.

3. Evaluate the alternatives against identified criteria.

4. Assess the risks involved with the decision.

5. Develop a plan of action and follow through.

Issues Affecting Helping

One's personal values and points of view can affect the helping process in an advisor/advisee relationship, particularly since most academic advisors work with a tremendously heterogeneous group of students from a wide variety of cultural and socioeconomic backgrounds and from many racial and age groups. It is important that we recognize this fact, or else those values and beliefs could seriously hamper our usefulness as advisors.

Personal values

A variety of personal values can affect an advising relationship. This includes "our attitudes and feelings about people, what is 'good' or 'bad,' what is acceptable or unacceptable, what is important for choices, and what makes people tick..." (Okun, 1992, p. 233). These values are intertwined with "beliefs about gender, family, money, politics, religion, work, race, authority and culture as well as with one's personal taste and lifestyle" (Okun, 1992, p. 234). These values are transmitted, either directly or indirectly, to our advisees. Consequently, it is essential that advisors become aware of their own value systems so that they don't impose them on the students they are trying to help.

Why is it important that you not try to impose your values on others?

- Does not encourage growth and independence of advises

- May result in submission to the advisor

- May result in withdrawal from the advisor

What should you do in a situation where you find it difficult to be genuine and non-judgmental with an advisee?

- Talk it out with the advisee

- Assist the student in finding another advisor

- Seek assistance from a colleague or supervisor in working with the student

Sexism

The significant changes that have occurred in the economic, social and legal position of women in the past 20 years have caused dramatic shifts in the traditional values, expectations and life goals of women and men. Some advisors may have difficulty adjusting to those changes, which in turn may affect how they work with their advisees. Sexist advising occurs when an advisor discourages either a female advisee from exploring a career in electrical engineering because that is a "male occupation" or a male advisee from pursuing a career in nursing because it is a "female occupation." It occurs when an advisor ignores an advisee's request to have classes completed by 2 p.m. so he or she can be home when children finish school.

Racism and ethnocentrism

Racist advising exists when advisors allow their biases about different ethnic groups to affect their relationships with advisees. It can take the form of discouraging (or not encouraging) black advisees from pursuing certain careers that require additional higher education, or assuming an Asian student can handle calculus because "all Asians are good at math," or simply treating advisees from different ethnic groups differently.

As advisors, it is important that we expand our interaction with students and colleagues from different backgrounds and cultures so as to increase our knowledge of those cultures. We must remember that there are many differences in values, attitudes and beliefs among groups as well as among individuals within groups. The more we know and understand, the better our relationships will be with our advisees.

Ageism

Ageism can be defined as "...imposing our own beliefs and values about what can or should be done at different ages onto other people" (Okun, 1992, p. 245). It can occur in advising relationships when we discourage (or don't encourage) an older student to consider graduate school or to pursue a career in law or medicine because they'll be "too old" when they finish. It can occur when we treat the 45-year-old advisee the same way we treat a 17-year-old advisee, ignoring the valuable life experiences they have to share. It is important that we be conscious of our own attitudes and beliefs and that we examine our stereotypical assumptions about "older" students.

The Advising Interview

"The advising process is a complex set of interactions that identifies a problem, provides and evaluates information, produces a tangible solution and implements the solution by taking action (Gordon, 1992, p. 51). Specific components of an advising interview and characteristics of each are as follows:

1. Open the interview
Begin the interview with an opening question or lead, such as "How can I help you" or "What's up?" If the student has made an appointment, be sure to have relevant information available (e.g., student file, catalog, etc.). Practice good communication skills so that you convey interest, openness and attention.

2. Identify the problem
Help the student to clarify the problem and to provide all relevant facts and information. Ask probing and open-ended questions. Restate the problem as a way of giving the student a chance to clarify, correct or add to the information.

3. Identify possible solutions
Ask the student for his or her ideas for solving the problem. Help the student generate additional or alternative solutions and focus on what, how, when and who might solve the problem. Identify any resources that might be needed. If more than one solution is suggested, discuss the implications for each.

4. Take action
Help the student identify specific action steps with a suggested order and time frame. Determine what follow-up is needed by the student and/or the advisor.

5. Summarize the transaction
Review what has transpired, including the action steps to be taken. Encourage future contact and make a definite appointment, if appropriate. Summarize the interview in the student's folder or record, being sure to include follow-up steps or assignments if any were identified. •

Bibliography

Adler, R., & Towne, N. (1975). *Looking out/looking in: Interpersonal communication.* San Francisco, CA: Rinehart Press.

Bolton, R. (1979). *People skills.* Englewood Cliffs, NJ: Prentice-Hall, Inc.

Burley-Allen, M. (1982). *Listening: The forgotten skill.* New York, NY: John Wiley and Sons, Inc.

Crockett, D. S. (Ed.). (1982). *Advising skills, techniques, and resources.* Iowa City, IA: American Testing Corporation.

Gordon, V. (1992). *Handbook of academic advising.* Westport, CT: Greenwood Press.

Okun, B. (1992). *Effective helping: Interviewing and counseling techniques.* Pacific Grove, CA: Brooks/Cole Publishing Co.

Vowell, F., Wachtel, E., Grites, T., & Rozzelle, B. (1992). *The NACADA advisor training manual.* Manhattan, KS: National Academic Advising Association.

Advising Undecided/Exploratory Students

Virginia Gordon, Ph.D.
Assistant Dean, Emerita, The Ohio State University

Two main themes will be addressed in this paper:

1. *Who are undecided students?* Undecided students comprise a heterogeneous population. Most undecided students are engaged in the normal development issues involved in making educational and career decisions.

2. *How can we advise undecided students effectively?* Special techniques and approaches can be used that lead to more effective advising and more positive student outcomes.

Characteristics of Undecided Students

There are as many definitions of undecided students as there are individual students. Undecided students may be defined as those who are unwilling, unable or unready to make educational and/or vocational decisions upon entering college (Gordon, 1984).

Another type is the student who enters college with a tentative decision that changes later. Some of these students may find the coursework in their chosen major uninteresting once they have been exposed to it. Some may find their major performance does not meet the expectations for certain majors (e.g., low math grades for a prospective business or engineering major). A third group of major-changers are those who are rejected for a variety of reasons from a selective or oversubscribed major.

Undecided students may be defined differently on individual campuses. Some campuses identify them through admissions. Others are identified through advising assignments or procedures. Others may be identified during the transition from one major to another. The names given administratively reveal the institution's attitude toward this special group (e.g., exploratory, pre-majors, open majors, general studies majors).

Why students are undecided

1. Most undecided students simply do not have enough information on which to base a sound educational or vocational decision. This information includes three areas: self-information, information about majors and/or information about occupations.

   Students need to identify and examine their personal strengths and honestly evaluate their limitations. Some may have so many interests, they cannot narrow them down to a manageable size. Others may not be able to express any interests because they lack experiences on which to base those interests. Some undecided students may not be sure of their abilities because they have not had an opportunity to test them or may be unwilling to take the risks necessary to find out. Many students have no clear sense of their values or what is important to them in a career.

   Many students do not have enough information about academic majors, curriculum or what is required to graduate with certain majors. They lack concrete information about different occupations, such as the tasks involved, entry requirements, salaries, job-market projections, etc.

   In addition, they lack knowledge about the relationships between academic majors and occupations. They often consider an educational and career choice the same. They need to learn that all majors do not lead to specific occupations, and those that don't are still viable paths to many interesting fields.

2. Many entering undecided student may not know how to make decisions. They may be dependent decision makers because they never had the opportunity to make decisions for themselves. Some may never have taken responsibility for decisions they made in the past. A few are not even aware that there is a decision-making process that can be learned and practiced effectively. They have not learned the skills necessary to implement this process.

3. Some undecided students are not ready to make educational or vocational decisions when they enter college. They may lack vocational maturity, or they may not have developed a vocational identity. They may not be able to picture themselves as a "lawyer" or a "banker" or "in advertising," etc.

4. A small number of students may be afraid to commit to a decision. These students may have difficulty in making a commitment to anything in their lives. They are fearful of the unknown or afraid to make the wrong choice. They are sometimes called indecisive students since they have difficulty making decisions about anything. They may need psychological help for a problem that can be debilitating.

5. Some undecided students simply do not feel pressure to decide. They have parental support for taking time to explore. They realize that they need more information before a sound decision can be made. A few students may even be apathetic. They are experiencing college and are in no hurry to make a commitment to a field of study.

6. Some students become undecided after their original choice of major is no longer viable or is thwarted. These "major-changers" may benefit from the same approaches used for entering undecided students; even though they have an established academic record, they may need additional help because they often have mixed feelings about the change.

Three Areas of Need for Undecided Students

The reasons that students are undecided can be summed up in three areas of need:

Informational deficits

Most students need information before making a sound choice of major or occupation. Not only do they lack information about their own interests, abilities and values, but they often need more concrete information about majors and career fields. They may not know the resources on campus where they can obtain the information they need to make a realistic choice.

Developmental deficits

Some students may need time to develop vocational maturity. They may be slower in accomplishing some of the developmental tasks that are essential for college students to complete, such as autonomy or identity development. They may lack appropriate decision-making experiences, may have counterproductive decision-making styles, or not know how to implement a decision once it is made.

Personal-social concerns

Undecided students may have conflicts that need to be resolved before they can progress in the exploration process. They may have a values-goal conflict where what they think is important does not fit with their goals (e.g., the social work major who wants a job that pays a large salary). They may have an interest-ability conflict where their interests and abilities don't match (e.g., a pre-med major who cannot pass chemistry). They may have a conflict with significant other people in their lives. They have difficulty separating the "shoulds" and "oughts" of others from their own.

Research-Based Characteristics of Undecided Students

Anxiety

Two groups of students have already been mentioned, the undecided student and the indecisive one. Both may be experiencing anxiety, but the type of anxiety is different.

Undecided students may be anxious because they have not made a choice. This is a normal anxiousness that is situation-specific.

Indecisive students have an anxiety that permeates their lives in general, and they have difficulty in reaching a decision about anything. These students have a debilitating anxiety and need to be referred for more long-term counseling.

Locus of control

Some undecided students have an external locus of control, that is they are not accustomed to taking responsibility for their decisions. They may perceive events as unrelated to their own behavior. Some have been dependent decision makers, and rely on others to continue making decisions for them. Until an internal locus of control is realized, they will have difficulty making decisions and taking full responsibility for them.

Identity

Some students are unclear as to who they are in a vocational sense. They are unable to relate personal characteristics to educational or occupational alternatives. There may be a normal developmental delay in establishing their identity, but in time it will develop. A few may have a concept of self that is shaky or distorted.

It is important to point out that many students who are ostensibly "decided" may also exhibit some of the characteristics that are outlined above. There may be "undecided" students who do not display any of the characteristics outlined. Each student must be viewed as an individual and approached in ways that help him or her and the advisor determine which variables apply.

Advising Strategies for Undecided Students

Advisor traits

Advisors of undecided students need certain traits that are not required for advising "decided" students.

- They need particular knowledge and skills, e.g., occupational information, counseling skills.

- They need to be generalists in the knowledge of academic programs, course requirements, and general curricular areas because undecided students often have two or more areas (often totally unrelated) that they wish to explore.

- Their attitudes toward undecidedness cannot be judgmental; undecidedness needs to be viewed as a normal developmental state in most students.

- They must be accessible. Accessibility is important because a continuous relationship needs to be established.

Advisor knowledge and skills

- Advisors must have the necessary general knowledge of academic options available on campus. They cannot be biased toward one discipline. Exploration needs to start where the students' interests begin.

- Advisors can use course exploration and scheduling to expose students to various alternatives, giving students the opportunity to test their interests and abilities in certain subjects.

- Advisors can teach schedule building as a process because careful scheduling can keep options open for a longer period of time. That is, common courses can be identified that cut across a variety of majors. Advisors can be interpreters of course requirements. Pre-scheduling is an important process as well, because this allows for more in-depth advising and reflection.

- Advisors can help students identify alternative majors with similar outcomes (e.g., there may be business-related majors outside the business college). A specific career goal can be attained by many educational paths in a variety of disciplines. A generalist advisor can often identify course requirements that overlap among alternative majors. In this way, careful scheduling can help keep various options open.

- Advisors can teach the decision-making process by helping students understand and use an orderly, logical sequence of steps. An advisor can also model the decision-making process by leading the student through a series of orderly steps during the advising exchange.

- Advisors need to use specially developed curricular materials that can help students see the differences and similarities between majors. These might include curriculum sheets for each major, lists of common general education courses across majors, and lists of how majors relate to interest areas (e.g., business, health professions, communications). Students should be encouraged to examine carefully the requirements for the junior and senior years, because this is where they can acquire a better understanding of what is involved. Constant updating ensures that the information is complete and accurate.

- Advisors must have good referral skills. Knowledge of campus resources that are relevant to a particular undecided student's need is not enough. Knowing when and how to refer are equally important. To ensure that a student follows through on a referral, an advisor can (a) explain the reason for the referral, (b) explain what can be expected when they arrive, and (c) define the precise task that needs to be completed. It is sometimes expedient to hand the student the phone to make an appointment in your presence. Always ask the student to return to you with the results of the referral contact.

- Advisors must create a comfortable environment so that students do not feel uncomfortable talking to an advisor about their undecidedness. They may feel they are the only ones experiencing this "problem." It is important that advisors convey feelings of openness, understanding and trust. When a student senses a caring, non-judgmental attitude, an ongoing helpful relationship can be established.

An Advising Model for Undecided Students

Advisors who follow a decision-making model when advising undecided students can ensure that all the necessary steps will be covered. The model below follows a sequence of steps that leads the student through an orderly decision-making process. This plan may be used in a 30-minute advising session or over an extended period of time.

Step 1: Help students analyze their situation

- How undecided is the student? (e.g., deciding between two alternatives, totally undecided).

- Why are they undecided? (The reasons they give will often suggest a place to start gathering information.)

- What majors are they considering? What majors have they eliminated? (If they can't answer either question, you can go through a complete list of your institution's majors and offer explanations of each; in this way you can help the student eliminate many majors.)

- Be sensitive to sex-role stereotyping in the alternatives they name.

- Listen for students' values; discuss how these might be important for identifying alternatives.

- A trusting advising relationship needs to be established. The first contact is critical.

Step 2: Help students organize a plan for exploring (information gathering phase)

- What type of information do they need (e.g., self-information, academic information, occupational information, decision-making information)?

- Devise a plan for gathering information (where? how? when?). To what campus resources do they need to be referred (e.g., people, libraries, computer systems, career center)?

- Establish a timeline for accomplishing the tasks in this step.

Step 3: Help students integrate information they have collected

- Integrate self-information (e.g., interests, abilities, values, experiences, skills) into possible majors/occupational fields.
- Help them understand academic and occupational relationships, including majors that lead to many occupational possibilities.
- Help them understand how different majors fit their values and goals.
- Broaden their horizons.
- Help them narrow down their options to two or three possibilities.

Step 4: Support students while they make decisions

- Offer feedback on how the decision-making process is progressing.
- Help identify external factors that need to be considered.
- Help students understand their decision-making style and how it affects the process.
- Support their decision once it is made.

Step 5: Help students initiate an action plan

- Help identify specific action steps to be taken.
- Help identify resources needed to take action.
- Help set up a realistic timetable for taking specific actions.
- Remind students that no plan is static; as changes take place, new decisions may need to be made.

Step 6: Encourage future contact

- Explain that you are available if they need to assess further or update their decision.
- Remind them that your role is one of support, that you are willing to act as a sounding board for future decisions and that you will provide continuity and stability as needed.

CASE STUDY

Anne is a second-term freshman who is undecided about a major and career field. In high school, Anne was very good in her math and science courses, but did not enjoy them as much as history and English. When she entered college she considered a pre-med major because of encouragement from her family and friends, who felt her science aptitude would make medicine a good field for her. She has also considered an English, journalism, biology or nursing major.

Anne has performed just above average in her math and chemistry courses her first term in college. She has received a grade of A in her humanities and social sciences courses and has enjoyed them very much. She particularly enjoyed psychology and a creative writing course that she took to fulfill general education requirements. Even if she continues her pre-med idea (which is becoming less interesting to her by the day), she still needs to select an academic major.

Anne comes to her advisor anxious and somewhat frustrated because she does not want to go home for the summer without a major. Her parents were delighted with her initial choice of pre-med, but will support her in any decision she makes. It is important to Anne that she please her parents. She wants to make them proud of her. Her brother graduated from medical school and is now a resident at a hospital in another state. Anne's sister is an engineering major and is a senior at another institution. She knows Anne would enjoy engineering as much as she does.

Anne has been so busy with her studies she has not had time to use any campus resources to help her choose a major. She is ready to take any steps to help her make a decision. How would you, as her advisor, help her begin the exploration process?

CASE STUDY

Matt entered college as a business major. His father, grandparents and uncles are all involved in a family business and he assumed he would continue the tradition. As he took the required courses for business, however, he did not feel his academic strengths and interests were met. He did not do well in math or accounting, and although he received a B in his first economics course, he did not enjoy it. Now as he progresses through his sophomore year, he is having real doubts about his choice of a business major.

Matt has been active in student government since his freshman year and was elected chair of several committees for his fraternity. He finds political science and history courses to be his best subjects. He has also enjoyed soliciting and writing advertising for the yearbook. His interests span so many areas that he is having difficulty identifying all the alternative majors that might be possible for him.

Matt is concerned about going home to talk to his father about the doubts he feels about the business major, but he is almost sure that he needs to change direction. As his advisor, how could you help him begin the exploration process? How would you help him resolve his dilemma with his father? •

Bibliography

Anderson, B. C., Creamer, D. G., & Cross, L. H. (1989). Undecided, multiple change, and decided students: How different are they? *NACADA Journal, 9*, 46-50.

Buescher, K. L., Johnston, J. A., Lucas, E. B., & Hughey, K. F. (1989). Early intervention with undecided college students. *Journal of College Student Development, 30*, 375-376.

Fuqua, D. R., & Hartman, B. W. (1983). Differential diagnosis and treatment for career indecision. *Personnel and Guidance Journal, 62*, 27-29.

Gordon, V. N. (1981). The undecided student: A developmental perspective. *Personnel and Guidance Journal, 59*, 433-439.

Gordon, V. N. (1984). *The undecided college student: An academic and career advising challenge.* Springfield, IL: Charles C. Thomas.

Gordon, V. N., & Steele, G. E. (1992). Advising major-changers: Students in transition. *NACADA Journal, 12*, 22-27.

Grites, T. L. (1981). Being "undecided" might be the best decision they could make. *The School Counselor, 29*, 41-46.

Hartman, B. W., Fuqua, D. R., & Blum, C. R. (1985). A path-analytic model of career indecision. *Vocational Guidance Quarterly, 33*, 231-240.

Holland, J. L., & Holland, J. E. (1977). Vocational indecision: More evidence and speculation. *Journal of Counseling Psychology, 24*, 404-415.

Krumboltz, J. D. (1992). The wisdom of indecision. *Journal of Vocational Behavior, 41*, 239-244.

Lewallen, W. (1993). The impact of being "undecided" on college-student persistence. *Journal of College Student Development, 34*, 103-112.

Lucas, M. S., & Epperson, D. L. (1990). Types of vocational undecidedness: A replication and refinement. *Journal of Counseling Psychology, 37*, 382-388.

Newman, J. L., Fuqua, D. R., & Minger, C. (1990). Further evidence for the use of career subtypes in defining career status. *Career Development Quarterly, 39*, 178-188.

Salomone, P. R. (1982). Difficult cases in career counseling: The indecisive client. *Personnel and Guidance Journal, 60*, 496-499.

Salomone, P. R., & McKenna, P. (1982). Difficult career counseling cases: Unrealistic vocational aspirations. *Personnel and Guidance Journal, 60*, 283-286.

Taylor, K. M. (1982). An investigation of vocational indecision in college students: Correlates and moderators. *Journal of Vocational Behavior, 21*, 318-329.

Theophilides, C., Terenzini, P. T., & Lorang, W. (1984). Freshman and sophomore experiences and change in major field. *Review of Higher Education, 7*, 261-278.

Titley, R. W., Titley, B., & Wolff, W. M. (1976). The major changers: Continuity or discontinuity in career decision process? *Journal of Vocational Behavior, 8*, 105-111.

Advising Graduate Students

Cheryl J. Polson, Ph.D.
Associate Professor, College of Education, Kansas State University

Research has consistently found that academic advisors are the most important reason why graduate students succeed to degree completion:

1. Numerous researchers have found that the quality of the interpersonal relationship between the advisor and the student is more important in determining whether a doctorate is received than academic ability based on GRE score or undergraduate GPA.

2. Existing research has found that a graduate student's relationship with the faculty advisor is regarded as the single most important aspect of the quality of their graduate experience.

3. Unfortunately, graduate students also report that the single most disappointing aspect of their graduate student experience is the quality of their relationship with their advisor.

4. The need for quality advising has been further documented by research in which graduate students were asked to select the student service they needed the most as they pursued their advanced degrees. Academic advising was reported as the number one service needed. Interestingly, this need was consistent across all age groups of advisees—those under 25, 25-32, 33-40, and 40 and over.

5. Seventy-eight percent of Polkosnik and Winston's sample (1986) indicated that a close personal relationship with their advisor was very important.

These findings clearly point to the difference the advising relationship can make—not only in a student's persistence through graduation but in the degree of satisfaction with graduate school experience.

Graduate students have multiple role and time commitments

Many graduate students return to campuses engaged in a variety of other roles beside those of student. They are frequently parents, spouses, full- or part-time employees, and active community volunteers and leaders.

These roles frequently require that the student prioritize obligations. The student role may not always get top billing. Advisors need to be aware of the multiple demands on graduate students, in addition to those commanded by the student role, and need to understand how these may impact the time the student can devote to completing degree programs. Realistic and attainable schedules must be established.

Graduate students bring a different quality and quantity of life experiences

Graduate students frequently bring to the institution a greater volume and different quality of life experiences than the traditional-age undergraduates.

This experience is a rich resource for learning, and often provides a foundation upon which to build new knowledge. It can also be a liability, in that life experiences have helped form the students' attitudes, values and beliefs. When views presented in the classroom conflict with long-held belief systems, students may be resistant. Advisors may need to encourage students to remain open and flexible to other views, as opposed to merely assisting them in dropping a class where their views conflict with the instructor's views.

Graduate students may be focused off-campus

They frequently live off-campus, are seldom aware of university-based student services and may find their support network in the community surrounding the institution.

Graduate students are often experiencing a variety of adult development tasks

The majority of these adult advisees are not in the process of identity formation, as are traditional-age undergraduates, but instead may be in the process of establishing new identities. It is important that graduate advisors become familiar with adult development theories and understand how the various life tasks/stages/phases will impact a students' academic career.

Frequently, graduate students have a clear educational goal in mind

Many graduate students seek advanced degrees to assist them with current challenges they face on the job or in their personal lives. Advisors should encourage them to look beyond their short-term work-related goals and explore how current activities relate to long-term goals. Equally important, advisors should help students evaluate how previous career and life decisions affect the viability of their current goals (i.e., do they have family obligations that restrict their mobility?).

Graduate students are consumers

They want their money's worth! They don't want to waste time. They expect their learning to be applicable to problems they confront on a daily basis.

Many of the characteristics listed above also describe adult undergraduate students who are entering (and re-entering) higher education today. But graduate students also bring unique advising concerns that relate specifically to the pursuit of advanced degrees.

The advising needs of graduate students differ for many reasons. It is difficult to establish universal "graduate student advisor guidelines" because the approaches to degree completion are varied (part-time versus full-time; on-campus versus off-campus), degree levels pursued vary (doctorate, master's, specialist's) and there are wide differences among academic disciplines in terms of content, research methodologies and desirable personality characteristics.

Continuous and Returning Graduate Students

There are two distinct groups of graduate students whose diverse nature and approach to graduate work warrant special attention. They are:

1. "Continuous" graduate students: advisees who enter graduate school immediately upon completion of undergraduate degree work.

2. "Returning" graduate students: advisees who are perhaps older, who haven't been enrolled in formal coursework for some time, and who are frequently employed part- or full-time.

The advising needs of continuous and returning graduate students differ in significant ways. These differences impact the activities of the advisor.

Characteristics of the continuous graduate student

1. They are familiar with the institution. They know the rules and regulations. They know where to go for what. (As a result, advisors need to spend less time helping them "negotiate the system.")

2. They are often beginning careers and may need more career counseling.

3. They frequently have less life and "real world" experiences.

4. They may need of assistance in gaining "real world" exposure.

5. They may not be torn by as many other demands as returning students.

Characteristics of the "returning" graduate student

Though some of the items listed below may also apply to the continuous graduate student, many are very descriptive of graduate students who have been away from the formal educational system for some time.

1. Many students at the master's and specialist levels (and some at the doctoral level) are part-time and frequently commute to campus (sometimes long distances).

This means there is little time for these students to take advantage of campus-based resources. Additionally, they may not be available for advising during the traditional graduate faculty office hours.

2. It is more difficult for these students to access "timely" information (such as deadlines for applying for financial aid, potential exam dates for GRE, application deadlines).

Where the continuous student probably has a resource network that helps them become aware of deadlines, the returning graduate student often relies on "fate" and calls or applies without awareness of clear established deadlines.

3. Unlike the continuous student who is familiar with the "system," returning graduate students may need more advisor assistance in "negotiating the system."

For example, the continuous student may be more likely to know about the institution's enrollment procedures, drop/add deadlines, financial aid availability and forms that must be completed at various times during the program. Until graduate students have "experienced" the institution, they may frequently rely on the faculty advisor to guide them through the maze.

4. These students may have rusty study skills and may need "refresher" courses. They are frequently less confident in their academic abilities and may have a fear of failure.

For example, many returning graduate students have not had to write academically since they were last enrolled. They may find they need assistance from advisors in locating a course to help them improve their writing skills.

5. Returning graduate students may require more advisor support, orientation and counseling.

For example, many graduate students report feeling lonely, isolated and frustrated with the graduate experience. In order to pursue an advanced degree, they may have left well-established support systems in another community. In instances such as this the advisor becomes the graduate student's institutional "lifeline."

Sometimes these learners feel frustrated with their loss of status at the institution. Some have left high-level positions of authority, only to be reduced to a lower status as "graduate students." This can create the need for some attitude adjustment. Again, advisors become critical in helping the student make this transition.

7. These students frequently have a higher stake in returning to school. They often have more invested, in time

and money. For example, some have left full-time, well-paying jobs to pursue degrees.

8. Some have put their lives (as well as those of their families) "on hold" until the degree is obtained.

Though it is important to understand these differences in working with graduate student advisees, there are some specific roles effective graduate student advisors play regardless of the students' orientation.

Stephen Brookfield, the author of *The Skillful Teacher*, believes it is very important that we look to our own experiences and reflect on them as we formulate our ideas about good teaching and advising. Advisors can either enhance the graduate experience or they can detract from the experience. If we are to retain graduate students until degree completion, it is important that we not only learn from our own experiences as graduate students, but that we broaden the role we play as advisors.

Five Essential Roles and Functions of Graduate Advisors

In *Developmental Academic Advising* (1986), Roger Winston and Mark Polkosnik outline the five essential roles and functions graduate student advisors must fulfill if they are to be effective: reliable information source, departmental socializer, advocate, role model and occupational socializer.

Reliable information source

There are a multitude of rules, regulations and deadlines to which graduate students need to be introduced. Although most graduate student handbooks outline these procedures, students haven't always read, understood or comprehended what has been presented.

Graduate students want information to be thorough, accurate and not just a "quick fix." They want to know not just the formal rules but the informal, unwritten ones as well. They often will seek to know what the rationale is behind the policies. Students don't have the "historical knowledge" that might help them better understand the established policies.

They want information in six areas: curriculum, careers, paperwork/logistics, financial support, time management and establishing realistic expectations.

Courses
Graduate students want information about:

1. Program requirements

2. Courses that will fit with their interests and career goals; courses that will maximize their career options

3. Course content

4. Courses available outside the department

5. Courses that will help them prepare for exams

6. Possible internship sites

7. Guidance in writing proposals, theses, dissertations

Careers
Research that has looked at the service needs of graduate students has found that the young, continuous graduate students want their advising to include information about:

1. Career strategies and planning

2. Availability of positions

3. Assistance in the job search

Paperwork/logistics
What needs to be done when? Deadlines for graduation, etc. They need help piloting their way through the system.

Financial support

1. Information about potential graduate assistantships available in and outside of the department

2. Information about external funding options

Time management

1. Need assistance balancing multiple roles.

2. A list of "things to do" isn't enough—they often need advisors to help them establish reasonable time limits and priorities. For example, students may need help with strategies for planning time to study for exams and strategies for conducting a review of the literature.

Expectations

1. Advisors must help advisees determine whether or not graduate school is the appropriate goal for them.

2. Advisors may be in the best position to know when advisees should be encouraged to explore other degree options or alternative career options.

3. Equally important, advisors must help students assess whether they can pass their exams.

Departmental socializer

Katz and Hartnett's well known book, *Scholars in the Making: The Development of Graduate and Professional Students* (1976), describes the loneliness, anxiety and role confusion graduate students experience due to the lack of rapport with the institution.

Another author terms this experience cultural discontinuity, describing graduate school as a new subculture that requires the student to assume new roles.

Some authors equate the graduate school experience to adolescence where the individual is trying on a new identity while being asked to conform to authority figures.

The key point to all of this is that advisors are central to the graduate student's transition into the institution and into the department. Graduate students who have relocated to pursue a degree program may not only lack local support systems, but are also entering a new role for which there are often unclear and unwritten rules. Advisors play a pivotal role in helping the student in this process.

In the role of departmental socializer advisors:

1. Provide help in understanding departmental politics. If faculty are competitive and lack shared purposes, it is important for students to understand departmental politics.

2. Provide opportunities for quality interaction, both inside and outside of the classroom. Research has consistently found that graduate students often enter degree programs with high expectations from the faculty/student relationship and consistently report disappointment in this aspect of their graduate work.

It is often up to the faculty advisor to initiate contact because new students may not be willing to take the risk. Students lack of knowledge of departmental "norms" may also make them reluctant to initiate contact.

Asking advisees to get a cup of coffee at the union or perhaps asking them to become involved in a research project are good ways to initiate this type of interaction.

Entering graduate advisees also need to be connected with established graduate students (those who already know the system and who can be good resources). Advisors often provide the linkage between these two groups of advisees.

All graduate students can benefit from such things as graduate student clubs or peer support groups for students who are at the same point in their graduate programs. Faculty advisors often ensure these clubs maintain their vitality.

Many departments offer new student orientations that are useful to the new student transitioning into graduate school. These orientations frequently involve all faculty and provide another effective way to socialize advisees.

Advocate

Graduate student advisors frequently get caught in the middle between the administration and the student while acting as the student's advocate. It may be difficult at times to interpret and respond to policies that may not seem beneficial or helpful to the student.

Therefore, the advocate role often involves the advisor in:

- Letting the student know there is someone out there "pulling" for him or her.
- Communicating that the student's talents and skills are valued.
- Providing support.
- Helping the student understand what to expect emotionally while completing the program.
- Extending the advising relationship beyond prescriptive advising issues. Allowing and encouraging the student to discuss issues that may not be directly linked to degree work but that impact performance (i.e., work commitments, family commitments). This may also involve discussing with students the life transitions that might have brought the student to the program and the issues that surround that return.

Role model

As a student's role model, the advisor helps the student learn professional terminology and helps the student "develop a vision of what scholars, researchers and professional practitioners should or should not be and do" (Winston & Polkosnik, 1988, p. 296).

Katz and Hartnett (1976) extends the advisor's function as a role model into the area he calls "careermanship," where advisees, whose employment goal is to remain in a higher education institution, learn how to politick, how to write grants and how to establish networks and perform other activities that may be critical to survival.

Winston and Polkosnik indicate there are several critical conditions which must be in place if an advisor is to serve as a role model. Advisors must not only be available to meet with students, but they must also convey a caring attitude. Advisors who serve as role models communicate that they are approachable. They also provide support for their advisees. Role models maintain consistent contact with their students throughout the degree program and demonstrate an interest in students as people.

Occupational socializer

In this role, advisors are involved in helping the student develop a sense of "professionalization" (Katz & Hartnett, 1976). Other labels have been assigned to this concept, such as helping students develop an "occupational identity" (Becker & Carper, 1956) and helping students develop a "professional self concept" (Pavalko & Holley, 1974).

Becker and Carper (1956) suggest that this is a four-step process.

1. **Development of the student's interests and skills.** This usually occurs during the first year in the program as the student becomes aware of the profession's literature and its approach to research. Students become more confident in their abilities and have a more accurate picture of the field.

2. **Acquisition of ideology.** After a period of questioning the degree program, the student decides to remain in the profession and adopts the fields' ideology for themselves.

3. **Internalization of motives.** During this stage the emphasis shifts towards employment. Advisees are more cognizant of the career choices available to them and become confident in their abilities as a member of their chosen profession.

4. Sponsorship. The advisor is central to this stage. Their role involves writing letters of recommendation—publicly recognizing the student as a viable contributor to the profession. The students' role is to then uphold the values of the profession, thus confirming their occupational identity.

Advisors must be involved in the student's development throughout the program if they are to uphold their sponsorship role. They must know the student's strengths and weaknesses, in order to be able to accurately represent the student when they receive inquiries.

The roles we have discussed are performed throughout the student's degree program. There do appear to be some key points in the advisees' career during which advisor intervention is critical. Various authors (Cox, 1992; Winston & Polkosnik, 1988) have provided their insights into these intervention points.

Selection/development of a program of study

1. Advisors should take into account students' interests, academic preparation, career goals and professional experiences while helping a student outline a program of study.

2. Advisors should keep in mind the student may still be in the career exploration mode. Courses selected might be designed to assist the student in exploring career options.

3. Advisors should encourage students to take a more active role in decision making.

4. Advisors should assess students' levels of intellectual and personal development and should identify courses that will strengthen their areas of weakness.

5. Advisors should help students identify courses that can enhance their chances for success in examinations and writing components (dissertation/thesis) of degree work.

Problems in classroom performance

1. Does the problem stem from a lack of preparation in the subject matter (e.g., inadequate undergraduate math sequence)? Is there a mismatch between the student and degree program?

2. If the problem stems from lack of appropriate academic preparation, advisors should assist the student in identifying appropriate "refresher" courses.

3. Advisors should help the student explore whether the problem stems from teaching/learning style preferences. For example: international students may have difficulty in highly interactive, seminar-type courses, or courses that are student-centered versus teacher-driven. Advisors should also provide students with suggestions on how to adapt their style to meet the teacher's expectations—or help them identify alternative course options if the problem appears too severe.

Comprehensive exams

1. The advisor should provide insight into the assessment process (be that oral exams, written and oral exams, etc.). Advisors can help students become aware of what they can expect during the exam process and what will be expected from them. Illustrate the positive aspects of the process (e.g., helps them bring closure to the coursework phase of the study; helps them synthesize large amounts of information they have read throughout the program).

2. Advisors can give clues as to how the student might prepare for the exam process (e.g., read over previous course notes, textbooks, exams).

3. Advisors can refer students to veteran students who have successfully completed this phase of their study.

4. Advisors should help eliminate potential anxiety by outlining the evaluation procedures (e.g., each committee member must read and assess written exams and may ask for a rewrite on some sections).

Dissertation

Bargar and Mayo-Chamberlain (1983) outline four steps to the dissertation phase—developing the topic, collecting the data, writing and oral defense—and provide clues as to what advisors should do at each phase.

1. Once a topic has been selected, advisors should reflect on how the student's committee will respond. Any potential resistance/objections from committee members should be explored with the student.

2. Advisors should encourage students to consult committee members throughout the proposal stage.

3. Advisors should help students establish appropriate and realistic timetables.

4. Advisors can suggest helpful ways to organize data and information. Advisors can also refer advisees to previous students who appeared to have developed successful techniques.

5. Advisors should critically review research findings with advisees, provide constructive feedback and consistently provide encouragement to help ensure completion.

6. Prior to the oral defense, advisors can explore the student's attitude about the process; discuss what can be expected to happen in the defense; explain the outside chairpersons role; provide encouragement about their ability to perform well; and explore areas in which the student might expect to be questioned.

7. During the exam process, the advisor can provide the student with nonverbal encouragement. Provide time following the exam for celebrating the moment with committee members or set aside time to debrief the student should the outcome not be positive.

8. Advisors should provide honest feedback about the student's performance.

Job placement

1. When possible, connect students with any potential networks that might help them attain employment.

2. Explore possible contacts with graduates of the program.

3. Help students identify professional organizations that provide placement service.

4. Refer students to local and regional chapters of professional organizations.

5. Make individual referrals.

6. Provide ongoing reassurance and supportive counseling.

Summary

Graduate student advisors play a pivotal role in ensuring that students persist to completion. The importance of the roles advisors play must not be overlooked. In summary, graduate advisors should encourage advising relationships that extend beyond merely the clerical functions. In doing so advisors should:

1. Be available to students.

2. Be current on the latest procedures and rules.

3. Serve as student advocates.

4. Build open, trusting relationships with advisees.

5. Encourage networking among graduate student advisees.

6. Help students establish realistic timetables and goals.

7. Provide constructive feedback about students' progress.

8. Extend the advising relationship to include the five roles and functions outlined by Winston and Polkosnik. •

Bibliography

Abedi, J., & Benkin, E. (1987). The effects of students' academic, financial, and demographic variables on time to the doctorate. *Research in Higher Education, 27*, 1, 3-14.

Baker, H. K. (1993). Counseling needs and graduate student characteristics. *Journal of College Student Development, 34*(1), 74-75.

Baker, H. K. (1992). Service needs of traditional age and adult graduate students. *NASPA Journal, 30(1)*, 20-29.

Bargar, R. R., & Mayo-Camberlain, J. (1983). Advisor and advisee issues in doctoral education. *Journal of Higher Education, 54*(4), 407-432.

Becker, J. S., & Carper, J. W. (1956). The development of identification with an occupation. *American Journal of Sociology, 6*, 289-298.

Beeler, K. D. (1991). Graduate student adjustment to academic life: A four-stage framework. *NASPA Journal, 28*(2) 163-171.

Berelson, B. (1960). *Graduate education in the United States.* New York: McGraw-Hill.

Berg, H. M., & Ferber, M. A. (1983). Men and women graduate students: Who succeeds and why? *Journal of Higher Education, 54*(6), 629-648.

Berger, B. A. (1992). Mentoring graduate students. *American Journal of Pharmaceutical Education, 56*, 79-82.

Bowen, W. G., & Rudenstine, N. L. (1992). *In pursuit of the Ph.D.* Princeton, NJ: Princeton University Press.

Brookfield, S. D. (1990). *The skillful teacher.* San Francisco: Jossey-Bass.

Brown, R. D. & Krager, L. A. (1985). Ethical issues in graduate education: Faculty and student responsibilities. *Journal of Higher Education, 56*(4), 403-417.

Butters, R. (Ed.). (1990). *Research on doctoral study: An annotated bibliography of doctoral dissertations on doctoral study.* Naples, FL: Creative Learning Services.

Clark, M. J. (1984). *Older and younger graduate students: A comparison of goals, grades, and GRE scores.* Princeton, NJ: Educational Testing Service. (ERIC Document Reproduction Service No. ED 245 645)

Council of Graduate Schools in the U.S. (1989). *Off-campus graduate education: A policy statement.* Washington, DC: Author. (ERIC Document Reproduction Service No. ED 331 417)

Cox, G. H., Jr. (October, 1992). *Enhancing graduate and professional advisement.* Paper presented at the 16th National Conference of the National Academic Advising Association, Atlanta, GA.

Criner, L. (February, 1991). *Self-direction for all-but-dissertation students: A model for the release of conviction, courage, and creative energy within.* Paper presented at the Fifth International Symposium on Adult Self-

Directed Learning. Norman: The Oklahoma Research Center for Continuing Professional and Higher Education, University of Oklahoma.

Dixon, C. (1993). Qualitative thoughts of the education doctoral process. *College Student Journal, 27*(2), 180-183.

Dyk, P. A. H. (1987). Graduate students' management of family and academic roles. *Family Relations, 36*, 329-332.

Egan, J. M. (1989). Graduate school and the self: A theoretical view of some negative effects of professional socialization. *Teaching Sociology, 17*, 200-208.

Ethington, C. A., & Smart, J. C. (1986). Persistence to graduate education. *Research in Higher Education, 24*(3), 287-303.

Girves, J. E., & Wemmerus, V. (1988). Developing models of graduate student degree progress. *Journal of Higher Education, 59*(2), 163-189.

Gunn, C. S., & Sanford, T. R. (1988). Doctoral student retention. *College and University, 63*(4), 374-382.

Jacks, P., Chubin, D. E., Porter, A. L., & Connolly, T. (1983). The ABCs of ABD: A study of incomplete doctorates. *Improving College and University Teaching, 3*, 74-81.

Katz, J., & Hartnett, R. T. (1976). *Scholars in the making: The development of graduate and professional students.* Cambridge, MA: Ballinger.

Kirk, J., & Wysocki, J. (1991). Factors influencing choice of graduate program and some implications for student advisement. *NACADA Journal, 11*(2), 14-20.

Kowalik, T. F. (1989). What we know about doctoral student persistence. *Innovative Higher Education, 13*(2), 163-171.

Kuh, G. D., & Thomas, M. L. (1983). The use of adult development theory with graduate students. *Journal of College Student Personnel, 24*(1), 12-19.

Lacefield, W. E., & Mahan, J. M. (1988). Factors influencing satisfaction of nontraditional students with mainstream graduate programs. *Educational Reseach Quarterly, 12*(2), 36-50.

Malaney, G. D. (1987). *A decade of research on graduate students: A review of the literature in academic journals.* Paper presented at the Annual Meeting of the Association for the Study of Higher Education, Baltimore, Maryland, November 21-27, 1987. (ERIC Document Reproduction Service No. ED 292 383)

Malaney, G. D. (1987). Why students pursue graduate education, how they find out about a program, and why they apply to a specific school. *College and University, 62*(3), 247-258.

Mallinckrodt, B., & Leong, F. T. L. (1992). International graduate students, stress, and social support. *Journal of College Student Development, 33*(1), 71-78.

McCaffrey, S. S., Miller, T. K., & Winston, R. B. (1984). Comparison of career maturity among graduate students and undergraduates. *Journal of College Student Personnel, 25*, 127-137.

Mooney, C. J. (1991, Jan. 16). The dissertation is still a valuable requirement, survey finds, but graduate students say they need better faculty advising. *The Chronicle of Higher Education*, pp. A15, A22.

Pavalko, R. M., & Holley, J. W. (1974). Determinants of a professional self-concept among graduate students. *Social Science Quarterly, 55*, 462-477.

Polkosnik, M. C., & Winston, R. B. (1986). Graduate students' views of their experiences. *The College Student Affairs Journal, 6*(3), 30-42.

Pruitt-Logan, A. S., & Isaac, P. D. (Eds.). (1995). Student services for the changing graduate student population. *New Directions for Student Services, No. 72.* San Francisco, Jossey-Bass.

Rimmer, S. M., Lammert, M., & McClain, P. (1982). An assessment of graduate student needs. *College Student Journal, 16*(2), 187-197.

Rosenblatt, H. S., & Christensen, C. (1993). "Welcome to the whole family": A graduate student orientation. *College Student Journal, 27*(4), 502-505.

Selke, M. J., & Wong, T. D. (1993). The mentoring-empowered model: Professional role functions in graduate student advisement. *NACADA Journal, 13*(2), 21-26.

Smart, J. C. (1987). Student satisfaction with graduate education. *Journal of College Student Personnel, 28*, 218-222.

Smith, E. P., & Davidson, W. S., II. (1992). Mentoring and the development of African-American graduate students. *Journal of College Student Development, 33*, 531-539.

Sorenson, G., & Kagan, D. (1967). Conflicts between doctoral candidates and their sponsors. *Journal of Higher Education, 38*, 17-24.

Tarule, J. M., Weathersby, R. (1979). Adult development and adult learning styles: The message for nontraditional graduate programs. *Alternative Higher Education, 4*(1), 11-23.

Urbano, M., & Jahns, I. (1986). A developmental approach to doctoral education. *Journal of Nursing Education, 25*(2), 76-78.

Vickio, C. J., & Tack, M. W. (1989). Orientation programming for graduate students: An institutional imperative. *NACADA Journal, 9*(2), 37-42.

Winston, R. B., Jr., & Polkosnik, M. C. (1988). Advising graduate and professional students. In R. B. Winston, Jr., T. K. Miller, S. C. Ender, T. J. Grites, & Associates (Eds.), *Developmental Academic Advising* (pp. 287-314). San Francisco: Jossey-Bass.

Advising Transfer Students

Thomas J. Kerr, Ph.D.
Associate Provost, Rowan College of New Jersey

Margaret C. "Peggy" King, Ed.D.
Assistant Dean for Student Development, Schenectady County
Community College

Introduction

"Education is, or should be, a seamless web" (Boyer, 1988, p. 36), an interconnecting system where qualified students can move systematically from one educational level to another or from one institution to another without unnecessary roadblocks in their way.

Transfer—the movement from an associate degree-granting institution to a baccalaureate degree-granting institution—is a defining characteristic of American higher education today. Yet while the process looks good on paper, that reality is that transferring is not necessarily a smooth process. Concerns about that reality prompted the American Council on Education to develop a policy statement entitled "Setting the National Agenda: Academic Achievement and Transfer." The preamble to that statement is as follows:

> Why a national agenda for academic achievement and transfer? Why now? Because we as a nation rely heavily on our higher education system to unlock the doors of opportunity, to foster equity, to promote success and encourage advancement by the full range of citizens. Because the quality of public life we seek requires a highly educated citizenry. Because our economic prosperity is uniquely dependent upon the effectiveness of our colleges and universities. Because as a nation, we continue to value fairness, decency and social justice.
>
> America's community colleges in particular embody our hopes for the future. For millions of students, they are the entry point to higher education and thus serve as the avenue to intellectual and economic growth. Entry to four-year colleges or universities by community college students...is central to the realization of equal opportunity in education. Community colleges and universities must strengthen their curricular and instructional links so that qualified students can transfer easily and routinely, with full expectation of success upon transfer (p. 1).

Two-year colleges enroll approximately 43 percent of the nation's undergraduates and 51 percent of all first-time entering freshmen (Boyer, 1988, p. 6). To be more specific, in 1988, community colleges enrolled 56 percent of Hispanic undergraduates, 54 percent of Native American undergraduates, 42 percent of black undergraduates, and 40 percent of Asian undergraduates (p. 9). These populations make up about 30 percent of community college enrollment. In California alone, about 80 percent of the under-represented ethnic minority students who are enrolled in postsecondary institutions are in the California community colleges (Kerschner, 1990).

Although many entering two-year college students do not want or need to go on to a four-year college to attain their career goals, we need to recognize that for others, transfer is appropriate and desirable. Research shows, however, that of those students who initially plan to transfer, many do not. Watkins, writing in the *Chronicle of Higher Education* (Feb. 7, 1990, p. A37), has estimated that while as many as one-third of the students in two-year colleges plan to continue their education in a four-year college or university, only 15 to 25 percent actually do so.

Other studies cited in the ACE paper indicate similar percentages. As we consider the fact that entry to four-year colleges and universities by community college students is central to the realization of access and equal opportunity in education, these statistics become a matter for concern. And they have implications for advising personnel at both the sending and receiving institutions.

Two-year college students do not transfer for many reasons, some of which are perfectly appropriate (e.g., career interests) and some of which may be beyond our control (e.g., money). Some do not transfer because of a lack of encouragement, because attending a four-year college has never been viewed as an option, or because of fear and low self-esteem. These are issues that must be addressed by those working at the two-year college level.

Advisors have a responsibility to identify, early in the process, qualified students who have yet to view transfer as an option, and to provide them with the support, encouragement and skills needed to explore such transfer opportunities successfully. Because many of these students may not be enrolled in traditional transfer programs, this may not be an easy process, but it is important, particularly in working with multicultural students.

Advisors at four-year institutions have a responsibility to be welcoming to transfer students, to get to know them as individuals with complex histories, to help them make the adjustments they will surely need to make, and to provide the support and encouragement many of them will need to be successful.

Advising at the Two-Year Level

Identifying and encouraging prospective transfer students

Many students enter two-year colleges with little or no self-esteem, with little support for continuing their education, and with few ideas about transfer options. As a result, it is incumbent upon faculty advisors to try to identify students with the potential for transfer, and to provide the support and encouragement needed for them to consider continuing their education. Such students can be identified in a number of ways:

- Review standardized/placement test scores

- Discuss students' interests and assessment of abilities.

- Discuss students' experiences in relationship to educational goals; identify any other academic preparation beyond high school

- Have students identify strengths

- Have students identify five reasons they have selected their particular major/career

- Monitor students' academic progress; recognize good academic performance

Once the advisor recognizes that a student is considering transfer, it is important to make sure that the student is in an appropriate degree program and that he or she understands the differences between transfer degrees (Associate in Arts, Associate in Science) and career degrees (Associate in Applied Science, Associate in Occupational Studies). Transfer degree programs parallel the first two years of a four-year program and include a significant number of liberal arts courses, while career programs provide practical courses designed to prepare students for employment. Although students can still transfer with an AAS or AOS degree, they will probably not be able to transfer the career-specific courses. Advisors must be able to explain the differences in what students can do with each specific degree.

Once students have made the decision to transfer and are enrolled in appropriate degree programs, the advisor must identify and monitor student progress in key courses critical for student success in the major. For example, students pursuing a major in engineering must do well in such courses as physics and calculus, and students interested in law must do well in English. If they experience difficulty in preparatory courses, a discussion about the appropriateness of their career choice would be in order.

Discussion Questions

1. Select two transfer degree programs with which you are familiar. What courses would you consider critical for student success in those majors and why?

2. List five transfer and five career programs at your institution that are not in your field and identify one resource person for each who could answer questions about the program.

3. For those programs in your field, identify the differences between one transfer and one career program, e.g., Business AS and Business AAS.

4. Identify potential career opportunities for graduates of a career program and graduates who go on to complete a four-year degree in your field.

Preparing for the transfer process

Students should be advised to follow a series of steps when preparing for transfer to a four-year college or university. These include:

- Attend a general information meeting or workshop on transfer

- Select an academic major

- Select a college(s)

- Speak with transfer admissions staff at the college(s) being considered

- Visit the campus(es)

- Request application materials from each school's office of admissions

- Request financial aid materials from each school's financial aid office

- If required, take the SAT or ACT

- Submit application(s) for admission and all other requested documents by the specified deadlines

- Submit appropriate applications for financial aid consideration

- Have an official transcript sent at the end of each term

- Submit the required admissions deposit

- Submit housing deposit if needed

- Arrange off-campus housing if needed

- Attend campus orientation program(s)

The earlier a student can identify prospective four-year schools, the better. Once this is done, the advisor can make students aware of articulation agreements and can review the courses required. If these agreements are not widely publicized and made available to faculty advisors, the student should be referred to the appropriate person on campus for that information.

Every campus has resource people and/or materials for transfer that students can utilize. These resources may include the following:

- A transfer counselor/advisor, someone who specializes in the transfer process and who is knowledgeable about transfer opportunities and application procedures

- A computerized career guidance system such as DISCOVER, which can help students gather information about schools and help them narrow down their choices based on information such as major, cost, location, etc.

- A collection of college catalogs and other printed resources such as *The College Handbook* or the *Guide to Four-Year College Majors*

- Articulation agreements

The advisor should be familiar with the resources available on his or her campus and their location so that students can be referred to them.

Discussion Questions

1. List articulation agreements your institution has with four-year colleges and universities. Are these agreements comprehensive for all majors or restricted to a few? Are different GPA's required beyond the core requirements specified in your degree program?

2. Where can you and/or your advisee go for more information on existing articulation agreements?

Writing Transfer Recommendations

Faculty advisors may be called upon to write recommendations for their advisees for transfer. By keeping records of contacts with advisees, faculty advisors will have appropriate information to include in those recommendations. That information typically includes the students' planned major, their GPA, their extracurricular activities and/or work experiences, and the advisor's personal recommendation (if you are comfortable making one).

Discussion Question

1. Writing recommendations for students you have gotten to know well and for students you feel confident will be successful is relatively easy. How would you respond to a request from a student you didn't know well and whose record was marginal? If you agreed to write a recommendation, what would you say?

Complications in Successful Transfer

The advisor has a responsibility to prepare students for some of the complications they may encounter either during the transfer process or when they arrive at the four-year campus. Consequently, knowledge of transfer issues at the major receiving institutions will be helpful. Those complications may include:

1. **Lack of a welcoming environment.** Some four-year institutions do not provide a welcoming environment for transfer students, particularly multicultural and adult students. If students chose to attend such institutions, the advisor has a responsibility to make the student aware of the environment and to discuss how the student might deal with it.

2. **Inequitable treatment.** At some four-year institutions, transfers are not treated the same as native juniors. They may be the last to register and the last to receive housing. The advisor should make students aware that they may encounter such situations and help the student plan how to deal with them. This may include identifying a contact person on the four-year campus who would be able to assist the student, or developing alternative plans such as other housing choices.

3. **Academic and articulation issues.** Some four-year institutions will not readily accept credits from two-year colleges; will accept credits as "electives" rather than as required courses; or will require students to test out of courses they have successfully completed. The advisor should make students aware that this may happen and discuss strategies for dealing with the situation. Again, having the name of a contact person on the four-year campus would be beneficial.

4. **Bureaucratic obstacles.** Four-year institutions often rely heavily on bureaucratic forms of management that can discourage students because of confusing rules, regulations and requirements. Insensitive or mechanical decision-making may ignore the complex histories of many transfer students and may thus deny opportunities to students who have the potential to succeed. Students need to be aware of this. They also need to be aware of admissions policies and deadlines, and need to learn that deadlines in a four-year school are generally not as flexible as they may be in a two-year setting.

5. **Inadequate support systems.** Some four-year colleges and universities are larger and more impersonal than community colleges, and may lack many of the support systems that exist on the two-year campus. Two-year college advisors need to prepare students for what they will encounter upon transferring. If possible, provide

linkages with former students who have transferred to an institution, or help the student make connections with appropriate staff at the four-year school. Encourage students to attend orientation programs at the four-year campus, reminding them that although they have college experience, they need to learn about their new campus. Encourage them to plan for how they will deal with support services that may be less intrusive or less well-developed.

6. **Age impediments.** As indicated earlier, some institutions are not receptive to returning adults. In addition to treating adults like traditional-age students, they may not have programs and services available at times adults need them. If adults choose to attend such institutions, they need to plan ahead about course scheduling and support services.

Discussion Questions

1. Identify one campus to which your graduates transfer. What resources are available on that campus to assist the student?

2. One way to help transfer students deal with the above issues is to connect them with former transfer students who have gone to a given institution. Identify steps you can take to match up current transfer students with those planning to transfer to the same institution.

3. How can you make your advisees aware of relevant academic policies and procedures at the four-year school?

Advising at the Four-Year Level

The role of articulation

The art of facilitating transfer consists of balancing coordination with institutional autonomy. Often this involves improvements in communications, expenditures of time and energy, and acceptance of some restrictions on a four-year institution's autonomy (Wechsler, 1989). The most critical barrier to transfer is not having a system or procedure in place that properly evaluates a student's past college performance; is consistent across the institution; and is continually evaluated and revised on a regular schedule.

In this regard, articulation, which is probably the most important component of transfer, ensures continuity in coursework transferred within and between institutions. Many attempts at transfer facilitation fail over the issue of articulation. The receiving four-year institution expects that a student's transfer coursework is adequate preparation for the next course in the sequence. Unless all parties are committed to clarifying the articulation process, it will not

work smoothly over the course of time. Students too often find that although they have been accepted to a four-year college or university and have gained degree credit for their completed work, these credits are considered elective rather than required courses and consequently they have to take additional requirements to complete a baccalaureate degree. This can be a significant barrier to transfer students.

Factors affecting the success of articulation

An articulation agreement, while important in transfer, will not be successful unless it is properly promoted, regularly updated and evaluated using student academic performance as the primary criterion.

Harold Wechsler's monograph, "The Transfer Challenge," documents a study conducted by the Association of American Colleges in the late 1980s. As part of the study, each participating institution was required to agree to a set of formal conditions that assumed that successful implementation of a transfer program required improved ongoing communication among institutional counterparts (administrators, faculty members, students and support personnel) as follows:

- Institution of formal arrangements for consultation and procedures for concluding agreements between presidents and chief academic officers of both the four-year institution and the two-year institution.

- Provision for regular meetings of admissions officers, academic counselors and financial aid officers at participating institutions.

- Formal and informal exchanges between the faculty of the institutions so that faculty members learn firsthand about the academic programs on each campus.

- Opportunity for students from cooperating institutions to spend time on each campus, talk with other students and attend classes.

- Regular consultations between staff members of learning development centers and advisors to share information and understanding of the special characteristics, attributes, problems and needs of transfer students.

How can we tell if an articulation agreement is successful? An obvious measure is the number of students who transfer from the participating schools. Quantity of students, however, is not the true measure for the success of an articulation agreement. What truly indicates the success of a program is the academic performance of the students once they have transferred. The advisor plays an important role in the ongoing evaluation of an agreement. Only after an agreement has been in existence for some time can its effectiveness be properly evaluated. It is not uncommon to modify initial judgments of course equivalency, when it becomes clear that course content does not properly prepare students for follow-up courses at the receiving institution. The advisor plays a key role in the constant "fine-tuning" of an active articulation agreement.

Discussion Questions

1. Where can you go to look at the past performance of students from a given college?

2. Are you aware of grading policies from your sending institutions? Is that important? Why? How can you get that information if it is not available?

After transfer: The first advising session

Advisors on four-year campuses cannot assume that because students have had college experience, they will be able to reach their potential immediately. Advising, as well as other support services, must be sensitized to the unique needs of transfer students if we are to expect them to be successful in the transition from one institution to another.

Transfer students are less likely to complete a degree (Pascarella, 1986; Trent & Medsker, 1968). Johnson (1987) found that transfer student persistence was strongly associated with perceptions of the work-relatedness of their degree, their integration, performance and satisfaction with their academic program, and their intent to continue in college. Academic advisors can have a direct impact on a student's integration into the new academic environment and consequently on student satisfaction with academic programs.

Advisors can ease the adjustment of the transfer student to the university by establishing a welcoming atmosphere. The initial advising sessions are critical, for the advisor will be called upon to provide an orientation to the new college or university, and to deal with special problems and concerns unique to transfer students. Although some students transfer by design, i.e., two-year to four-year, others transfer because their original plans did not work out. These students will be particularly anxious about starting off well at a new school.

The following are topics that the advisor might consider covering with the student during the first advising session:

- Introductions and getting to know the student as an individual

- Discussion about the student's educational and career plans

- Discussion of how courses completed fit into the four-year program

- Discussion of the differences between the two-year and four-year institution

- Discussion of the student's needs and the resources available on campus to help meet those needs

Discussion Questions

1. Identify five differences between a transfer student and an entering freshman.

2. What challenges do these differences present to you as an advisor?

3. Give an example of a student who has transferred to your institution without the appropriate background/coursework for the major they have selected. What did you do? What could you have done?

Evaluation of credentials/proper placement

The existence of an articulation agreement, if it in fact does exist, does not reduce the importance of academic advising for the transfer student. The transfer student—like the freshman student—brings special advising issues that must be addressed by the advisor.

If the transfer evaluation has been completed: have courses been examined and determined to be "equivalent" because the content is identical? Will the material presented in a particular course provide the academic skills and competencies necessary for the student to be successful in a higher level course? It is not in the best interest of the student to grant equivalent credit unless the academic competency necessary to complete the next level course has been achieved.

Constant evaluation and review of the academic records of students who come from feeder schools over time will quickly provide the advisor with hard facts on whether courses were evaluated for content or "competency." Articulation agreements must be viewed as dynamic—and must be reviewed and monitored as curricula are revised and new courses are developed.

Prior to advising the new transfer student, the advisor needs to examine the student's past academic records critically. The transcript will provide indications of the student's strengths, weaknesses and areas of interest. The transcript and supporting documents can also provide early identification of a student's special abilities or problems (e.g., returning adults, students with learning disabilities).

The most compelling issue for transfer students is "how long will it take to complete degree requirements?" Therefore, early in the advising process, advisors should plan to discuss with students which credits have transferred and how these credits apply toward graduation requirements.

Advisors should also explain why certain courses do not transfer and should explain how to appeal the transfer evaluation.

Discussion Questions

1. Identify at least five courses the student must have completed at the two-year college in order to move into required courses for the junior year.

2. Are you aware of course sequencing issues within the student's major? Give an example of how the timing of when a required course is completed would impact a student's graduation date.

3. What are the critical/key courses in your program for a student's success?

Academic policies and procedures

Transfer students feel a great deal of pressure as soon as they arrive at the four-year institution. They must make important decisions about courses, programs and activities before they are familiar with the college or university. Unless there is adequate information provided to them, they often assume that academic procedures in such areas as grading, withdrawals, academic standards, etc., will be the same as those of their previous schools.

As institutions become larger, they often must rely on bureaucratic forms of management that can discourage students with confusing and conflicting rules, regulations and requirements and may create barriers to success. Consider the following: A student failed in the first college experience and was dismissed. Ten years later the student returned to a community college and completed an associate degree, showing high motivation and earning excellent grades. If overall grade point average is used as the criteria for admission to the four-year school, a qualified student could be denied admission.

One way to address this issue is to provide transfer students with information that makes the transition to the new environment easier. Such information could include: a transfer brochure, curriculum guides for the student's major, information sheets on academic advising and tutorial services, information about financial aid available for transfers, how-to-register bulletins, career counseling information, and so forth.

Even more important, however, is the academic advising the transfer student receives. Beal and Noel (1980), reporting on a national survey conducted by the American College Testing Program and the National Center for Higher Education Management Systems, noted that "inadequate academic advising" emerged as the strongest negative factor in student retention, while "a caring attitude of faculty and staff" and "high quality of advising" emerged among the strongest positive factors (pp. 44-45). Kemerer (1985) has stated, "Virtually every study of retention has shown that a well-developed advising program is an important retention strategy. Advisors who are knowledgeable, enthusiastic, and like working with students can often make the difference between a potential dropout and a persister" (p. 8).

Discussion Questions

1. Transfer students typically come from institutions with less rigid academic policies and procedures. How can you prepare them for what they will experience at your institution?

2. Does your institution have any of the following unique academic policies and procedures? How can you make the student aware of them?

- GPA within major that is different from the school GPA

- Minimum level of credits at certain academic level, e.g., 12 credits at C or better

- Only ___ credits of D grades can count toward the degree regardless of the overall GPA

- If a student fails the same course more than twice they will be automatically suspended

- A time limit on degree completion

- A time limit for withdrawals before a grade must be submitted

Supporting resources

Academic advising may be the only structured service on the campus that provides a student with the opportunity to interact with a concerned representative of the institution. Because of this, academic advisors play a key role in helping students become integrated within the academic and social systems on campus, which in turn contributes to student growth, satisfaction and persistence. Advising can therefore be viewed as the hub of the student service wheel, providing the linkages with other support services such as career planning, counseling, financial aid and tutoring (King, 1987).

Transfer students often feel like the "odd man out" because they have lost the opportunity to establish a network of friends and acquaintances. Institutions are careful to develop opportunities for freshmen to become "connected," because research supports the need to provide these connections. Tinto (1987) pointed out that the rate of student departure from higher education systems is highest during the first year of college (p. 21) and is particularly high during the first six weeks of the student's first term (p. 49).

Tinto goes on to postulate that transfer students experience many difficulties in adjusting to a new campus because they are rarely given an orientation to academic programs and services. As a result, transfer students face an important disadvantage when compared to students who begin as freshmen. It is expected that freshmen must adjust to greater academic demands than they have experienced before, and they are provided with extensive orientation and support systems, special freshman seminars, peer advising, student organizations, study skill seminars, tutoring, etc. They have opportunities to explore educational and social offerings of the university community, to establish friendships and to become familiar with the campus milieu. If we are serious about promoting transfer, should not these same opportunities be provided to the transfer population?

Discussion Questions

1. What resources exist on your campus to assist transfer students in assimilating into your institution, e.g., transfer newsletter, transfer student lunches with prior transfers, mentoring program, transfer student directory? What resources should be developed? Who should have responsibility?

2. Does your institution have a separate orientation for transfers? What is included? What should be included? Are you involved? Should you be?

3. What academic and social opportunities exist for students to interact with the faculty outside the classroom? What should exist?

4. How can you facilitate a transfer student's participation in activities? Why is that important?

5. How can you facilitate a transfer student's interaction with faculty or with graduate students with similar interests? Why is that important?

Special issues for the nontraditional transfer student

The term "nontraditional student" encompasses a variety of student populations: multicultural students, international students, women, adults, single parents and those with disabilities. Each of these populations brings unique characteristics and special needs to any campus.

Many nontraditional transfer students have complex histories and personal circumstances that impact their ability to be successful in college. They may be single parents; they may have been forced to make a career change due to layoff or injury; they may be in recovery; they may be adjusting to a different culture with different forms of communication; or they may have been in prison.

Whatever the history, it is important for the faculty advisor to learn about and understand that history and to recognize that the student brings valuable experiences that will bear on decision making. Whenever possible, the advisor needs to be available at times convenient for the student, particularly for those working full time, or those with children. The advisor also needs to recognize the other commitments nontraditional students have that may affect their availability for classes.

Discussion Questions

1. Does your institution hold faculty development workshops that deal with issues related to nontraditional transfer students? When are they offered?

2. Who would you categorize as a nontraditional transfer student at your institution? What are the unique characteristics they bring to your campus? What are their special needs? How is your institution addressing those needs? How can you address them? What else could be done?

Assisting students with career planning

The baccalaureate degree is only one step in the continuum of goals for students attending institutions of higher education. Does the college or university have a responsibility to assist students with life after they receive their four-year degree? If so, what is the role of the academic advisor in the process?

Career advising, whether for a professional position or for graduate school, is an important part of academic advising because students are concerned about their work life after college. Helping students assess their needs and helping them understand the career decision-making process are important advisor responsibilities. Career advising includes helping students explore or confirm academic choices and helping them understand the occupational implications (direct or indirect) of the academic decisions they are considering or have made (Gordon, 1990).

To achieve this objective, advisors must be knowledgeable not only about the academic and occupational relationships within specialized areas, but also about career resources on campus so that appropriate referrals may be made. Referring students to appropriate resources on campus in a timely way is an important aspect of career advising.

Academic advising and career advising are closely linked together. Pascarella and Terenzini (1991) found that a student's choice of academic major influences the college experience. They indicate that skills learned in a major relate indirectly to job fit and satisfaction. Development of materials relating to the integration of academic and career information to assist students will require a cooperative effort, and advisors have an obligation to help students clarify their values and set goals that may relate to career and life planning.

Discussion Questions

1. Does your institution have a program to prepare students for the world of work, e.g., résumé writing, interview skills, understanding corporate culture? What offices have that responsibility?

2. Are workshops required before students can access job placement opportunities on campus?

3. Does your institution provide opportunities for co-op and internship experiences? How do students access these opportunities?

4. As an academic advisor, what do you see your role as in preparing students for employment?

5. Is there a program or service on your campus to assist students in the application process for graduate school? Who has that responsibility?

6. What are the steps in the transfer process from baccalaureate institution to graduate school?

7. What do you see as your role in encouraging graduates to pursue continuing education opportunities? •

Bibliography

American Council on Education. (1991). *Setting the national agenda: Academic achievement and transfer.* Washington, DC: Author.

Beal, P. E., & Noel, L. (1980). *What works in student retention: The report of a joint project of the American College Testing Program and the National Center for Higher Education Management Systems.* Iowa City, IA: ACT and NCHEMS.

Boyer, E. L. (1988). *Building communities: A vision for a new century.* Washington, DC: American Association for Community and Junior Colleges.

Gordon, V. N. (1990) *Handbook of academic advising.* Westport, CT: Greenwood Press.

Johnson, W., & Packer, A. (1987). *Workforce 2000: Work and workers for the twenty-first century.* Indianapolis, IN: Hudson Institute.

Kemerer, F. R. (1985). The role of deans, department chairs and faculty in enrollment management. *College Board Review, 134*, 4-8.

King, M. C. (1993). *Academic advising, retention, and transfer. New Directions for Community Colleges, No. 82.* San Francisco: Jossey-Bass.

Pascarella, E. T. (1986). Long-term persistence of two-year college students. *Research in Higher Education, 24*(1), 47-71.

Pascarella, E. T., & Terenzini, P. T. (1991). *How college affects students.* San Francisco: Jossey-Bass.

Tinto, V. (1987). *Leaving college: Rethinking the causes and cures of student attrition.* Chicago: University of Chicago Press.

Trent, J., & Medsker, L. (1968). Beyond high school: A psychological study of 10,000 high school graduates. San Francisco: Jossey-Bass.

Watkins, B. T. (1990). Two-year institutions under pressure to ease transfers. *Chronicle of Higher Education, 36*(21), A1, A37-38.

Wechsler, H. (1989). *The transfer challenge: Removing barriers, maintaining commitment.* Washington, DC: Association of American Colleges.

Advising Students of Color

Thomas Brown
Dean of Advising Services, St. Mary's College of California

Mario Rivas, Ph.D.
Director of the Advising Center and Director of the Learning Assistance Center,
San Francisco State University

An earlier version of this article appeared in New Directions for Community Colleges, No. 82. Copyright 1993, Jossey-Bass, Inc.

Introduction

As academic advisors, we will achieve success in supporting the educational development of multicultural populations only when we are aware of difference and recognize that difference is a fact of the human experience; when we become proficient in identifying and using advising methods that are appropriate for and effective with the diverse student constituencies we serve; when we become aware of how our individual expectations and assumptions affect our work with students of color, and, most critically, when we understand and commit to the principle that students of color, like all students, are capable of achieving growth and success in the postsecondary environment if we care and respond to them in appropriate ways.

Multicultural populations in education

In *Guess Who's Coming to College: Your Students in 1990*, Harold Hodgkinson (1983) suggested that American colleges and universities were systematically ignoring the rapidly increasing percentage of minorities in American life. He went on to charge that higher education structures had been weak in planning for future generations of college students, who would increasingly be black, Asian, Hispanic and Native American (persons of color/ethnic minorities).

In our society, general trends influence local action, and the trends are clear. According to a U.S. Census Bureau projection, between 1995 and 2025, the white population will increase by 17.8 percent. During the same period, the black population will increase by 45.8 percent, American Indian by 50.6 percent, Hispanic by 103 percent, and Asian by 164 percent (Source: U.S. Census Bureau, *Current Population Reports*, pp. 25-26). Projections for the year 2000 point out that Asians, blacks, Hispanics and American Indians will comprise 33.5 percent of school age children (Kominski & Adams,1991). In her remarks to the 14th conference of the National Academic Advising Association, Blandina Cardenas-Ramirez, former director of the American Council on Education (ACE) Office of Minority Concerns, pointed out that at least 50 percent of the K-12 students in 25 of the nation's largest cities are Asian, black or Latino.

Why focus on multicultural advising?

Each year, the American Council on Education (ACE) produces a Status Report on Minorities in Higher Education. The 1993 report points out that even as the proportion of blacks and Latinos in the U.S. population continues to increase, they continue to be underrepresented in higher education. In 1992, only 33.8 percent of African-American and 37.1 percent of Hispanic high school graduates ages 18 to 24 were enrolled in a college or university compared with 42.2 percent of whites (Carter & Wilson, 1994). Only 19 states indicated gains in both the number and proportion of bachelor's degrees earned by American Indians and that progress was offset by declines in several key western and southwestern states, such as California, New Mexico and Texas, where the numbers declined by 4.4 percent, 21.8 percent and 17.1 percent, respectively (Carter & Wilson, 1994). Finally, while Asian Americans as a group continue to participate and succeed in higher education at levels that exceed even the white population, there are ethnic groups within the Asian Pacific Islander category whose achievement and success does not support the myth of Asians as a "model minority" for whom no additional efforts need to made to provide access or assistance in postsecondary education.

Access to higher education continues to be problematic for American Indian, black and Hispanic/Latino students. Even when they are admitted to college, attrition studies find them withdrawing at higher rates, and they are far less likely to achieve their educational goals than their Asian or white peers. The attrition rate of these students is not only a personal tragedy for them and the communities that need their skills so desperately, it is also a significant loss of human capital for a nation that can ill afford to lose the vast potential represented in this growing proportion of its population.

Extrapolating from the ACE Annual Report of 1994, if 10 black and Hispanic students enter elementary school, about 6.5 will graduate from high school. Of this 6.5, about 2 will enter college and less than one will graduate. These statistics point to the critical challenge posed to higher education to respond effectively to the academic development needs of students of color.

Advising as a key link in persistence and success of students of color

Alexander Astin (1985), David Crockett (1985) and Vincent Tinto (1987) are among those who have identified academic advising and academic advisors as the key links between students, our curricula and colleges. No single student service is mentioned more in retention research as an effective means of promoting student retention and success than academic advising (Thomas, 1990). A major study of attrition in the nation's public colleges and universities (Cowart, 1987) found that inadequate academic advising ranked number one among negative institutional characteristics related to attrition. The same study also found that a "caring attitude of faculty and staff" and "consistent high quality advising" were among the most frequently cited institutional characteristics that enhanced retention. Cowart concluded that institutions that are most successful in retaining students are those that have made improvements in academic advising.

Tinto (1987) demonstrated that incongruence, or the mismatch between students' expectations of an institution and their experiences, was a major factor in student attrition. When institutions place much or all of the burden for changing on students who are most like those they have traditionally served, they limit the range of minority students they can serve responsibly. (Skinner & Richardson, 1988.)

With regard to ethnic minorities, faculty advisors are on the front lines of American higher education. Levin and Levin (1991) reviewed research and intervention programs for minority students, and their findings supported the earlier work of Astin (1985), who observed that "quality interaction with faculty seems to be more important than any other single college factor in determining minority student persistence" (p. 324). Faculty advisors are key sources of information, guidance and support for students. It is important, therefore, that they be fully aware of the skills, attitudes and behaviors required if they are to respond effectively to the educational needs of an increasingly diverse student population.

Challenges in Multicultural Advising

Advisors need to have a knowledge base in the following areas:

1. Understanding the experiences of multicultural students in higher education

2. Understanding culture and diversity within culture

3. Understanding how cultural difference can undermine effective communication in an advising relationship

Understanding the multicultural student experience in higher education

"Minority" students for the first time

Augustine Pounds (1987) observed that "For some black students, enrolling in college is the first time they have lived or learned in an integrated environment" (p. 27). Deborah W. LaCounte (1987) noted that for American Indian students, many of whom attended high schools on reservations that were 98 percent Indian, enrollment in college is frequently the first long-term exposure to a non-Indian environment. Thus, it is not until they enroll in college that many students of color experience what it means to be a "minority" in American society (Brown & Rivas, 1995). Many come from communities in which their ethnic group may have been a majority. Perhaps they attended high schools where there was a critical mass of persons from backgrounds similar to theirs or where there was a variety of different ethnic groups.

The success of women who have attended women's colleges or blacks who have attended historically black colleges and universities (HBCUs) attests to what can happen in an environment where students are not just given an equal opportunity, but where everything and everyone affirms them and the feasibility of their goals. The academic advisor serves as a key connection between such students and environments that may seem alien or even hostile. The advisor can help students develop trusting relationships with peers, faculty and staff.

To be designated a "minority" student on many campuses is to be assumed to be "underprepared," "at-risk" or even "inferior." On the other hand, to be identified as an "Asian" student is to find oneself confronting frequently unrealistic expectations of success and/or stereotypical notions of the fields or careers for which one is best suited.

In a society that proclaims their inadequacy in so many ways, these students may avoid becoming fully engaged in their academic work as one way of avoiding the pain of failing and the double bind of confirming one's inferiority through failing at a task (C. Steele, 1992). Many students of color are "ego involved," in that they compare themselves to some idealized vision or norm and conclude that they do not measure up. The challenge for academic advisors is to encourage these students to be task involved and assist them to break down the various tasks of college into doable components so they will be able to measure and experience, in concrete, tangible ways, their progress toward goal achievement.

Role models and mentors

Many students of color come from family backgrounds with little direct experience with higher education, and for these students, advisors are crucial sources of guidance, information and support. All students need mentors, but these mentors do not necessarily have to be of the same ethnicity. Data from the National Research Council indicate that while there has been progress in the numbers of ethnic minorities achieving doctorates, most notably among American Indians and Asians, we are still some distance from the day when there will be sufficient numbers of minority role models to mentor the growing numbers of students of color. All advisors must hold themselves accountable for supporting all students in the campus communities and should seek to develop the skills and behaviors needed to do so.

When students are asked why they have been successful, they frequently recall some person in their campus community who recognized their potential and took an active, personal interest in supporting their social and academic integration. Whether students have a disability or learn differently; whether they are Asian, American Indian, black, Latino or white; whether they are heterosexual, gay or lesbian, they must not be made to feel marginal in our campus communities if they are to achieve their personal, educational and career goals.

Marginalization and attachment

Vincent Tinto (1987) observed that the closer one is to the center of the intellectual and social life in a college or university, the more likely one is to experience a sense of connection and resultant commitment to remain in that institutional environment. When a student perceives herself to be on the periphery, the greater the likelihood that she will experience a sense of disconnection and apartness. In fact, a student can consciously or unconsciously move away from the intellectual center of institutional life because she feels isolated and marginalized. While she may feel a strong sense of attachment to her immediate group, there is not necessarily a commitment to the institution as a whole and dropping out is one result. Affiliations with significant members of the campus community (e.g., faculty advisors, peers, mentors) can counter the social isolation experienced by students of color.

Social and academic integration issues are important for students of color, but successful social integration does not necessarily support success in academic areas. In fact, the converse is all too frequently the case. Students must adjust to the academic milieu to achieve their goals; in this regard, faculty advisors are best equipped to help students of color to gain a mastery of the ins and outs of the college/university.

Understanding culture and diversity

Diversity within diversity

Allen Ivey (1981), former president of the American Psychological Association Division of Counseling Psychology, has argued that it may be unethical to counsel a person with a different cultural background than one's own without appropriate information and sensitivity. It is also inappropriate to generalize broad knowledge about cultural groups to all individual group members. Academic advisors must take Ivey's words to heart in that they too must become familiar with the "person" of the ethnic minority student whom they are advising.

Advising needs will differ based on the individual backgrounds and experiences of students. For instance, who is the "Hispanic" you are advising? Is she a first-generation Mexican-American from a rural background, a recent arrival from Puerto Rico or a fourth generation Cuban-American? Is the "Asian American" you have seated in front of you a Vietnamese who fled to the U.S. at the time of the American withdrawal from Saigon, or has his Hmong family been lingering in the refugee camps of Bangkok for the past decade awaiting permission to emigrate? Is the "Native American" you're preparing to advise a product of a suburban experience, or has she lived her entire life on a reservation? Is the "black" student you are scheduled to meet next week the first in his family to go to college, a Haitian refugee or the product of an affluent professional family? Suc (1981) cautioned not to generalize any generic cultural variables to all individuals within the groups with which we work. Effective cross cultural advisors must be aware of *diversity within diversity* (Brown & Rivas, 1993). It is important, therefore, to make distinctions based on socioeconomic class, educational background, family structure, gender, and previous experiences with academic advising.

All ethnic groups within the U.S. are an aggregation of many distinct subgroups. Despite similarities, there are many ways in which these subgroups are distinct from one another in terms of language, culture and socio-economic status. For example, there is a tendency, perpetuated by stories in the media of the remarkable success of many Asian American students, to view Asians as a monolithic "model minority" group that need not be the focus of any special attention in higher education. There are more than 30 nations of the Asian Pacific and in these nations there is significant diversity. The U.S. Census Bureau's *Current Population Reports* list the following Asian groups: Chinese, Filipino, Japanese, Asian Indian, Korean, Vietnamese, Laotian, Thai, Hmong, Pakistani, Hawaiian, Samoan and Guamanian. Within these groups, further distinctions must be made and understood. For example, the Philippines are a collection of some 7,000 islands where 111 languages are spoken.

In Taiwan, there are differences between Chinese who have lived there for generations and those who fled to the island nation following the communist takeover in 1948. There are significant differences between Vietnamese whose families migrated to the U.S. in the mid-1970s and those who arrived during later migrations (referred to as "refugee waves" by Kiang and Wai-Fun Lee, 1993). These diverse backgrounds and experiences impact students and affect their readiness to pursue a higher education program and be involved fully in pursuit of their goals. For example, while some Asian students may be hesitant to be confrontational (Japan, Indonesia), students from more competitive environments may be less reticent about challenging authority figures (e.g., Hong Kong, Taiwan).

There are more than 20 Spanish-speaking countries in the Western hemisphere, and many Latinos tend to identify based on their country of origin. Frequently, identification as "Latino" or "Hispanic" is used in relation to others who are not Spanish-speaking.

The Mexican American population is by far the largest, having constituted 60 percent of the total Hispanic student population in 1990; Puerto Ricans were 12 percent of the Hispanic population and "Other Hispanics" constituted 22 percent. Cuban-origin Hispanics comprise the smallest proportion, with less than 5 percent of the total.

GROUP	POPULATION (IN MILLIONS)	PERCENTAGES
All Hispanic	22,354	100.00
Mexican origin	13,296	60.40
Puerto Rican	2,727	12.20
Other Hispanic	5,086	22.80
Cuban	1,043	4.70

(Jorge Chapa and Richard R. Valencia, Latino Population Growth, Demographic Characteristics, and Educational Stagnation: An Examination of Recent Trends. Hispanic Journal of Behavioral Sciences, Vol. 15 No. 2, May 1993, 165-187.)

While the majority of black persons living in the U.S. are descendants of Africans brought to the U.S. during the 400 years of the slave trade, there are others (and depending on geographic region of the country, quite a few others) who trace their recent roots to the islands of the Caribbean (Jamaica, Haiti) or who are on student visas from the nations of Africa. Within these groups, there will be distinctions between the first waves of wealthier, more Americanized immigrants, such as Haitians who fled in the 1950s, and many of the "boat people" who are fleeing in the 1990s. In still other instances, students are of Hispanic origin and will tend to identify as Cuban, Puerto Rican or Belizian rather than as "black."

Many of the latter groups of individuals spent their formative years in environments where blacks were in the majority and held power. When Sidney Poitier was once asked where his remarkable "dignity" came from, he responded that he had grown up in the Caribbean and "had a chance to develop a sense of self" before encountering racial prejudice when coming to the U.S. Poitier continued, "I had the circumstance to develop a feeling of self without having to deal with racism that early." He concluded by noting that if he had been raised in the U.S., where people of his age and race are constantly being told that they are inferior, "I don't know if I would have had the strength to succeed" (Oakland Tribune, November 1, 1991).

There are some 545 American Indian tribes recognized by the federal government. (Klein, 1993), and there are about 250 languages spoken by North American Indians (Native American Connections, Volume 2, No. 2, 1994). Indians identify with specific groups, and some groups, for example the Apache, do not consider those who are not members of their tribe to be Indians. Only 27.3 percent of American Indian students who enter college ever earn their degrees and more than 50 percent leave college in the first year (Wells, 1989).

Thompson (1990) pointed out that this may be attributable to the fact that many are the first in their families to attend college and there is "no tradition of support, encouragement or even understanding the pressures of college attendance" (p. 245).

Falicov (1982) advises that broad cultural generalizations often do not do justice to regional, generational, socio-economic or other distinctions within specific ethnic groups. Advisors must avoid the tendency to economize on the energy that is required to understand diversity within diversity and strive to see the individual student. Otherwise, the result is generalization and stereotyping.

Identity development and world view
For effective communication with students of color, advisors should understand how students' social development can impact their ability to interact with an advisor of a different socio-cultural background. Ibrahim (1985) observed that it is important to understand the cultural values and world views of students if we are to understand the culturally different client. Sue (1981), in turn, noted that for minorities in America, their world view is shaped by racism and the subordinate position assigned to them in society. Advisors cannot work with black students [and other students of color] in a meaningful and effective manner unless they understand their philosophical assumptions and life experiences (McEwen, Roper, Bryant, & Langa, 1990).

With regard to the growth and development needs of students of color, Doris Wright (1987) charged that "current models of student development fail to account for the influence of culture on the developmental process and result in a fundamental lack of understanding of minority students" (p. 10). There are a number of ethnic identity models that have been developed and these can help advisors to better understand and effectively respond to students of color (Atkinson, Morten, & Sue, 1979; Cross, 1971; Ruiz, 1990). These models all clarify the impact of being socialized in a hostile environment, and point out that there are passages/stages that ethnic minorities undergo in developing a strong sense and acceptance of self and others.

A basic theme of ethnic minority identity models is that students go through a developmental "encounter" stage where they are likely to be less receptive to communication with those outside their own ethnic group. This stage is generally followed by a transitional phase that leads to an internalization or resolution phase where the person of color is "self appreciating, group appreciating and selectively appreciating of others," (Atkinson, Morten, & Sue, 1983). There is considerable research showing that students of color often prefer working with helping professionals who share their ethnicity. Sanchez and Atkinson (1983) found this to be the case for Mexican-American students, while Johnson and Lashley (1989) obtained similar data for Native American students. Pomales, Claiborn and LaFramboise (1986) observed that black students see a "culturally sensitive" counselor as more competent than a "culture blind" counselor.

The effective multicultural advisor must be willing to respect and support the social identity development of students of color. For example, this may mean not responding defensively to a black student who is in the angry "encounter" stage of development (Cross, 1971) and who may display overt hostility and resistance to the most culturally sensitive professional of different ethnicity. Shelby Steele (1990) has noted that to be black in America is to be a member of this nation's most despised and denigrated group. Advisors must recognize that many students of color have been expected to learn and develop in hostile environments (Wright, 1987). A single positive encounter with an aware advisor could be the catalyst that facilitates student development toward internalization of self-acceptance and full engagement in the academic enterprise.

To support students of color in their development, the academic advisor must familiarize him or herself with the various resources on campus that can assist/support students' development. The following are offered as examples:

- Advisors must become aware of resources on campus and in the community that will contribute to the identity development of minority students.

- Advisors must familiarize themselves with courses that include a focus on the history, achievements and challenges confronted by individuals from minority backgrounds. They should also examine their own attitudes toward ethnic studies courses and learn more about these courses and what they offer students and students of color, in particular.

- Effective advisors must learn about campus organizations and programs that will allow minority students to become involved, develop leadership capabilities, and contribute to a campus environment in which the many cultures that comprise these communities can be understood and respected. Frequently organizations like the Black Students Union, MEChA, or the Asian Pacific Club provide a primary source of networking, social/academic support and leadership development opportunities for minority students on predominantly white campuses.

- Advisors must seek out and encourage students' involvement with role models and mentors within the campus community and the community at large. (Possible mentors and role models include faculty, staff, alumni, upper division student and graduate students.)

- Advisors must also understand the importance of addressing students' needs that may not focus on issues of race. For example, a 10-year study of black student use of services at Michigan State University found that students frequently came to their advisors seeking help with financial problems, issues of academic adjustment and concerns about on- and off-campus living conditions. When students experience advisors as competent to respond to their immediate needs, and when their advisors are genuine and caring, there is a greater likelihood that the advisor will be able to use this initial rapport as the foundation for dealing with more significant, long-term issues of academic integration and achievement.

It is also essential for advisors to appraise their own identity development within a pluralistic society in order to understand the concept of individual perceptions of reality (world view) associated with models of minority identity development. Ponterotto (1988), citing Wrenn (1985), asked, "what pragmatic use will a counselor's understanding of the client's racial consciousness level foster, if the counselor himself/herself is racially 'unconscious' and culturally encapsulated?" (p. 147). For example, an Asian American or Hispanic advisor should reflect on his or her ethnicity, *vis a vis* ethnic identity development, to be aware of potential emotional conflicts that could hinder effective communication with students of color. Specific to white advisors, who comprise the greater number of advising professionals, there are white identity models that can assist these individuals to explore their own ethnicity as a member of the white race in order to reveal emotional and attitudinal obstacles to effective communication (Hardiman, 1982; Helms, 1985).

Although we all may wish for an America in which people are judged by the content of their character, the reality is that experiences of racism and prejudice shape many perceptions and attitudes. As professionals, all advisors must be willing to face this reality and act to have a positive impact on individuals and systems.

Understanding how advisor ethnicity and socialization can undermine effectiveness

Value conflicts in advising

For advisors to succeed in cross-cultural advising interactions, they must become knowledgeable about how diversity is expressed in advising and how cultural differences between the advisor and the student can undermine the advising encounter. Furthermore, advisors must commit to developing sensitivity, concern and the ability to address the developmental issues that students of color bring with them to college—issues ranging from emerging pride in their ethnic identity to the potentially paralyzing effects of societal racism and discrimination. This latter point is important because students' personal development has a direct impact on their readiness to pursue academic and intellectual goals (Schein, Laff, & Allen, 1987).

Much has been written about how cultural differences can undermine communication (Sue, 1981; Pederson, 1985; McGoldrick, Pierce, & Giordano, 1982; Tannen, 1990). Specifically, Sue and Sue (1990) have identified sources of conflict and misinterpretations in counseling interactions when there are differences in the cultural backgrounds of the counselor and counselee. Much in the Sues' model applies to the work of academic advisors. Indeed, many of the examples they use, as well as others in the counseling literature, describe academic advising situations.

Sue and Sue offer a number of generic characteristics of counseling among which are the following:

1. Participants use standard English.

2. Participants emphasize verbal communication.

3. Participants focus on long-range goals.

4. The processes are often ambiguous and open to interpretation.

5. Interactions are based on openness and the willingness of the client to share personal/intimate information with the counselor.

6. The process focuses on the needs of the individual.

They also describe "Third World group variables" that relate to counseling Asians, blacks, Hispanics and Native Americans. These differ from the *generic characteristics of counseling* that are associated with white middle class values in that:

1. "Standard" English may be the second language.

2. The client is action-oriented and focuses on immediate, short-range, "present time" goals.

3. The client requires a more concrete, structured tangible approach.

4. The client's interests are likely to be family-centered, group-oriented, and/or based on cooperative, not competitive individualism.

Advisors must be aware of potential incongruencies in the communication process when advising ethnically diverse students, because cultural differences often lead to miscommunication, misunderstanding and a lack of engagement.

On the whole, people of color are likely to have had limited experiences with counseling/advising interactions (Vontress, 1981; Sue & Sue, 1990). Therefore, when engaged in cross-cultural communication, "[advisors] should be especially aware that the assumption that there is a common ground of shared expectancies is probably incorrect" (Yuen & Tinsley, 1981, p. 69). Among the generic characteristics of counseling is the expectation that interactions will be based on openness and the willingness of the [advisee] to share personal and intimate information with the [advisor]. In contrast, for Asians and Hispanics, discussing personal issues beyond the boundaries of the family or community can be perceived as a betrayal of the entities that they customarily turn to for advice, support and assistance.

Past experiences with racism and prejudice cause many people of color to be distrustful of persons from different backgrounds. In advising, this mistrust often produces hesitancy to disclose personal information. The experiences of students may suggest that bureaucracies and their agents, in this instance the advisor, do not have their best interests at heart and are seeking to frustrate their goal achievement rather than supporting and advancing it. These students may have concerns about being misunderstood, hurt, or taken advantage of if personal information is disclosed

(Ridley, 1984). When one has had a history of strained relations with the Bureau of Indian Affairs, U.S. Health and Human Services, Immigration and Naturalization, or any number of other bureaucratic agencies and their representatives, it is reasonable to expect reluctance to participate openly in an advising encounter.

It is essential for advisors to structure advising sessions to clarify the purposes, goals and methods of academic advising so as to reduce advisee hesitancy. For example, the advisor should begin by inquiring about the student's prior advising experiences and his or her level of satisfaction with them. If the advisor concludes that the student is unfamiliar with advising, she or he will want to define advising, academic planning and the decision-making process; outline roles and responsibilities; and discuss what may be gained from talking about issues and problems. It is particularly important to set forth the confidential nature of advising and the fact that nothing can legally be shared with anyone, inside or outside the institution, who does not have a legitimate need to know, without the express consent of the advisee.

Another characteristic of advising that may be in conflict with the cultural experiences of many students of color is that advising is often non-directive. An egalitarian presumption underlying advising calls for the advisor to set forth a range of alternatives while the advisee makes the final decision about an appropriate course of action. This perspective is often at odds with role-relationship experiences that stress hierarchical patterns of interaction and deference to authority.

Many students of color come from family situations where roles are well defined and expectations clear. For example, Vietnamese children are taught from an early age to listen to authority figures and speak only when asked to do so. Advice, questions and opinions are not encouraged (Do, 1983). Likewise, Attneave (1982) observed that in most American Indian and Alaskan Native social settings, the dominant person is expected to be active and the subordinate person shows respect by quiet attentiveness. Similar dynamics of interaction with authority figures have also been observed for Latinos (Bernal & Flores-Ortiz, 1984), rural blacks (Vontress, 1981) and Puerto Ricans (Garcia-Preto, 1982). In a study of counseling style preferences, Exum and Lau (1988) found that Chinese students rated the directive approach more positively than a non-directive style. Similarly, Ruiz and Casas (1981) highlighted the importance of using a directive approach when engaging Chicano college students. The unwillingness of the advisor to accept the role of providing direction may be unsettling to many students of color and leave them confused, disoriented and dissatisfied with the advising encounter. This

may be one of the reasons why students of color underutilize student services.

In setting forth Third World group variable for counseling, Sue and Sue (1990) identified the need that many people of color have for concrete, tangible, structured approaches to addressing and resolving issues and problems. Many students of color see advisors as "experts" (i.e., authority figures) who have the "right" answers and "know" what they should do. The nondirective approach that underlies current advising practices may not prove satisfying to these students.

Terry O'Bannion, a leading advocate of developmental advising whose "hierarchy of advising" guides the work of many advisors, asked in his remarks to the 1987 National Academic Advising Association Conference , "Aren't there times when advisors know what is best of students, and when they do, don't they have a responsibility to share insights and experiences with students?" Effective multicultural advising often requires advisors to adjust their advising strategies to accommodate the need many students of color have for the concrete, tangible responses they expect from their advisors. This adjustment may be particularly important in early advising interactions, when student expectations are that advisors will provide some clear direction.

Faculty advising assumptions

The expectations that faculty advisors have of students of color can often undermine their faith that they have the ability to succeed and consequently can decrease the amount of effort these students commit toward achieving their academic goals. More tragically, the expectations that faculty have of students of color can also lessen the inclination of faculty to invest the necessary time and effort necessary to help these students succeed in college.

Faculty and advisor expectations can be of varying types, but basically revolve around expecting too little or too much. Frequently, for example, faculty assume that black, Latino and American Indian students are all special admission and lack the requisite preparation, skills and motivation to succeed in college. When lower expectations are communicated by a significant person in the learning environment, e.g., a faculty member or advisor, the student's level of self-doubt may increase or the student's doubt about the sincerity and helpfulness of the faculty advisor may be heightened. While it is true that many students of color attended high schools where they could not get ready for college, and thus may lack a solid foundation of skills to compete with the average student, this does not mean that all students of color fit this profile. Faculty/advisors must "expend the energy needed to make distinctions" about who the student is and what his or her specific needs in advising are.

Expectations about Asian students are of a different but no less damaging nature. Too often, faculty advisors see these students as uniformly competent, and therefore not in need of outreach, support and guidance. Students from this group who indeed require assistance too often do not receive guidance (1) because they lack the confidence to reach out and (2) do not see the faculty advisor as a welcoming resource. Again, it is important to make distinctions among individuals within groups in order to ensure that we are effectively assisting those students who require our support.

Beyond Engagement: Promoting Academic Achievement and Success

Historical perspectives: Redefining success

In his remarks to the 1989 ACE conference on Educating One Third of a Nation, Maricopa Community College Vice-Chancellor Alfredo de los Santos pointed out that in the 1960s and 1970s, the issue for students of color related to increasing opportunities for them to access higher educational opportunities; in the 1970s and 1980s, educational institutions turned their attention to retention; and for the 1990s, the issues for students of color will be achieving excellence and success.

While access and retention remain important issues, advisors must challenge ethnic minority students to strive to higher levels of competence and achievement. Asian, black, brown and Native American students must be encouraged to see education as a social responsibility to themselves and to their communities and to our nation (Wright, 1987), a responsibility that calls for individual discipline and strength of purpose. Jaime Escalante, whose story was told in the film, *Stand and Deliver*, inspires and motivates his students by telling them that "Success is a victory. It is a big bonus to your community and to your last name." The Escalante equation: "Determination + Discipline + Hard Work = Success." Like Jaime Escalante, advisors must learn how to motivate students of color so as to increase the students' abilities to success in college.

Following specific advising models

An effective way for advisors to promote achievement and success of students of color is for advisors to have a "guiding" model or models to use in their day-to-day advising work. A model is recommended because it provides the advisor with (1) a "concrete approach" for how to work with students and (2) a "jumping-off point" toward eventually developing a systematic repertoire for advising students of color.

We recommend that a developmental model of advising

be followed, because such a framework is based on the notion that students are involved in a process of development in college (Brown & Rivas, 1994). Specific to students of color, we suggest that there are three primary areas of development that are important for an advisor to be especially concerned with in order to help students maximize achievement and success: (1) the role of attributions with regard to the development of confidence; (2) the role of skills in the development of a greater sense of confidence and competence; (3) the important role of increasing student awareness and utilization of the wide range of resources within the campus community (social and academic integration). One theme that these three areas have in common is the requirement that a student gain more information regarding important developmental processes that he or she is involved in.

Attribution theory as a guide for the work of the advisor

A model that we have found useful to guide advising work with students of color with regard to overcoming negative attributions of ability is Bernard Weiner's (1984) Attribution Theory of Achievement and Emotion. Weiner's theory outlines significant variables that strengthen and/or undermine achievement when individuals are involved in tasks that call for skill development. The variables that Weiner delineates are individual's attributions (perceptions) of ability, attributions of task difficulty and attributions about the relationship of effort to outcome.

According to Weiner, all of the above variables influence how confident a person feels as well as how hard a person works toward desired goals. For example, self-attributions of low ability (e.g., ability to write research papers) combined with attributions of high task difficulty (learning to write research papers is a next to impossible task) lead to low goal expectancy (I will never to able to pass this course and complete my major). These attributions, in turn, undermine effort or "trying" behaviors. Conversely, if a person sees the self as high in ability and faced with a doable task, the thought will be "I can do it," and, therefore, "I will succeed." These attributions motivate the individual to work diligently toward the achievement of desired goals.

Weiner cites extensive research indicating that low ability attributions are accompanied by feelings of shame and doubt and that high task difficulty attributions are accompanied by feelings of helplessness and hopelessness. For example, if an ethnic minority student perceives the self as having low ability in a particular task(s), the accompanying feelings are very likely to be doubt and shame; also, if a student perceives the tasks (demands) of college to be overly difficult, there is likelihood that the student may feel a sense of helplessness and hopelessness toward the possibility of accomplishing the task. These feelings, needless to say, are not congruent with those of confidence, i.e., pride, assuredness, self-efficacy and hope.

With regard to attributions, it has been the authors' experience that many students of color are caught up in entanglement of negative attributions as well as their accompanying negative feelings. This entanglement often undermines students' development in a variety of key areas, including the development of a confident and positive approach to self vis-a-vis the tasks of college. The authors have also found that the experience of these undermining thoughts and feelings are clearly related to students not succeeding and eventually leaving college.

With regard to not succeeding, the scenario is very often one of "I really don't have what it takes (low ability attribution), and, even if I wanted to, college is too difficult for me to really do well." These thoughts lead to feelings of doubt, a sense of hopelessness, and often to thoughts and behaviors about giving up.

Weiner's solution for how to help individuals overcome negative attributions and their accompanying negative feelings is to suggest that persons change the way they perceive and think about particular achievement tasks. There are two areas that Weiner focuses on in proposing how to change negative attributions: (1) change the way task-difficulty is appraised and (2) reinforce more "effort-leads-to-outcome" attributions. By way of example, if a student sees the task of college as being too difficult, what must be done in advising is to help the student "re-frame" the way the task-difficulty of college is perceived by helping the student to divide the work of college into doable parts (tasks), i.e., work that is more manageable. Once the student sees doable tasks, the advisor's job is to reinforce the idea that with persistent effort the student will be able to master the demands of college and succeed.

Continuing with attributions, it has been the authors' experience that too often the tasks of college are not perceived clearly and/or realistically and that the role of effort is too often underplayed and/or overplayed. Specific to task-difficulty, many college tasks are very often viewed by students of color as being too demanding. Whether this demand involves taking a statistics course, learning to write research papers or learning how to read and comprehend college-level material at a high level of effectiveness, students of color too often do not have a clear perception of the difficulty level. To combat these undermining attributions whenever they occur, advisors must challenge the lack of clarity in students of color while helping these students develop a clearer picture of the tasks of college as well as what each student must think and do to undertake these

challenges. Changing negative attributions into confident behavior and perceptions is one of the main jobs of the advisor when working with students of color.

The role of skill development in building confidence

The development and/or enhancement of skills is one of the primary challenges that faces students of color in their quest to achieve success in college. The formula is straightforward: students of color need to be given concrete guidance as to the skills they need to succeed in college and they must also be advised into learning experiences that will assist them with their skills development needs.

Rivas (1988, 1990) has developed a task-focused academic advising model, the Zero-100 Percent Competence Method, that supports students as they focus on the skill demands of college. Central to this approach is the message that the student must develop competence (White, 1959) in college and in satisfying the human "need to know" (Maslow, 1968). The method has six steps to assist the advisor to organize, strategize and effectively approach educational challenges when advising students:

1. Review the student's academic record and learning history, looking for strengths/insights, weaknesses/lack of insights.

2. Define the student's personal, educational and career goals and related skills that must be developed to achieve these goals.

3. Assess the student's initial skill level (zero-100 percent) in those areas identified as essential to achievement.

4. Establish standards of excellence (zero-100 percent) that the student will work toward in each of the identified skill areas.

5. Identify curricular, co-curricular, and community learning experiences that will assist the student to develop skills and achieve desired goals.

6. As part of an ongoing advising relationship, review and evaluate progress toward goal achievement and skill development.

There are two important requisites, however, that the advisor should consider when using this approach: (1) be straightforward about the need for the student to realistically appraise his or her skill level vis-a-vis the demands of college and future careers and (2) effectively communicate a sincere commitment to advise and support the student's work toward skill development. To assist a student in this process, which can be threatening, the student is encouraged to focus on the task of becoming skillful (task-involved) versus comparing self to real or imagined "others" in a particular group (ego-involved) (Nicholls, 1984). Comparing self to others, especially when skills are low, can lead to feelings of shame, doubt, hopelessness, or helplessness. These negative feelings can undermine efforts to develop competence (Weiner, 1985).

Once the student has realistically appraised his or her skill levels, the advisor helps the student plan an academic program to achieve desired competency levels. For example, a student who is ill at ease participating in class or speaking in public could take a speech course to learn how to organize presentations, be more comfortable talking before a group, or effectively support an argument with details and facts. As the student takes classes, the advisor and student are able to verify the student's initial self-appraisal and make appropriate changes in the student's academic program. For example, a student who rated herself a 40 in oral communication might discover that she has strengths that would lead to a higher skill rating (possibly 60) because she has excellent stage presence, but that to effectively make that stage presence work she needs to improve on her level of preparation, research and practice before making a presentation.

The Advisor: Commitment to Make a Difference

One of the key ingredients of the advisor's work with students of color is the level of care and commitment toward making a difference in the lives of these students. This care and commitment has the following components:

1. A time component that calls for the advisor to devote a significant amount of time to students' development in college.

2. A personal involvement component that calls for the advisor to continue working with students though at times not reinforced for making the effort.

3. A skill component that asks that the advisor commit to becoming a skillful and successful academic advisor with students of color.

Why is advisor commitment so important? After all, isn't it up to the student to rise to the occasion and make effective use of the faculty member in order to secure the knowledge and insights necessary to succeed in college? Yes, by all means; however, these admonitions are ideals far removed from the reality of our current statistics that show too few ethnic minorities succeeding in college. Too few of these students are "connecting" to college. In the authors' minds, this "lack of connecting" comes down to the individual experiences of students with faculty advisors. Can we make a difference? Yes! And how do we make a difference? First, by committing to this goal.

As previously noted, very often the student of color is wary of "where" the faculty advisor is "coming from." Students are concerned about the sincerity and genuineness extended by the advisor. This doubt on the part of students of color has many origins, extending from the general "You are a different human being to me and, therefore, you can't really care," to "It's just your job and you're not really interested in me," finally to "I am a person of color and generally people don't really care about me and you're probably like all the rest."

If faculty advisors can work through this wariness, the next phase of the advisor's work can commence: getting into the particulars of each student's issues. The particulars, in turn, are only the initial phase because once we get to know a student from a social-cultural perspective, and a learning perspective, then we can begin to introduce the student to the work of college. Ideally, faculty advisors should commit to a developmental working through, challenging and supporting, of the three, four or five years of college that the student of color will undertake. This is a commitment to sticking with the student; a commitment to seeing the student through to the end, or let us say the beginning, because what follows is graduate study, professional school or work in a society that so desperately needs the leadership skills of more and more ethnic minority persons.

Summary

The effective multicultural and pluralistic advisor is aware of cultural difference and is sensitive to his or her own biases. Such an individual understands the basis of difference and recognizes that acknowledging difference is not a negative thing, but a reality of the human experience. Such an advisor commits herself or himself to difference and moves toward becoming a multicultural person. The effective cross-cultural/pluralistic advisor must examine personal attitudes and beliefs, while recognizing the need to increase knowledge and information about the groups she or he interacts with. An advisor cannot expect to wake up one morning with pluralistic sensitivities; it takes effort (reading, interacting and sharing with colleagues of color or with pluralistic backgrounds/experiences). Finally, in order to be effective cross cultural and pluralistic professionals, advisors must look at their repertoires of advising skills and apply innovative strategies to support the success of increasingly diverse student populations.

Academic advisors are the key links between students of color and higher education. When these advisors are culturally sensitive, willing to go the extra mile in support of students, challenge students to excel rather than merely persist, and give students concrete, tangible strategies to take responsibility for their own learning and achievement, they will make a difference for these students, for their institutions and for society. •

Bibliography

Astin, A. (1985). *Achieving educational excellence.* San Francisco: Jossey-Bass.

Atkinson, D. R., Morten, G., & Sue, D. W. (1983). *Counseling American minorities.* Dubuque, IA: Wm. C. Brown.

Attneave, C. (1982). American Indians and Alaska native families: Immigrants in their own homeland. In McGoldrick, M., Pierce, J., and Giordano, J. *Ethnicity and Family Therapy.* New York: Guilford Press.

Bernal, G., & Flores-Ortiz, Y. (1984) Latino families in therapy: Engagement and evaluation. *Journal of Marital and Family Therapy, 8*(3), 357-365.

Brown, T., & Rivas, M. (1993). Advising multicultural populations for achievement and success. In M. King, *Academic advising: Organizing and delivering services for student success.* San Francisco: Jossey-Bass.

Brown, T., & Rivas, M. (1995). Pluralistic advising: Facilitating the development and achievement of first-year students of color. In *First-year academic advising: Patterns in the present, pathways to the future* (pp. 121-137). University of South Carolina: National Resource Center for the Freshman-Year Experience and Students in Transition.

Brown, T., & Rivas, M. (1994). The prescriptive relationship in academic advising as an appropriate developmental intervention with multicultural populations. *NACADA Journal, 14*(2), 108-11.

Bynum, Alvin S. (1987). *Black students—white counselor: Developing effective relationships.* Indianapolis, IN: Alexandria Books.

Carter, D. J., & Wilson, R. (1994). *Minorities in higher education: Twelfth annual status report.* Washington, DC: American Council on Education.

Crockett, D. (1985). Academic advising. In L. Noel, R. Levitz, D. Saluri, & Associates. *Increasing student retention.* San Francisco: Jossey-Bass.

Cross, W. E. (1970). The Negro-to-black conversion experience: Toward a psychology of black liberation. *Black World, 20,* 13-27.

Do, V. T. (1983). Cultural differences: Implications in the education of Vietnamese students in U. S. schools. In V. A. Smith, & M. B. Dixon (Eds.), *Second lives: The contemporary immigrant/refugee experience in Orange County.* Costa Mesa, CA: South Coast Repertory.

Ender, S. C., Winston, Jr., R. B., & Miller, T. K. (1984). Academic advising reconsidered. In R. B. Winston, T. K. Miller, S. C. Ender, T. J. Grites, & Associates. *Developmental academic advising.* San Francisco: Jossey-Bass.

Exum, H. A., & Lau, E. Y. (1988). Counseling style preference of Chinese college students. *Journal of Multicultural Psychology, 1,* 84-91.

Falicov, C. (1982). Mexican families. In M. McGoldrick, J. Pierce, & J. Giordano, *Ethnicity and family therapy.* New York: Guilford Press.

Garcia-Preto, N. (1982). Puerto Rican families. In M. McGoldrick, J. Pierce, & J. Giodano, *Ethnicity and family therapy.* New York: Guilford Press.

Hardiman, R. (1982). White identity development: A process model for describing the racial consciousness of white Americans. *Dissertation Abstracts International, 43,* 104A.

Helms, J. E. (1984). Toward a theoretical explanation of the effects of race on counseling: A black and white model. *The Counseling Psychologist, 12*(4), 153-165.

Hodgkinson, H. L. (1983). *Guess who's coming to college: Your students in 1990.* Washington, DC: National Institute of Independent Colleges and Universities.

Ibrahim, F. A., (1985). Effective cross-cultural counseling and psychotherapy: A framework. *The Counseling Psychologist, 3,* 625-638.

Ivey, A. (1981). Foreword. In D. W. Sue, *Counseling the culturally different* (2nd ed.) New York: John Wiley and Sons.

Johnson, M. E., & Lashley, K. H. (1989). Influence of Native American's cultural commitment preferences for counselor ethnicity and expectations for counseling. *Journal of Multicultural Counseling, 17,* 115-122.

Kiang, P. N., & Wai-Fun Lee, V. (1993). Exclusion or contribution, in *The state of Asian Pacific America.* Los Angeles, CA: UCLA Asian American Studies Center.

Klein, B. (1993). *Reference encyclopedia of American Indians.* New York: Todd Publications.

Kominski, R., & Adams, A. (1991, October). *School enrollment: Social and economic characteristics of students.* Washington, DC: U.S. Bureau of the Census.

La Counte, D. W. (1987). American Indian students in college. In D. J. Wright (Ed.), *Responding to the needs of today's minority students. New Directions for Student Services, No. 38.* San Francisco: Jossey-Bass.

Levin, M. E., & Levin, J. R. (1991). A critical examination of academic retention programs for at-risk minority college students. *Journal of College Student Development, 32,* 323-334.

Maslow, A. H. (1968). *Toward a psychology of being.* Princeton, NJ: Van Nostrand.

McEwen, M. K., Roper, L. D., Bryant, D. R., & Langa, M. J. (1990). Incorporating the development of African-American students into psychosocial theories of student development. *Journal of College Student Development, 31,* 429-436.

McGoldrick, M., Pierce, J., & Giordano, J. (1982). *Ethnicity and family therapy.* New York: Guilford Press.

Nicholls, J. G. (1984). Achievement motivation: Conceptions of personality, objective experience, task choice, and performance. *Psychological Review, 91*(3), 328-346.

Pederson, P., Darguns, J., Lonner, W., & Trimble, J. (1981). *Counseling across cultures.* Hawaii: University of Hawaii Press.

Pomales, J., Claiborn, C. D., & LaFramboise, T. D. (1986). Effects of black students' racial identity on perceptions of white counselors varying in cultural sensitivity. *Journal of Counseling Psychology, 34,* 123-131.

Ponterotto, J. G. (1988). Racial consciousness development among white counselor trainees: A stage model. *Journal of Multicultural Psychology, 16,* 146-156.

Pounds, A. W. (1987). Black students' needs on predominantly white campuses. In D. J. Wright (ed.), Responding to the needs of today's minority students. *New Directions for Student Services, No. 38.* San Francisco: Jossey-Bass.

Ridley, C. R. (1984). Clinical treatment of the nondisclosing black client. *American Psychologist, 39,* 1234-1244.

Rivas, M. (1988) *An exploratory study of a group intervention for underprepared ethnic minority students entering college.* Unpublished doctoral dissertation, University of Minnesota.

Rivas, M. (1990, October 16) *Zero to 100 percent advising method: A task focused academic advising model to empower students to take responsibility for their own learning, achievement and success.* Paper presented at the National Academic Advising Association Conference, Anaheim, CA.

Ruiz, A. S. (1990). Ethnic identity: Crisis and resolution. *Journal of Multicultural Counseling and Development, 18*, 29-40.

Ruiz, R., & Casas, J. (1981). Culturally relevant and behavioristic counseling for Chicano college students. In P. Pederson, J. Darguns, W. Lonner, & J. Trimble, *Counseling across cultures.* Hawaii: University of Hawaii Press.

Sanchez, A, & Atkinson, D. R. (1983). Mexican-American cultural commitment, preference for counselor ethnicity, and willingness to use counseling. *Journal of Counseling Psychology, 30*, 215-220.

Schein, H. K., Laff, N. S., & Allen, D. R. (1987). *Giving advice to students: A road map for college professionals.* Alexandria, WV: American Association for Counseling and Development.

Skinner, E., & Richardson, R. (1988, May/June). Making it in a majority university. *Change.*

Steele, C. (1992, April). Race and the schooling of black Americans. *Atlantic Monthly,* 68-78.

Steele, S. (1990). *The content of our character: A new vision of race in America.* New York: St. Martin's Press.

Sue, D. W. (1981). *Counseling the culturally different.* New York: John Wiley and Sons.

Sue, D. W., & Sue, D. (1990). *Counseling the culturally different.* New York: John Wiley and Sons.

Tannen, D. (1990). *You just don't understand.* New York: Ballantine.

Thomas, R. O. (1990). Programs and activities for improved retention. In D. Hossler, J. P. Bean, & Associates. *The strategic management of college enrollments.* San Francisco: Jossey-Bass.

Thompson, G. E. (1990). Access versus success: The Native American Indian community college student.. *Community/Junior College,* 14, 239-250.

Tinto, V. (1987, October 9) *The educational roots of effective retention.* Paper presented at the National Academic Advising Association Conference, Miami, FL.

Vontress, C. (1981). Racial and ethnic barriers in counseling, In P. Pederson, J. Draguns, W. Lonner, & J. Trimble, *Counseling across cultures.* Hawaii: University of Hawaii Press.

Weiner, B. (1985). An attributional theory of achievement motivation and emotion. *Psychological Review, 92*(4), 548-573.

Wells, R. (1989). *The forgotten minority: Native Americans in higher education.* Saint Lawrence Press.

White, R. W. (1959). Motivation reconsidered: The concept of competence. *Psychological Review, 66*(5), 297-333.

Wrenn, C. G. (1985). Afterward: The culturally encapsulated counselor revisited. In P. Peterson (ed.), *Handbook of cross-cultural counseling and therapy.* Westport, CT: Greenwood Press.

Wright, D. J. (Ed.) (1987). Responding to the needs of today's minority students. *New Directions for Student Services, No. 38.* San Francisco: Jossey-Bass.

Yuen R. K. W., & Tinsley, H. E. A. (1981). International and American students' expectancies about counseling, *Journal of Counseling Psychology. 28*(1), 66-69.

Advising Adult Learners

Cheryl J. Polson, Ph.D.
Associate Professor, College of Education, Kansas State University

Defining the Adult Learner

We all know who adult learners are. They are the students who sit in the front row of class; the ones who remember when John F. Kennedy was president; the ones who get mad when the instructor doesn't show up for class; the ones whose favorite sweatshirt is older than some of their classmates.

Numerous labels (nontraditional students, older-than-average, re-entry, stop-outs) have been assigned to the student population that typically includes people who:

1. Have been away from the formal educational system for some time

2. Have established their own homes and assumed roles other than student

3. Have been employed—many in full-time positions

4. Are older than 25

5. Have been actively involved in community and/or church activities

6. Are seldom on-campus residents

7. May not attend college full-time while completing their degree

I will refer to this clientele as the adult learner. Existing research-based literature pertaining to the adult learner in higher education has specifically designated this population as 25 years old and older (Kasworm, 1990).

As the above descriptors imply, adult students differ from traditional-aged students in their academic and life involvements. They are diverse and cannot be treated as a single entity. Because there is no single definition of what an adult learner is, there can be no universal statements about what characterizes all adult learners. However, it is possible to describe some general attributes.

Characteristics of Adult Learners

Multiple role and time commitments
Adults are engaged in multiple roles that impact both the time and the energy they can devote to their role as students.

College is not a full-time occupation for adults. It is often a secondary role to that of being a parent, a spouse, an employee and/or a community leader. Adulthood requires many decisions where students have to prioritize their obligations, and attending class will not always come out on top.

For example, if students must choose between meeting a critical, unexpected project deadline for work and attending class—work may win out. Or if they must choose between being at the emergency room with a child or class, they may not be in class. However, advisors must openly discuss the potential consequences of the advisee's choosing to miss a class. Advisors should also discuss the attendance and examination policies of instructors.

Advisors need to be aware of the pressures and demands of these roles and commitments. As they help adults plan their academic schedules, advisors may want to ask students what other roles they might be balancing and how these might impact the time they can devote to completing coursework. This will encourage advisees to establish a realistic schedule at which they can succeed.

Advisors also need to know the students' time and/or geographical restraints that may limit the options for course selection (i.e., evening or weekend). Additionally, they need to identify alternatives to the on-campus course, especially those delivered via distance technology.

Quality and quantity of life experiences
Adults have a greater volume and a different quality of experiences than the traditional student. This experience base can be an asset and a liability. It provides a rich resource for learning and a foundation upon which to build new knowledge, and it gives them a "hook" on which to hang new information.

But these experiences can also create barriers to learning. Adults' attitudes, values and beliefs are established as a result of their experiences. Adults filter material that is presented through their own life experience—rejecting some things and accepting others. This may lead to close-mindedness, which can be a barrier to learning. Adults can be very resistant to accepting alternative views provided by instructors, especially when it means giving up long-held assumptions. This can be very painful.

In these situations, advisors need to encourage adults to remain open and flexible to others' views. They should not merely assist the student in dropping a class. Advising adults is further complicated by the number of informal learning experiences adult students have had. They have learned informally through on-the-job training, through talking with friends, through observation and through trial and error. This does not mean they have learned everything completely, or even correctly, but it does mean adults will have established some preconceptions that may need to be addressed. If these preconceptions are not addressed in the classroom, the advisor may end up dealing with the consequences. Adults may also believe that through these experiences they have already mastered the content of required courses, and may feel as though they should not have to take these courses.

Off-campus direction

Adult advisees are less concerned with on-campus activities than the traditional-age student. Campuses have found that even when activities are specifically geared toward this student population, attendance rates are low. The adult students' interaction with the institution is often limited to their time in the classroom and with their advisor. An advisor plays a central role in ensuring that the student feels connected to the institution. It is not uncommon for the adult student's advisor to be the student's primary link to campus. Advisor access is critical.

Adults find their support and service network in the community surrounding the institution. Several things contribute to this situation. On many campuses, student services have been designed specifically for traditional-age students. For example, many career placement centers are geared toward students who are entering their first career and not towards students who may have been employed for 15 years and are seeking career advancement or are retooling for another career. It is helpful when advisors develop resource directories that include agencies that can effectively assist the adult student, for example: lists of child care providers, lists of financial institutions that provide educational loans, lists of reputable counselors and names of agencies that provide time and stress management workshops.

The majority of adults live off-campus. This impacts not only the number of courses but the type of courses they can take. For example, the time adults have to complete assignments—specifically those that require library, lab or computers—may be impacted by their commute to and from campus. Advisors need to encourage advisees to consider this factor when selecting courses.

Developmental tasks of adult students

Traditional students enter college dealing with the transition from late adolescence to young adulthood. They have a commonality of age and of developmental issues. Many are in the process of identity formation. On the other hand, adult students are experiencing a variety of developmental stages and phases. Unlike their younger counterparts, they are often in the process of establishing a new identity. Recent research (Breese & O'Toole, 1994) has documented that a return to the student role often serves as a bridge from one identity to another.

When working with adults, it is helpful if advisors understand adult development theories. This will assist them in recognizing possible life challenges and issues their advisees may be confronting. Additionally, it is important to remember that adult students enter higher education having been influenced by a variety of economic and social forces. For example, think of how different campus experiences might have been for a returning adult student whose initial college experience was during the campus unrest of the 1970s and the adult student who attended college in the 1980s. The student's expectations of the advising process might differ greatly based on these previous experiences.

Clear educational goals

Adults frequently come to the advising session with a clear educational goal in mind. As we have already discussed, this is often the goal that triggered their return. However, this does not imply that they require less advising assistance in education and career planning. For example, adults will frequently choose programs that they feel will assist them with the current challenges they confront on the job or in their personal lives. To help them establish personal and vocational goals, these advisees must be encouraged to look beyond their short-term work-related goals and to explore how current activities relate to long-term goals. Advisors must also help these students realistically evaluate how their previous career and life decisions affect the viability of their current goals (e.g., do they have family obligations that restrict their mobility?).

Advisors need to help adults examine their pre-enrollment career choices and, if appropriate, investigate alternative careers. For example, if the advisee has chosen to return to a degree program in which he or she originally enrolled as a late adolescent, the advisee may have misconceptions about the viability of that degree in today's job market. These students may then need assistance in identifying existing skills that are transferable to alternative career options. Locating vocational options that build on the student's assets (e.g., problem-solving abilities) and recognizing liabilities (e.g., health problems) will be important. Advisors should also help students realistically assess whether or not they can devote the time and energy the degree program will require. Adults take the advising process seriously and expect advisors to assist them in accomplishing their goals most expediently.

Consumer-oriented

Adults are more likely to be paying for their own educations. Their decision to spend money on education is usually at the expense of someone or something else—the new car or the family vacation. Adults view education from a consumer point of view—they want their money's worth. They seek coursework or a degree from the institution that provides the best product and service. Questions they might want an advisor to address include:

- Can I complete the entire degree at convenient times?
- How many previous credits will transfer?
- Will my previous college-level life experience be assessed?
- Are the services I need available at convenient times and locations?
- Will I be able to apply what I am learning to my job?

Adult students set high standards for themselves, advisors and faculty. They don't want to waste time. For example, they get angry when a faculty member doesn't show up for class or office hours, especially when they may have taken vacation time to attend or perhaps paid a babysitter to watch their children. These advisees are very task oriented. They want and expect their learning to be applicable to problems they confront on a daily basis. Advisors are often the recipients of student frustration when they find themselves enrolled in courses that are not meeting their needs or appear to be irrelevant to their goals. It is important for advisors to understand the learning goals of the various courses and the rationale for including them in the curriculum. By sharing this broader vision with the advisee, the advisor can have a positive effect on student motivation.

Advising Issues and Strategies

Advisors of adults need to know they want the same things out of the advising relationship that younger students want. They want advisors to be accessible, up-to-date and able to dispense accurate information. However, adults have unique concerns that co-exist with the traditional-age student, concerns that should be addressed by different advising strategies.

Identify motivation for returning to formal education
Adults frequently return to college in response to some life transition. In fact, it is often these life transitions that triggered their return. For example, some may be returning as a result of being fired, some may have recently become divorced and others may have planned the transition in response to the launching of their last child into school. Advisors may want to encourage advisees to discuss their transition(s) by directly asking what motivated them to enroll. They may also want to ensure that the student's return was not a snap decision in response to a crisis, but one that has been well thought out.

Sometimes adults in transition become immobilized and fail to see options. When appropriate, advisors should help these students explore options available to them that may or may not include a return to school. For example, an individual who has been laid off or perhaps passed over for a promotion may believe the only way to get ahead is to get a college degree. This assumption may or may not be true, and advisors will need to assist the advisee in exploring this issue.

Since the transition into college will add to the stress of existing transitions, it is important that these advisees be encouraged to discuss how their personal and situational constraints will impact their transition to college. For example, a female, single parent's return may have been triggered by a recent divorce. Although eager to learn, some barriers may get in her way. These may include financial and child care responsibilities. As a single parent, both may interfere with her ability to focus her attention on her studies. During the initial advising session, the advisee should be urged to explore how the transition to school will alter her life. How prepared is she for the changes this transition will create?

Potential liabilities such as strained family and personal relationships, increased financial concerns and the stress generated by the need to balance a variety of roles should be discussed. This reality check should be balanced by the advisor's discussion of the strengths an adult learner brings to college (knowledge of world of work, previous experience). Equally important, advisors should examine how the student role will be impacted by the transition that has triggered the return to school.

Nancy Schlossberg has been involved in writing two books that advisors may find exceptionally helpful in understanding adult transitions. *Counseling Adults in Transition* (Schlossberg, Waters, & Goodman, 1995) helps readers identify the factors that impact transitions and provides a conceptual overview of the transition process. *Improving Higher Education Environments for Adults* (1989) focuses on the transitions adults face as they return to higher education environments.

Familiarize adults with educational policies, routines and resources
Many adults are returning to college after a prolonged absence and are frequently unfamiliar with institutional routines. Unfamiliarity with a complicated system can be frustrating and sometimes costly to adults who feel "time is running out." Advisors should help adult advisees become aware of the institutional system and help them negotiate institutional red tape when outdated policies and procedures create barriers to learning.

Older advisees may be hesitant to seek help (often believing they should be able to handle the problem themselves) and when they do, it is often too late. This is further compounded by their off-campus focus, which often leaves them unaware of existing campus resources that could help them attain the academic survival skills they need to be successful.

When appropriate, advisors need to know where to refer adult students for:

- Study skills courses or individual tutoring

- Test-taking seminars

- Writing, reading, math refresher courses

- Time and stress management workshops

Appropriate referrals to other trusted sources who are good at working with adults can be important to this clientele. But many adult students are unable to access campus-based services because they often work full time and cannot come to campus during traditional office hours. This situation is further complicated when learners live long distances from the institution and special trips are required. Therefore, advisors should be aware of local community resources to which the student can be referred.

Determine dispositional barriers

Adults may have previous negative experiences with formal education. Frequently, these experiences have eroded their self-confidence. Adult advisees may not only be embarrassed by their previous performance, but may also be anxious over their readiness for college. Many fear failure. This fear is compounded by the fact that they may feel "too old to learn." K. Patricia Cross refers to these attitudes and self-perceptions about oneself as a learner as "dispositional barriers." It is important that advisors assess these barriers up front.

Advisors can identify dispositional barriers by asking students to discuss previous educational experiences. How they are feeling about beginning or returning to college?

To eliminate barriers, advisors might want to encourage advisees to explore how they may be different now than they were when they first attended college. Some points that might be made include:

- They have clearer educational goals and are more serious about their education.

- They have an experience base from which to draw.

- They are more mature.

Although it is most critical for this issue to be discussed during the first advising sessions, advisors may need to deal with the ramifications of a poor self-concept throughout the student's college experience.

Remembering how a poor self-concept can contribute to the stress advisees experience in college and the pressure they put on themselves as learners will help the advisor be more patient and tolerant.

Assess previous experiences

Most adult advisees feel a sense of urgency about completing their degrees in the shortest time possible. As a result, they become frustrated when they are asked to sit through courses where they have already mastered the content. Advisors need to ask adult advisees to discuss what previous educational experiences they have had. For example, some advisees will have taken courses from other institutions that were not transferable. Others will have had on-the-job training or will have attended intensive workshops or seminars sponsored by their companies. Others have extensive volunteer experience. The advisor may want to ask the student to write an educational history to help identify possible college-level learning the student has already acquired.

Additionally, advisors need to be aware of their institution's policies and procedures for prior learning assessment. Some institutions have comprehensive assessment centers, but the majority rely on traditional assessment methods such as departmental exemption tests and CLEP (College Level Examination Program) exams. If no prior learning assessment system is in place, the advisor may be asked to guide the adult student to the resource people who can make such assessments possible.

The benefits of assessing an adult advisee's prior learning are many. They are able to begin their college experience at an appropriate point; they have an increased confidence in their ability to succeed; and they see immediate progress toward their goals.

Provide ongoing support

Advisors are frequently the adult student's institutional "lifeline" for continued support and encouragement. Some adult students will enter college despite opposition from family, friends and/or co-workers. If these students are to persist, it is often up to the advisor to help balance the stress with support. Additionally, advisors may need to be aware of the potential guilt the adult learner experiences for disrupting the family's lifestyle.

Advisors should urge adult students to talk about their "cheerleaders" (those people who are pulling for them, encouraging them and who want them to succeed) and their "toxics" (those individuals who may sabotage their efforts to get their degree). This information will help the advisor know what type of support the student will need throughout the program. For example, if an advisee indicates she has little or no support from her family and spouse, the advisor knows there may be very little room for negotiating who performs household duties. Though the family may tolerate the mother's return to school, they will continue to expect her to maintain the household as she has always done. In this situation, the advisor may want to refer the student to an adult learner support group. Additionally, the advisor may suggest, if she is financially able to do so, hiring someone to assist her around the house.

Adult learners find great support from their peers who are also pursuing degrees. Advisors should, whenever possible, try to link entering adult students with other adult learners. Providing this peer connection may also be critical to an adult student's continuation. Establishing a telephone peer mentoring program may be helpful to these advisees.

Advisors also need to remember, however, that most of the adult students' support network will exist outside of the institution—in the form of spouses, children, employers and co-workers. These people can be significant sources of advice, encouragement and reassurance, even though they may feel threatened at first by the student's enrollment. They may not understand the system, or they may fear that their loved one will change as a result of the enrollment. To help diminish their concerns, advisors should encourage adult students to involve their families or friends in campus activities. It is important that they be included in the students' new world.

Advisors will sometimes recognize that their advisees have counseling needs that they have not been trained to meet. Referrals to campus-based counseling centers or reputable counselors found within the community should be made in these instances.

Conclusion

To summarize, the following points should be considered when working with adult learners.

1. Adults bring special needs to the campus that the advisor must address if the student is to be retained.

2. Adults are a heterogeneous group of students about which few generalizations can be made.

3. Adults have multiple role commitments that may detract from their educational experiences.

4. Adults bring varied life experiences that should be acknowledged within and outside the classroom. These experiences are a double-edged sword. They can be an asset to learning, or they can be a deterrent to learning.

5. Adults tend not to identify closely with the institution and often utilize resources and services available off-campus.

6. Adults frequently have clear goals and a consumer orientation. They set high standards for themselves and the institution.

7. Adults often return to campus as a result of major life transitions that may impact the success of their return.

8. Adults frequently have little experience with higher education, and if they do have experience it may not be recent.

9. Adults sometimes bring "baggage" with them from past negative experiences in formal education. The resulting lack of self-confidence may prevent them from persisting through degree completion.

10. Adults want to expedite their degree completion and get frustrated when they are made to take courses with content they have already mastered. Their prior learning must be assessed.

11. Adults frequently return to campus without support from spouses, family, co-workers and friends. This opposition must be balanced by institutional support. •

Bibliography

Ackell, E. F., Epps, R. G., Sharp, N. A., & Sparks, H. L. (1982). Adapting the university to adult students: A developmental perspective. *Continuum, 46*, 30-35.

Aslanian, C. B. (Anticipated publication date January 1997). *Adult learning in America: Why and how adults go back to school.* New York: College Board

Bonham, L. A., & Luckie, J. I. (1993). Taking a break in schooling: Why community college students stop out. *Community College Journal of Research and Practice, 17*(3), 257-270.

Breese, J. R., & O'Toole, R. (1994). Adult women students: Development of a transitional status. *Journal of College Student Personnel, 35*(3), 183-189.

Chickering, A. W., & Associates. (1981). *The modern American college. Responding to the new realities of diverse students and a changing society.* San Francisco: Jossey-Bass.

Dean, G. J., Eriksen, J. P., & Lindamood, S. A. (1987). Adults in mid-career change: Case studies for advisors. *NACADA Journal, 7*(2), 16-26.

Grites, T. J. (1982). Advising for special populations. In R. B. Winston, Jr., S. C. Ender, & T. K. Miller (Eds.), *Developmental approaches to academic advising. New Directions for Student Services No. 17.* San Francisco: Jossey-Bass.

Hughes, R. (1983). The nontraditional student in higher education: A synthesis of the literature. *NASPA Journal, 20*(3), 51-64.

Kasworm, C. E. (1990). Adult undergraduates in higher education: A review of past research perspectives. *Review of Educational Research, 60*(3), 345-372.

Kasworm, C. (1994). *Adult undergraduate students: Patterns of learning involvement.* Report on a Field-Initiated Research Grant submitted to the OERI, Dept. of Education, Washington, DC, Knoxville, TN: College of Education, 347 pp.

Lea, H. D., & Leibowitz, Z. B. (Eds.). (1992). *Adult career development. Concepts, issues and practices.* Alexandria, VA: National Career Development Association.

Mackeracher, D. (1996). *Making sense of adult learning.* Toronto: Culture Concepts, Inc.

Polson, C. J. (1993). *Teaching adult students.* (Idea Paper No. 29). Manhattan, KS: Center for Faculty Evaluation and Development.

Polson, C. J. (1994). Developmental advising for nontraditional students. *Adult Learning, 6*(1), 22-21, 28.

Polson, C. J. (1994). O'Banion's advising model and the adult student. *NACADA Journal, 14*(2), 96-102.

Richter-Antion, D. (1986). Qualitative differences between adult and younger students. *NASPA Journal, 25*(3), 58-62.

Saunders, S. A., & Ervin, L. (1988). Meeting the special advising needs of students. In R. B. Winston, Jr., T. K. Miller, S. C. Ender, T. J. Grites, & Associates (Eds.), *Developmental academic advising: Addressing students' educational, career, and personal needs.* San Francisco: Jossey-Bass.

Schlossberg, N. K., Waters, E. B., & Goodman, J. (1995) (2nd ed.). *Counseling adults in transition: Linking practice with theory.* NY: Springer.

Schlossberg, N. K., Lynch, A. Q., & Chickering, A. W. (1989). *Improving higher education environments for adults.* San Francisco: Jossey-Bass.

Simosko, S., & Associates. (1988). *Assessing learning. ACAEL handbook for faculty.* Columbia, MD: Council for Adult and Experiential Learning.

Thon, A. J. (1984). Responding to the nonacademic needs of adult students. *NASPA Journal, 21*(4), 28-35.

West, L. (1996). *Beyond fragments: Adult motivation and higher education.* Bristol, PA: Taylor & Francis.

Whitaker, U. (1989). *Assessing learning: Standards, principles & procedures.* Philadelphia, PA: Council for Adult and Experiential Learning.

Developing an Advising Portfolio

Faye Vowell, Ph.D.
Dean, School of Library and Information Management, Emporia State University

Evaluation, assessment and accountability are concepts that faculty, administrators, legislators and students are finding to be of continuing importance as we move toward the 21st century. Much of the evaluation of advising that is done takes the form of surveys of advisee satisfaction with advising. This article will propose an alternative or supplement to the advisor survey.

The Rationale for Creating an Advising Portfolio

Portfolios have become a standard in the movements to assess outcomes of student learning and the quality of teaching. But little has been done to apply the experience gained in these areas to assessment of advising. As Peter Seldin notes in Chapter 1 of *Successful Use of Teaching Portfolios* (1991), faculty members could prepare portfolios to "spell out for the record, the hard evidence and specific data about their teaching effectiveness. This is a clear advantage when an evaluation committee examines academic credentials for tenure and promotion decisions. Or they might do so in order to provide the needed structure for self-reflection about areas of their teaching needing improvement."

These uses of portfolios are equally relevant to advising; in fact, Susan Frost makes as strong a case for advising as for teaching in her 1991 AAHE ERIC monograph (1991). Both external and internal concerns are especially important to faculty members whose advising is counted as a part of their faculty load.

Many arguments about the usefulness of teaching portfolios are pertinent to a discussion of advising portfolios. For example, consider the points made by Edgerton, Hutchings, and Quinlan (1991); I have inserted *advising* in the place of *teaching* inside brackets.

1. Portfolios provide documented evidence of [advising] that is connected to the specifics and contexts of what is being taught.

2. They go beyond exclusive reliance on student rating because they include a range of evidence from a variety of sources such as…samples of student work, self-reflections, reports on [advising] research, and faculty development programs.

3. In the process of selecting and organizing their portfolio material, faculty think hard about their [advising], a practice that is likely to lead to improvement in [advising] performance.

4. In deciding what should go into a portfolio and how it should be evaluated, institutions necessarily must address the question of what is effective [advising] and what standards should drive campus [advising] practice.

5. Portfolios are a step toward a more public, professional view of [advising]. They reflect [advising] as a scholarly activity.

One use of advising portfolios is public or external. Portfolios document faculty development. If your annual performance evaluation shows a need or desire to improve in the area of advising, a portfolio could document and direct your efforts. It furnishes the hard evidence and specific data that chairs and deans often want to see.

At the same time, advising portfolios are responsive to continuous quality improvement (CQI) or total quality management (TQM) concerns. Both are based on the premises that if you focus on the process of an activity you can improve performance, and that any activity can continually be improved. Again, advising portfolios furnish the hard evidence and specific data desired in CQI and TQM processes to document improvement.

Closely related to TQM and CQI is the concern for outcomes assessment. Often, outcomes assessment has focused on student learning, but increasingly accrediting agencies and governing boards are requiring assessment to be practiced more broadly. In times of scarce financial resources, the more specific outcomes you can document, the more likely you are to retain a program or a position.

A final externally motivated reason to compile an advising portfolio is that it addresses faculty recognition issues, ranging from retention and promotion issues to tenure and merit pay. At milestones in faculty members' lives, when they are called upon to demonstrate excellence in the areas of teaching, research and service, it is important to document excellence in advising. This is especially true in institutions that consider advising as part of teaching responsibilities, or in disciplines or schools where student retention is a primary concern.

An advising portfolio is also an appropriate vehicle for internal concerns, such as self-improvement. It enables you to gather data, evaluate it and measure improvement for yourself. When you carefully consider an advising concern in such a context, you can often see connections and draw conclusions not evident from a less systematic consideration.

A second internal rationale for advising portfolios is that they provide an advising tool for individual students. Students and advisors who view advising as a developmental process for both the student and the advisor may collaborate by analyzing the process to see what worked well and what did not. The portfolio contains data that document the success of the process. Both the advisee and the advisor can examine the contents and reflect on the growth that took place.

An advising portfolio is a system of measurement that allows for pluralistic and multiple ways of knowing and being. As such, it reflects the complexity of life and better meets the needs of diverse faculty.

In addition, an advising portfolio is cost-effective and makes use of a wide variety of previously existing assessment activities. It uses multiple measures as a basis for evaluation. It disrupts faculty work patterns minimally. Finally, it generates valid information that can enhance advising.

The Contents of an Advising Portfolio

The contents of an advising portfolio will depend on its purpose. You might first think of creating a working portfolio out of which you will select certain artifacts as you compile other portfolios for more specific uses.

A working portfolio is a compilation of all artifacts you think might be important. The following items might be included:

Roles, responsibilities and goals

- A copy of the institutional mission statement, the advising mission statement and a job description
- A statement of your advising philosophy
- A reflective statement of advising goals and approaches
- A list of current advisees as well as numbers of advisees for the past five years

Annotated advising materials

- Lists of referral sources
- Lists of books and articles you use in advising and recommend to students
- Non-print resources
- Descriptions of how you use computers and other technology in advising
- Entries in an advising journal
- Periodic self-evaluations
- Reference materials

Documentation of student learning

- Student notes and comments
- Videotapes of advising sessions
- Written evaluations by peers who observe your advising

interactions
- Anecdotal entries on specific advising sessions
- Materials that you develop for working with specific students
- Self-reflective essays by advisees and advisor
- Pre- and post-scores on standardized student attitude and self-concept instruments

Evaluations of advising

- Summarized advisee evaluations of advising, including response rate and written comments and overall ratings
- Results of advisee exit interviews and focus group evaluation sessions
- Unsolicited letters from advisees
- Comments from peer observers or colleagues who also advise
- Letter from chairperson or director of advising with first-hand knowledge of your advising
- Letter from a colleague or mentor who has worked with you on improving certain aspects of your advising or who has viewed materials you have developed for advising

Contributions to institution or profession

- Service on advising committees
- Assistance to colleagues on advising
- Reviews of advising materials and publications
- Scholarly publications in advising journals or articles on advising in disciplinary journals
- Work on advising revision or development
- Funding or equipment obtained for advising programs
- Training presentations for advisors

Activities to improve advising

- Participation in advising seminars or professional meetings
- Advisor training program design
- Use of new methods or strategies in advising and assessing advising
- Descriptions of advising improvement projects developed or carried out
- Participation in advising listservs

Honors or recognition

- Advising awards from department, school, NACADA or discipline-based organizations

- Invitations to consult, give workshops, write articles based on your reputation as an advisor
- Requests for advice on advising by committees or other organized groups (This list is adapted from Waterman, 1993 as cited in Braskamp and Ory, 1994.)

From the materials in your working portfolio, you could compile two basic kinds of portfolios: one for summative evaluation and one for formative evaluation.

The portfolio created to meet formative evaluation needs of faculty development, continuous quality improvement, outcomes assessment or self-improvement is formulated to demonstrate change. It should document a process. To do so, it should contain artifacts that illustrate personal and academic growth, capability, connections in learning and reflections on student growth. Artifacts such as anecdotal entries summarizing the content of a series of advising sessions and self-reflective essays are most often found in this kind of portfolio.

A portfolio can also be compiled to meet summative evaluation purposes such as tenure, promotion, merit pay and student retention. They are also increasingly used to select outstanding advisors for such competitions as the ACT/NACADA Awards or the Freshman Year Experience Awards. These portfolios demonstrate excellence, capability, level of achievement and attainment of appropriate skill levels. Such portfolios document a snapshot rather than a process, and contain artifacts such as honors, awards and published articles and reviews.

Portfolios can be used as a part of your credentials in a job search. If advising is an important role of faculty at the institution to which you are applying, you could submit an advising portfolio in conjunction with a teaching portfolio to demonstrate your superior qualifications. This kind of evidence is becoming increasingly desirable, especially for schools whose primary mission is teaching or for whom student retention and satisfaction are issues.

Constructing an advising portfolio

The process of constructing an advising portfolio described below is a common-sense one that mirrors the process you would go through to analyze any complex activity.

1. **Determine the purpose of your portfolio.** Will it be summative or formative? Who will be your audience? What is the specific motivating event that occasioned your use of the portfolio? What goals should you set?

2. **Determine your outcomes and standards of measurement.** How will you measure success? How will you know if you have met your goals? Are your goals capable of being measured by quantifiable means? By qualitative means? Is there someone who can help you establish good evaluative measures? What artifacts does it make the most sense to collect?

3. **Outline the process you will follow.** How will you go about collecting the artifacts you will use? What kind of timeline makes sense? Are there other people who will be involved in gathering artifacts? Do you need to do any information gathering in order to begin or to analyze the data you gather?

4. **Implement the process you have outlined.** Collect the artifacts to document the fulfillment of your goals or purpose. You may have to make adjustments in your timelines or in the artifacts you collect.

5. **Evaluate your portfolio of artifacts.** If you have decided on the standard you will use to measure success, the process may be relatively easy. Often, however, you may find that measurement is more complex than you thought. It is frequently good to work with a colleague to discuss the portfolio items and the evaluation process. You might ask a colleague to be an "expert external evaluator" to ascertain the extent to which your artifacts demonstrate you have met your goals.

6. **Use the information or knowledge you have gained to enhance your advising.** This is a crucial aspect of the assessment of advising. Most often we attempt to measure something, but do nothing with the results we obtain. When we act on the knowledge we have gained, we complete the cycle and are ready to move on to assess another area.

Additional Considerations

Several other issues are worth thinking about when you decide to use an advising portfolio. First, begin with a pilot effort. By working on a small-scale effort first, you can become comfortable with the process and gain confidence in its effectiveness. You will also learn how you function in the process. For example, you may tend to procrastinate in gathering data or in seeking help from colleagues. If you know you are inclined to act in this way, you can build in safeguards for the next time you assemble a portfolio.

You should also consider how you will build support for a portfolio effort among your colleagues and advisees. Your colleagues will be interested or perhaps threatened by your efforts if the use of portfolios is not standard on your campus. Consider the ways in which they may come into contact with your portfolio efforts. Will you call on them to help you evaluate the success of your efforts? Will you ask them to critique an advising video, look at your advising handouts, or give you advice about someone on campus with expertise in an area you will need? Will they sit on the promotion and tenure committee that will examine your portfolio and make a judgment as to its merits?

In addition, you will need to gain the support of your chairperson if you plan to submit a portfolio for faculty evaluation in areas such as retention, tenure, promotion and merit pay. As Seldin (1993) observes, "It is of special importance that a periodic, written exchange of views between the chair and the professor take place about (1) [advising] responsibilities; (2) other duties related to [advising]; (3) the general content and structure of the portfolio; and (4) how [advising] performance is to be reported." (I have substituted the word *advising* for *teaching* in the above quotation.)

He goes on to point out that the chair may not understand why certain areas he or she considers important are not addressed if he or she is not kept abreast of the purpose and structure of the portfolio.

To create a climate of support and acceptance of portfolio assessment of advising, you may want to discuss the topic at a department meeting, make a presentation on the subject at a faculty seminar, provide a bibliography of background articles and books for colleagues interested in the area, or just talk about the concept over coffee or lunch with other faculty.

You may be so persuaded by the usefulness of advising portfolios that you may want all faculty at your institution to become aware of them. Seldin (1993) advances the following guidelines that should be helpful in creating an institutional climate of acceptance. They are based on his work (1991) as well as that of Edgerton, Hutchings and Quinlan (1991); Millis (1991); and O'Neil and Wright (1992).

1. The portfolio concept must be presented in a candid, complete and clear way to every faculty member and administrator.

2. Professors must have a significant hand in both the development and the operation of the portfolio program. They must feel, with justification, that they "own" the program.

3. The primary purpose of the portfolio program should be to improve the quality of [advising].

4. The institution's most respected faculty should be involved from the outset. That means the best advisors, because their participation attracts other faculty to the program. It also means admired advisors who are also prominent researchers, because their participation will signal both the value of portfolios and their willingness to go public with the scholarship of their [advising].

5. The portfolio should be field tested on a handful of prestigious professors. The fact that faculty leaders are willing to try the concept will not be lost on others.

6. Top-level administrators must give their active support to the portfolio concept. They must be publicly committed to the program and provide whatever resources are necessary so it operates effectively.

7. Sufficient time must be allowed for acceptance and implementation. Use the time to modify procedures, standards and techniques. But keep moving forward. Don't allow the portfolio concept to stall in a futile search for perfection.

8. The portfolio approach must not be forced on anyone. It is much better to use faculty volunteers.

9. If portfolios are used for personnel decisions, or for determining [advising] award winners, all professors must know the criteria and standards by which portfolios will be evaluated. And those who evaluate portfolios must be clear on those criteria and standards and abide by them.

10. It is wise to allow room for individual differences in developing portfolios. Disciplines differ. So do styles of [advising].

11. Encourage collaboration. A mentor from the same discipline can provide special insights and understandings as well as departmental practices in dealing with portfolios. On the other hand, a mentor from a different discipline can often help clarify the institution's viewpoint, the "big picture." That can be significant because portfolios submitted for personnel decisions will be read by faculty from other disciplines.

A Three-Step Process

The process of compiling an advising portfolio can be thought of as having three parts: collection, selection and reflection. Collection is a primary activity; items may be collected systematically for inclusion in a working portfolio or collected as need dictates for a special purpose portfolio. Selection takes place when you create a special purpose portfolio and decide to include specific artifacts to document attaining a specific goal. Reflection is probably the most challenging part of the process. After you have articulated your purpose, collected your data and analyzed your data to evaluate how closely you are meeting your purpose, you need to think reflectively about what you have learned or can learn from the process. Reflection can ready you to act on the knowledge you gain.

Collaboration With Colleagues

There is no one best way to structure collaboration in setting up an advising portfolio. The method that you choose will probably grow out of your own personal preferences and the culture of your discipline and institution. Collaboration can take three general forms.

You may choose to work with one colleague over the period of a semester or a year, sitting in on advising sessions and meeting periodically to discuss advising and portfolio contents. Usually this person will be your peer and will understand the issues that you face as an advisor.

Another fruitful collaboration is when a younger advisor works with a more experienced colleague who can give advice about advising situations and direction in assembling the portfolio.

Advising portfolios can also reflect the advising of an entire department or academic unit as a part of an accreditation self study or program review. Here, all the faculty in the department might engage in the creation of the portfolio. This discussion is itself a way to focus attention on advising and ensure that it continues to improve.

Overview of a Sample Self-Improvement Portfolio

Purpose
To improve my referral skills. This is a formative evaluation and I want to show change and growth.

Outcome and standards
I will have been successful in this portfolio endeavor if the result is that I feel more comfortable with referring students. A second measure of the success of the endeavor will be if I achieve good results from my referrals—if students follow through and get the help I recommend for them.

Collection of artifacts
The artifacts I will include in my portfolio include a list of referral sources with their names, phone numbers and addresses, a description of their services, and their hours of operation. I will include anecdotal entries about when and how I referred specific students and what the outcome was. I will keep a journal setting out goals in working with specific students. I will also write a self-reflective essay that analyzes my goals, my experience with students and the information in my journal. Finally, I will include student evaluations that have specific questions about referral.

Process
I will first make a list of referral sources I think my students will need. Then I will visit those sources to get first-hand experience of what those referrals will be like for a student. I will begin to set up a network of support across campus. I will collect materials from each source that I might hand out to my students. These visits will allow me to compile my list of referral sources and to gain a sense of the currency of their services.

Second, I will try to articulate my level of comfort with referring students and deciding when to refer. I will do this using a combination of journal writing, asking myself what issues I am uncomfortable dealing with and why. Then I will discuss with a colleague his or her comfort level and share my own, asking for feedback.

Next, I will begin to get a sense of what the school's and department's expectations of my role in referral should be. I will also increase my knowledge of student development theory, so I will be able to make some judgments about the developmental levels of students. I will then try to write down my general philosophy of when and how to refer students. I will share this philosophy with a colleague and ask for feedback.

Now I need to apply my general philosophy to specific situations. I will view a video in which an advisor refers a student and discuss it with a colleague and then I will role play a referral situation with a colleague and analyze that interaction.

The next step is to use my new-found skills with my student advisees. When I do this, I will describe the experience in my journal and ask the students for feedback on the referral experience.

Finally, I will reflect on the artifacts I have collected for my portfolio and will write a final essay pulling all the information together and evaluating the experience.

Evaluation
When the portfolio is complete, I will share it with a colleague and ask him or her to discuss it with me. I want to have a conversation about my goals and the extent to which the artifacts in my portfolio document whether I have met my goals. Are there measurable outcomes to show improvement?

Application
I will now try to use the insights gained in creating the portfolio and discussing it with a colleague to continue positive referral activities and alter less positive ones. I also need to decide if my referral skills are at the level I desire or whether I need to continue working on them. •

Bibliography

Braskamp, L. A., & Ory, J. C. (1994). *Assessing faculty work: Enhancing individual and institutional performance.* San Francisco: Jossey-Bass.

Frost, S. H. (1991). Academic advising for student success: A system of shared responsibility. *AAHE-ERIC Higher Education Report*, 3. Washington, DC: The George Washington University, School of Education and Human Development.

Edgerton, R., Hutchings, P., & Quinlan, K. (1991). *The teaching portfolio: Capturing the scholarship in teaching.* Washington, DC: American Association for Higher Education.

Hutchings, P., & Marchese, T. (1990). Watching assessment, questions, stories, prospects. *Change, 22*(5), 12-38.

Millis, B. (1991). Putting the teaching portfolio in context. In K. Zahorski (Ed.), *To improve the academy.* Stillwater, OK: POD/New Forums Press.

O'Neil, C., & Wright, A. (1992). *Recording teaching accomplishment: A Dalhousie guide to the teaching dossier* (2d ed). Halifax, NS: Office of Instructional Development and Technology, Dalhousie University.

Payne, D. E., Vowell, F. N., & Black, L. C. (1991). Assessment approaches in evaluation processes. *NCA Quarterly, 66*(2), 444-50.

Payne, D. E., Vowell, F. N., & Black, L. C. (1992). Assessing student academic achievement in the context of the criteria for accreditation. In *A collection of papers on self-study and institutional improvement* (pp. 174-80). Chicago: North Central Association.

Seldin, P. (1993). *Successful use of teaching portfolios.* Bolton, MA: Anker.

Seldin, P. (1991). *The teaching portfolio: A practical guide to improved performance and promotion/tenure decisions.* Bolton, MA: Anker Publishing.

Waterman, M. A. (1993). *Items that might be included in a teaching dossier.* Unpublished manuscript, Harvard Medical School.

Ethics and Values in Academic Advising

Marc Lowenstein, Ph.D.
Assistant Vice President for Academic Affairs, Richard Stockton College of New Jersey

Fundamental Concepts

Why is ethics important for advisors?

Academic advising is a powerful activity. The potential to do good for students is great, and so is the potential to do harm. This power needs to be wielded with care, and with thoughtfulness.

Faculty advisors, in particular, may not ordinarily think of advising as one of their one or two top priorities, and so even though they may perform well, they may not attend very much to the ethical dimension of the activity. However, advising routinely presents some important ethical opportunities and pitfalls.

Any activity (such as advising) in which one is trying directly to help others raises ethical challenges, because these others may have something to say about the help being offered. (A faculty member writing a book does not face these problems because the book has no opinion about how it should be written.) The problems referred to are similar to those faced by physicians in treating patients.

Ethical Basics

The ethical point of view

We say a person is taking an ethical point of view when he or she approaches a situation from a disinterested rather than a selfish perspective, asking not just what is best for me but what is, simply, best. The ethical point of view may be said to be "objective," because it is the point of view that an impartial observer would bring to the situation. No one is likely to do good ethical thinking for very long unless he or she takes an ethical point of view.

Situations arise in life where it will turn out that the course of action that is ethically best conflicts with the purely self-interested course of action. Many of our heroes are people who maintained an ethical point of view in such situations. Fortunately, these situations are not everyday experiences for academic advisors!

Ethical absolutism and relativism

But how can we talk about ethics; how can we hope to find absolute answers—isn't it really just a matter of personal opinion?

This is a question much discussed by philosophers. Fortunately, we do not have to resolve it in order to proceed. Maybe there is an ultimate moral truth and maybe there isn't—and even if there is, we may or may not know

what it is. The ethical explorations in this article begin with some basic ideas that we can probably all agree with regardless of what else we believe in. And we will go on to explore some ethical problems that academic advisors need to deal with regardless of their philosophical views on relativism. We will use a method that doesn't assume any absolute standard, or even assume that there is such a standard.

A starting point: Four ethical ideals

All the ethical thinking in this article is derived from the four basic ethical ideals listed here. They are concepts that most people will probably agree are good values to work from. They don't make specific reference to academic advising, since they apply to any area of work or life. Shortly we'll get on to seeing how these ideals apply to academic advising.

The four ideals are:

1. **Beneficence** (literally, doing good). This means, bringing about the most benefit and the least harm that one possibly can. In calculating how much benefit and harm we are creating we must take into account the impact on all affected persons, and we must look not only at immediate effects but at the long term as well. Sometimes the effects of our actions are remote in time or place, but they're still ethically relevant.

2. **Justice** (or fairness). Treat all individuals equally, granting no one rights or privileges that are not granted to all. "Equally" doesn't always have to mean "the same." It's not unjust to have men and women use different public rest rooms—but it is unjust if the two separate facilities are built so that it's much more likely for one sex to have to wait in line than the other! Any exception to equal treatment requires special justification.

3. **Respect for persons.** Treat individuals as ends in themselves, never merely as means to your or anyone else's ends. Treat them as rational, autonomous agents in their own right, not as things to be manipulated. Some specific ideas follow from this: tell people the truth, which they need if they are to make decisions; respect their privacy; support their autonomy.

4. **Fidelity.** Live up to commitments that you have made, whether explicitly or implicitly. Explicit commitments are usually apparent—such as promises and contracts. Implicit commitments occur when you take on a role that brings with it certain responsibilities, even though you may not be aware of these at the time.

Three important points about the four ideals:

1. Think of them as prima facie, not absolute, obligations. That means, we are saying each of them is a good ideal to try to live up to; we are not saying that it is never right to act in a contrary manner.

2. The reason that you may need to act contrary to one of the ideals is that they can conflict with each other—and when they do, something has to give.

3. Think of situations in which different combinations of the four ideals can conflict with each other. Beneficence in particular may conflict with some of the other ideals (though they can also conflict with each other), because it is the only one that evaluates our actions according to their consequences. For example, keeping promises is right (according to fidelity), whether or not we like the consequences of doing so. Similarly for justice and respect for persons. In medical ethics, the potential conflict between beneficence (the physician's desire to bring about good consequences for the patient) and respect for persons (in this case the patient's claim of autonomy regardless of whether the consequences are good for him) lies behind many agonizing dilemmas. Philosophers refer to an idea like beneficence as "consequentialist," and to an idea like respect for persons that doesn't depend on consequences as "non-consequentialist."

Ethical Principles for Advisors

If we adopt the four ethical ideals that we have discussed, we can derive the following as ethical principles that academic advisors should follow in practice. In each case, we briefly explain the principle and show which ideals it is derived from.

In examining each principle, try to imagine behavior that would count as a violation of it. Also, try to think of situations where obeying the principle might make it difficult to obey another principle.

1. **Maximize educational benefit to the advisee.** Seek for him or her the best learning experiences, courses and programs of study given his or her particular characteristics. In the advising arena, beneficence applies to thinking about the student's overall academic enterprise, and about individual decisions such as whether she should drop a course or study with a certain professor.

2. **Treat all students equitably.** Here we are applying the ideal of justice. Don't play favorites or grant special privileges. That doesn't mean treating all students the same, because their needs are different. But it means (for example) not expending more energy on one advi-see than another because she is more likeable. This principle not only directs you not to render unequal treatment; it also means that you should strive to see that the institution does not treat students inequitably.

3. **Enhance the advisee's ability to make decisions.** This principle is a consequence of the autonomy component of respect for persons. Notice that in order to do this we will probably have to permit the advisee to make decisions. It means that the student's wishes and preferences have to be respected. These wishes may not be in accord with your own assessment of what the student needs.

4. **Tell the advisee the truth.** Tell others the truth as well, but respect confidentiality. The potential for ticklish situations is more immediately obvious in this case than with some of the other principles. Respect for persons supports both your advisee's interest in the confidentiality of his talk with you and other college officials' interest in having the whole truth to support the decisions they may need to make about the advisee.

5. **Advocate for the advisee with other offices when warranted.** Fidelity to your commitment to the advisee demands some measure of advocacy. Sometimes your support will be necessary to win for the student a favorable decision from another office that is consistent with institutional policy but might not happen without a little agitation. This principle, though, tends to be more easily outweighed than others when conflicts arise.

6. **Support the educational philosophy and policies of the institution.** There is room for disagreement within a university, and (one hopes) legitimate channels for expressing disagreement. But your meeting with an advisee is not the time to say that you disagree with the math requirement. As a thinking person you have a right to your own philosophy. But ultimately if your philosophy and the university's cannot be reconciled, and you cannot refrain from saying so, you may be obliged to say it somewhere else. The point is not that you will be fired, but that fidelity imposes an ethical obligation on you.

7. **Maintain the credibility of the advising program.** You represent the program every time you talk to anyone—student, faculty, staff, parent. People's willingness to believe other advisors is partly in your hands; hence, so is the program's effectiveness. This is a matter of fidelity to the program, but also relates to beneficence: it's an example of the sort of long-term thinking required by that ideal.

8. **Accord colleagues appropriate professional courtesy.** No matter what you may secretly think of them, do not

belittle or disparage other faculty and staff when talking to advisees. An institution where this rule is not followed is one where no one retains credibility and students do not respect faculty. Beneficence obliges you not to contribute to such a state of affairs.

Applications of Ethical Principles

In this section we look at two different levels at which academic advisors will apply ethical principles. At the basic level, the principles dictate some minimum standards of conduct that characterize an ethical advisor. At the next level, we look at how the principles are used in solving ethical problems that advisors encounter. We will also take a brief look at how ethical principles relate to the model of developmental academic advising, and help to provide a foundation for that model.

Minimum standards of conduct

If you follow the ethical principles that we have discussed, here are some of the characteristics of the way you will conduct yourself as an academic advisor.

1. Do not exploit your unequal relationship with the advisee. There is a very large power differential in an advisor/advisee relationship, as indeed there is in a teacher/student relationship. The advisor must resist any inclination to take advantage of this differential for her or his personal advantage. This includes, but is not limited to, the area of sexuality.

   Discussion question. Does this mean advisor and advisee shouldn't go have a cup of coffee together? How about a beer (if the student is of age)?

2. Be available to your advisees. Keep office hours and keep appointments. Some faculty who would never think of skipping a class are less conscientious about their advising obligations, and this is wrong. Be on time, too. Among all the obvious reasons for this imperative, it's worth remembering that you are, or can be, a role model for your advisees.

3. Know the information that you need in order to give useful advice. This is actually a little surprising to some people: we are saying you have an ethical obligation to be well informed about the details of the rules and requirements that apply to your students. Ignorance or impatience with those details is not amusing; it is irresponsible. Recall that the ethical principle of truthtelling was based on the fact that advisees, as autonomous agents, need correct information with which to make decisions. You must give it to them (or know where they can get it).

4. Meet deadlines. Your duty of fidelity includes an obligation not to disadvantage your advisee through failure to process paper on time.

5. Do not discriminate against students for irrelevant reasons. Race, religion, gender—we know it is unjust to favor one student over another on these bases. But there may be others that are less obvious. You may find one student more personally (not to mention sexually) attractive than another. Or you like his politics better than hers; or you enjoy chatting with her about the fact that you've both been to Rome. None of these is a legitimate reason for serving one of your advisees more conscientiously or energetically than the other.

   Discussion question. Suppose a student has chronically missed appointments, or has been irresponsible in some other way—does that justify differential treatment by you?

6. Do not limit advising to the quick signature. You're tired, you've seen 30 students today, you desperately want to go home, and here's Bill, your last appointment, saying, "I've picked my courses; you can just sign this and I'll be out of here." Signing isn't advising. You have an obligation to do better by Bill than he's asking for. (Of course there could be contexts in which you have reason to trust that Bill's choices are appropriate, and maybe you talked to him yesterday, but that's a special case.)

7. Do not malign colleagues. The temptations are legion. The advisor of record for the student you're informally talking to seems to have made a foolish mistake. The instructor in a course your advisee is considering taking is someone you don't consider up-to-date in his discipline. Part of you wants to say to the student, "Stay away from this incompetent!" But you must control the impulse. Questioning of professional competence among colleagues can have a very serious affect on students. It undercuts the credibility and stature of the entire faculty or staff, and in a way that of the institution itself. You can find another way to encourage the student to take a different course.

   Discussion question. Isn't it dishonest to withhold from the student your true feelings or your real reasons?

   Discussion question. List all the reasons you can think of why you might want to advise a student against taking a class with a particular professor. In each case, do you think it might be unethical to tell the student? Or might there be an ethical and an unethical way of doing it?

Ethical dilemmas in advising

Sometimes we encounter ethical problems where just having principles to work with doesn't seem enough—we still have a dilemma. In ethics a dilemma isn't just any problem; it's a problem caused by there being two arguments, supporting opposite or incompatible courses of action, that seem to be equally valid. Dilemmas are what make ethics difficult.

Why are there ethical dilemmas? Our values, or our principles, give us rules to live by. But sometimes in a complicated situation, one rule tells us to do one thing and another rule tells us to do just the opposite.

This phenomenon is the source of the agonizing problems of medical ethics that have received much attention in recent years. Beneficence and respect for persons clash when a physician thinks she can benefit a patient with a particular treatment but the patient won't agree to it. Beneficence and justice collide in many tough decisions about how to allocate scarce medical resources. Though issues in academic advising are not usually matters of immediate life and death, the dilemmas involved are actually quite similar.

Ethics and developmental advising

Some of the ethical concepts that we have been discussing suggest that developmental advising is not only a good strategy but an ethical obligation.

Ethical Principles 1 (maximize educational benefit) and 3 (enhance decision-making ability) both argue for an approach to advising that goes beyond providing accurate information about course requirements and advice about sequencing. If an advisor does not use the advising encounter to help the student grow as planner and decision maker, then the advisor is not merely failing to be as good an advisor as he might be, he is being a less ethical advisor than he should be.

This distinction is worth noting. Some advisors will be perfectly willing to accept as part of their self-image that they're not the best advisors around, but much less comfortable with the notion that their practice has ethical shortcomings. •

Bibliography

Cahn, S. (1986). *Saints and scamps: Ethics in academia.* Totowa, NJ: Rowman and Littlefield.

Council for the Advancement of Standards for Student Services/Development Programs. (1988). *Standards and guidelines.* College Park, MD: Author. Reprinted in *NACADA Journal, 10*(1), 52-60.

Lowenstein, M., & T. Grites. (1993). Ethics in academic advising. *NACADA Journal, 13*(1), 53-61.

Pojman, L. (1990). *Ethics: Discovering right and wrong.* Belmont, CA: Wadsworth.

Rachels, J. (1993). *The elements of moral philosophy.* New York: McGraw Hill.

Ruggiero, V. (1984). *The moral imperative: An introduction to ethical judgment.* Palo Alto, CA: Mayfield Publishing Co.

Thiroux, J. (1990). *Ethics: Theory and practice* (4th ed.). New York: MacMillan.

Toulmin, S. (1981). The tyranny of principles. *Hastings Center Report 11*(6), 31-39.

Legal Issues in Academic Advising

Susan J. Daniell, Ed.D.
Associate Registrar and Director of Admissions, Gainesville College

Awareness of Legal Issues in Academic Advising

Many factors have contributed to increasing amounts of higher education litigation in recent years. Among them: (1) society as a whole has become more and more litigious; (2) increasingly, pressure is exerted on students (on themselves or by external forces) to achieve high grades, awards, degrees and the like; and (3) students have become more consumer-oriented—they expect to receive high-quality "products" (education and services) for their costly "investments" (tuition and effort).

Because of the potential for litigation related to the provision of educational experiences, virtually all segments of the academy now need to be aware of legal issues related to their roles and responsibilities as agents of their institutions. Those providing academic advising to students are no exception. In fact, due to the complexity of their multiple roles, faculty advisors perhaps have a greater need to be well-informed on issues related to the discharge of their responsibilities.

Is academic advising a high-risk activity legally? Practitioners, scholars and legal experts agree that advising should not be viewed as a high-risk endeavor. Although the courts are generally reluctant to enter into the academic arena, judicial intervention is apparent in response to educational actions and decisions that are clearly arbitrary, negligent or capricious, or abridge a student's protected rights. Thus, although not high risk, academic advising is an activity that can be the object of litigation.

Awareness of basic legal issues of academic advising should not have as its purpose avoidance of litigation, but instead should be viewed as a mechanism that allows the faculty advisor to function as a more effective, competent and ethical resource to students. The potential end result is an enhanced relationship between faculty advisor and student as they engage in academic advising as a shared responsibility.

The following information is offered as educational advice, not legal advice. The information contained in this paper should not replace the advice of institutional legal counsel if situations arise in connection with academic advising that are of a legal nature or that are of significant concern to faculty advisors or institutional administrators.

Legal Relationships in the Advising Setting

Students enrolled in institutions of higher education are engaged in several different legal "relationships" with their institutions. The three relationships most often resulting from a student's enrollment are contractual, constitutional and statutory.

The contractual relationship defines the rights and responsibilities of both the student and the institution. Both public and private institutions are engaged in contractual relationships with students. Students enrolled in public colleges and universities continue to enjoy the protections provided them by the Constitution of the United States. Students at private institutions are not guaranteed Constitutional protections by their institutions. This is the one relationship that differs for public and private colleges and universities. Statutory relationships afford students rights based on enactments of federal and state laws or statutes.

The three relationships will be discussed as they affect students, advisors and institutions.

Contractual Relationships

What constitutes a contract?

The contractual relationship, which defines the rights and responsibilities of both students and institutions, generally affects the advisor-advisee relationship more so than do constitutional and statutory relationships. For the vast majority of institutions, the contractual relationship ensues when the student matriculates and pays institutional fees.

Generally, the contractual relationship implies that if a student matriculates, pay fees, maintains the required academic standard of performance, abides by institutional rules and regulations and fulfills all curricular requirements, then the institution will award the earned degree. It is worthy to note that courts do not apply strict contract law when interpreting contractual relationships between institutions and students.

For the institution, the terms of the contract may be found in various institutional publications—catalogs, recruitment brochures, handbooks, departmental or major guides, etc.—unless a statement in the publication asserts that no contract can be implied by information contained in the publication. In addition to expressed contractual terms (publications, documents, etc.), terms and conditions of the contract may be implied. Generally institutions are required to abide by their established policies, rules and regulations, and to "deliver" on promised services. Failure to do so may result in allegations of breach of contract.

Students also have a role in the contractual relationship. They are bound to abide by rules, regulations and policies established by the institution. Catalogs should clearly state students' responsibility for being aware of institutional standards, policies and procedures, rules and regulations, important dates, and the like. Even so, advisors and institutional mechanisms should exert extraordinary effort to inform students of important information and details.

Advisor communications as a part of the contractual relationship

Academic advisors are "agents" of the institution and cannot disclaim their responsibilities as such. Although the concept of shared responsibility characterizes the advising relationship, and although academic advising is just that—advice giving—students should be able to rely on the accuracy of information provided them by their advisors.

Statements made by competent, authorized officials (i.e., academic advisors) given responsibility to do so can create terms the institution must fulfill. Advisors must exercise care in what they communicate, because the potential exists for verbal communications to be interpreted as implying promises the institution must fulfill.

It is recommended that advisors keep anecdotal notes of communications and meetings with advises. Such notes are not considered a part of a student's official file but can serve to avoid potential misunderstandings and misinformation.

It is imperative as well that advisors understand the "parameters of their discretion." In other words, to what extent can the advisor make changes to curricular requirements, authorize exceptions to institutional policies, procedures, rules and regulations, or otherwise deviate from written or implied requirements or processes adhered to by the institution?

Institutional changes as related to the contractual relationship

Institutions of higher education may make changes to their curriculum, curricular requirements, academic standards, policies, procedures and related academic areas. As long as such changes are designed to fulfill the institution's educational responsibilities, are not arbitrary and do not cause students significant harm, they are usually not viewed as breaches of an existing contact. However, arbitrary changes that clearly serve no educational function have, in many instances, been seen by the courts as a breach of contract.

In regard to institutional changes, it is incumbent on faculty advisors to exercise efforts to stay abreast of such changes so that they in turn may accurately inform their advisees of the changes. It is imperative that institutions and their agents exercise extraordinary efforts to apprise students of changes made, so that students are not disadvantaged by the changes.

Statutory Relationships

Title VI, Title IX and Section 504

Many federal and state statutes also affect students enrolled in institutions of higher education. These statutes (or laws) offer students significant rights and protections. Details on several federal statutes follow, but it is important to note that each of the 50 states has different laws governing institution-student relationships in that state. As a result, faculty advisors are well-advised to seek information from their institution's administrators regarding the existence of local (state) statutes that might affect the advisor-advisee relationship.

Several federal laws have direct bearing on institutions of higher education. In many cases, these enactments are key considerations in the academic advising process. For the most part, these statutes, which stem primarily from the Civil Rights movement of the 1960s, prohibit different types of discrimination. Failure to comply with these federal statutes could result in loss of federal funding for the institution, and further, could result in an academic advisor being held personally liable for damages.

A prohibition against discrimination on the basis of race, color or national origin forms the basis of Title VI of the Civil Rights Act of 1964. In effect, Title VI mandates that advisors should not treat students differently (from other students) on the basis of their race, color or national origin. All students must be given equal opportunity to participate in the courses, programs or activities of an institution.

Title IX of the Education Amendments of 1974 prohibits discrimination in programs, activities and services on the basis of sex or gender. The regulation basically mandates that typical sex role stereotypes must be eliminated. Regardless of gender, all students should be afforded the same rights to register for courses, participate in activities and avail themselves of institutional services.

Although Title IX does not specifically mention sexual harassment of students, the statute clearly protects students against such abuses. In many instances, allegations of violations of Title IX regulations have addressed the arena of college athletics and the opportunities, or lack thereof, for women to participate in collegiate athletics.

Section 504 of the Rehabilitation Act of 1973 strictly prohibits discrimination against individuals on the basis of one's handicapping condition. The regulation recognizes a handicapping condition as either physical or mental. The statute states that "otherwise qualified" individuals may not be discriminated against on the basis of a physical or mental impairment. The regulations mandate that classes, advisors and institutional programs and services must be made accessible to handicapped students.

The recent advent of the Americans with Disabilities Act has also altered the manner in which institutions interact with their students (and employees, as well). The act requires every college and university to have a named individual on campus to interpret the act locally, and to monitor institutional compliance with the provisions of the act. Again, faculty advisors are well-advised to seek out information on how the Americans with Disabilities Act is interpreted and applied on campus.

Family Educational Rights and Privacy Act of 1974
Students' rights to access their educational records and the guarantee of privacy of those records is assured by the Family Educational Rights and Privacy Act, more commonly referred to as the Buckley Amendment. Many educators consider the Buckley Amendment to be one of the most important statutes for an academic advisor to know thoroughly.

The statute "generally gives students a guaranteed right to inspect most of their records." It also prohibits the disclosing of information from a student's record without the student's written consent. The statute requires institutions to have a written policy specifying how the statute is interpreted and applied at that particular institution. Specifically, the institution must specify its policy regarding disclosure of information.

While the institution's policy regulates what information is disclosed and how it is disclosed, most institutions do not disclose student record information without written consent to do so. Most institutions do, however, disclose general information commonly referred to as "directory information." Such "directory information" generally includes such items as name, address, telephone number, dates of attendance, major, participation in officially recognized activities and degrees and awards earned.

It is absolutely imperative that faculty advisors know how the Buckley Amendment is interpreted on campus, and specifically, what information may be disclosed without the student's written permission, how students may give permission for information to be released, and the name of the campus administrator responsible for compliance with regulations of the policy.

If there is any question in the faculty advisor's mind about the appropriateness of sharing student record information, the advisor should have the student give written permission. The student must be told that he or she can revoke the permission at any time. All written documentation of this nature should immediately be placed in the student's file.

Faculty advisors often find themselves in the situation of dealing with a parent or other significant individual who is "demanding" information on a student. If the situation

cannot be dealt with to the parent's satisfaction, the advisor should refer the individual to the institution's registrar or other administrator on campus who has the authority to handle such situations.

Although the Buckley Amendment does allow a student access to his or her advising file, it is important to note that personal notes the faculty advisor may have made as a result of advising contacts are not considered a part of the "official" file, and thus, the student is excluded from access to these anecdotal notes.

The Family Educational Rights and Privacy Act does guarantee confidentiality of student information, but it also recognizes the advisor's right and need for "privileged communication." In an effort to help students, an advisor may discuss confidential information with other "appropriate" individuals who have legitimate educational interests in it. Faculty advisors should exercise extreme caution in discussing such information with institutional colleagues or administrators and should do so only in the student's best interest and with individuals for compelling educational reasons.

Although students' communications with their faculty advisors are considered confidential, there may, on rare occasions, arise circumstances that compel the advisor to violate the confidence. For example, if a student discloses to the advisor an intention to inflict harm on self or others, the advisor has an obligation to disclose such information to appropriate officials. It is advisable to err on the side of safety when making the decision whether or not to violate a student's confidence.

As stated earlier, violations of federal statutes can result in loss of federal funding for the institution. It is important for advisors to realize that they may be held personally liable for a Civil Rights violation if they do indeed violate student's rights guaranteed by federal statute. Questions regarding the appropriateness of actions regarding federal statutes should be discussed in detail with the campus administrator given responsibility for compliance with those statutes.

Constitutional Relationships

In addition to contractual and statutory relationships, students enrolled in public institutions of higher education also have a constitutional relationship with their institution. Most of the personal rights guaranteed to individuals are found in the amendments to the United States Constitution. But the same constitutional privileges do not always apply to students enrolled in private institutions. Faculty advisors in private institutions should seek out information regarding how their institution views the granting of constitutional privileges to students.

Faculty advisors at public institutions should be attentive to the First, Fourth and Fourteenth Amendments of the Constitution. Although these amendments are generally more applicable to the social or disciplinary settings of higher education, they may also be encountered in the advising setting.

The First Amendment protects speech (no matter how offensive), press, religion and the right to assembly. The Fourth Amendment safeguards students against illegal search and seizure, while the Fourteenth Amendment guarantees due process and equal protection under the law. Equal protection means that if one student is treated differently from another, there must be some rational reason for the different treatment. For example, in establishing the criteria for an internship, an institution can require specific coursework as a prerequisite or a minimum grade point average. However, the institution cannot restrict eligibility solely on the basis of ethnicity, gender or similar considerations.

Just as with statutory relationships, faculty advisors should exercise great care so as not to violate a student's protected constitutional freedoms. Again, advisors may be held personally liable for violations of students' rights guaranteed by the First, Fourth and Fourteenth Amendments.

Tort Liability

Educators, including faculty advisors, are expected to conduct themselves as "reasonable and prudent persons" and not to harm the person, property or reputation of others. The four basic "Duties of Educators" are: (1) to act as a reasonable and prudent person given the circumstances; (2) to provide adequate and appropriate supervision; (3) to provide proper instruction; and (4) to maintain all equipment and facilities in a reasonable state of repair.

These widely accepted "duties" are applicable to individuals throughout the academy, including those individuals who provide academic advising to students. Failure to adhere to these standards can result in tort litigation.

If a civil wrong is committed it is referred to as a tort. By definition, a tort is "a wrongful injury resulting from the breach of a legal duty." If the courts determine that such a wrong has indeed occurred, they will provide a "remedy" to the "injured" student in the form of "damages." For the most part this simply means the student will be compensated monetarily for wrongs suffered. The most common torts in the academic arena are negligence and defamation.

Negligence

Negligence is defined in legal terms as "the omission to do something that a reasonable person, guided by those ordinary considerations that ordinarily regulate human affairs, would do, or the doing of something that a reasonable and prudent person would not do." Simply put, negligence is "conduct of an individual that falls below a prescribed standard for the protection of others."

In the advising setting, negligence may take the form of either sanctioning certain advisee actions (for example, course selection, course withdrawal, etc.), or failing to properly inform the advisee of certain requirements, regulations, policies, responsibilities, and the like. While students must assume responsibility for advising, they should be able to rely on the accuracy of advice given them by individuals appointed by the institution as competent to provide such academic advice. If, as a result of poor advising, a student is required to take additional coursework or is otherwise hindered from progressing toward his or her educational goals, the tort of negligence may be alleged by the student.

Defamation

Defamation is written (libel) or verbal (slander) communication that results in an "injury" being suffered by an individual. Defamation results when a false statement is maliciously made about an individual to a third party. Advisors should refrain from making statements (written or verbal) about students that will knowingly harm the student's good name or reputation. Statements to third parties should be made only within the sphere of the faculty advisor's responsibilities and with no malice intended.

Academic advisors often find themselves in positions to make recommendations for students for jobs or admission to graduate school. While the requests are usually made of the faculty advisor by the student, the advisor may find it difficult to speak on the student's behalf in "glowing" terms. In such instances, remarks should be restricted to facts, should not imply assumptions and should not offer unsolicited information or opinions.

Personal liability

To be held personally liable, an advisor must personally commit a tort. Very generally, if advisors act within the scope of their responsibilities, exercise good professional judgment and make every attempt to provide sound, accurate information, they will avoid potential allegations of negligence and defamation by their advisees. To limit their liability, academic advisors should conduct themselves as "reasonable and prudent persons" and exert genuine efforts to act in the best interest of the advisee.

Given the potential for involvement in litigation, many educators wonder whether it is advisable to purchase personal professional liability insurance. Many professional organizations and associations make available liability policies designed to protect educators from suffering catastrophic monetary loses in the event of a court judgment asserting liability. While this is not intended to endorse the purchase of such a policy, faculty advisors may want to consider one benefit of having personal professional liability coverage. In the event of a lawsuit, having one's own liability policy might provide funds for one to hire legal counsel of one's own choosing, instead of relying solely on counsel that may (or may not) be provided by the institution or governing board of the institution.

Summary

Although the "risks" incurred by faculty advisors in the scope of their advising responsibilities may be considered of significant proportion, the opinion remains that, in and of itself, academic advising is not a high-risk activity legally. The courts have made it clear that they are reluctant to enter into the academic arena—they prefer to leave educational decisions to educators. They have, however, demonstrated that judicial interference is warranted and appropriate in instances where an institution or agent of the institution has treated students arbitrarily or capriciously, or in a manner that abridges their contractual, statutory or constitutional rights.

Participation in advisor training, asking questions regarding potentially litigious situations, keeping oneself informed of institutional requirements and policies, and consulting institutional legal counsel if necessary, are several ways faculty advisors can avoid litigation. Creating a climate on campus that reduces the incentives for legalism should be the goal of all institutional personnel—administrators, faculty and staff. •

Bibliography

Advising: Know the law. (1993). *Recruitment and retention in higher education, 7*(3), 1-3.

Bad advice can end up in court. (1987). *Perspective, 2*(4), 1-3.

Barr, M. J. (Ed.). (1988). *Student services and the law.* San Francisco: Jossey-Bass.

Bickel, R. D. (1986). *The college administrator and the courts: Basic casebook.* Asheville: College Administration Publications. (Quarterly Issues).

Crockett, D. S. (Ed.). (1987). *Advising skills, techniques, and resources.* Iowa City, IA: ACT.

Gehring, D. D. (1984). Legal issues in academic advising. In R. B. Winston, T. K. Miller, S. C. Ender, T. W. Grites, & Associates (Eds.), *Developmental academic advising* (pp. 381-411). San Francisco: Jossey-Bass.

Hollander, P. A., Young, D. P., & Gehring, D. D. (1985). *A practical guide to legal issues affecting college teachers.* Asheville: College Administration Publications.

Johnson, T. P. (1993). Managing student records: The courts and the Family Educational Rights and Privacy Act of 1974. *West's Educational Law Quarterly, 2*(2), 260-76.

Kaplin, W. A. (1986). *The law of higher education.* San Francisco: Jossey Bass.

King, R. D. (1992). Trends in defamation law: Let the advisor beware. *NACADA Journal, 12*(1), 34-41.

Lowenstein, M., & Grites, T. J. (1993). Ethics in academic advising. *NACADA Journal, 13*(1), 53-61.

Parents' rights under the Family Educational Rights and Privacy Act of 1974. (1985). *Lex Collegi, 8*(4), 1-5.

Young, D. P. (1986). *The college student and the courts: Cases and commentary.* Asheville: College Administration Publications. (Quarterly Issues).

Young, D. P. (1982). Legal issues regarding academic advising. *NACADA Journal, 2*(2), 41-45.

Zirkel, P. A. (1991). Academic misadvice. *The Department Chair, 2*(1), 1, 14-15.

Group Session Evaluation Form

Note to Participant. Please complete this evaluation of Academic Advising for Student Success and Retention and give it to your group leader at the conclusion of the program. Your comments and reactions are of great value in planning future sessions of the program.

1. What is your overall rating of the program? (circle one)

    6   5   4   3   2   1
    (High)   (Low)

2. Which part of the program did you find to be the **most** valuable, and why?

3. Which part of the program did you find to be the **least** valuable, and why?

4. Would you recommend Academic Advising for Student Success and Retention to colleagues at your institution:

    Strongly? ___   Moderately? ___   Not at all? ___

5. Was the program:

    Too long? ___   Too short? ___   About right? ___

6. Was the group leader's presentation effective? (circle one)

    6   5   4   3   2   1
    (High)   (Low)

7. What would you suggest to improve how this program is presented at your institution?

8. What additional topics not covered in the program do you wish had been given some attention?

9. Please list some advising topics you'd like to work on further in follow-up sessions:

10. What benefits did you receive from participating in the program?

11. What aspects of the program speak most directly to your experience as an advisor?

12. Select the category that best fits you:

    Professional advisor ____   Administrator ____   Faculty ____

13. Other comments?

14. [Optional institutional question to be asked by your group leader]